"Nicola Hanefeld embarks on an impressive and in-depth search for records of her family, which leads her to the Arolsen Archives. She unfolds a touching and revealing picture of her forebears with the documents she discovers there. Nicola interweaves her research experience with the dark chapters of persecution, imprisonment, and murder during the Nazi regime. The narrative reveals a striking understanding of where hatred, antisemitism, and racism can lead."

–Franziska Schubert, archivist, Arolsen Archives, Bad Arolsen, Germany[1]

---

1. The Arolsen Archives: an internationally governed centre for documentation, information, and research on Nazi persecution, forced labour and the Holocaust in Nazi Germany and its occupied regions. These archives grew from the ITS (International Tracing Service) after World War II.

THE UNSPEAKABLE

BREAKING MY FAMILY'S SILENCE SURROUNDING THE HOLOCAUST

NICOLA HANEFELD

ISBN 9789493322950 (ebook)

ISBN 9789493322943 (paperback)

ISBN 9789493322967 (hardcover)

Publisher: Amsterdam Publishers, The Netherlands

info@amsterdampublishers.com

The Unspeakable is part of the series Holocaust Heritage

Copyright © Nicola Hanefeld, 2025

Cover image: Marianne Vogel, the author's grandmother with her children. Photo: Bruno Vogel, the author's grandfather, 1931.

All Rights Reserved. No part of this publication may be reproduced or transmitted in any form or by any means, electronic or mechanical, including photocopy, recording or any other information storage and retrieval system, without prior permission in writing from the publisher.

CONTENTS

Preface	ix
Foreword by Peter Richard Pinard	xiii
Prologue	1
1. Dawn	7
2. The Black Forest	13
3. The person who wrote this book	23
4. Letters	27
5. Bruno	50
6. Marianne	71
7. Irma	79
8. Grete	91
Photos	111
9. Eva	130
10. Else	144
11. HPV: My father	160
12. Therese	207
13. Johanna and Martha	214
14. The Wilhelm family	223
15. Melitta	252
16. Opava	258
17. Julia and Nicola	267
18. Connecting links	285
Epilogue	297
Appendices	305
Literature and sources	309
Acknowledgments	313
About the Author	319
Amsterdam Publishers Holocaust Library	321

Dedicated to the memory of my relatives Therese, Grete and Else

It is the duty of the writer to report a terrible truth, and the duty of the reader to learn it. Anyone who turns away, closes his eyes and passes by, violates the memory of the murdered.

Wassili Grossmann[1]

---

1. Wassili Grossman, 'The Hell of Treblinka', in *The Road: Short Fiction and Essays*, pos 2217 (chapter 1, paragraph 106).

PREFACE

At some point in their lives, often later on, many people become interested in where they came from and who their ancestors were. How did one's relatives live years ago and what life-changing decisions did they have to make? How does that relate to me today? This book dives deeply and painfully into the long-unspoken past of one side of my family and tries to answer those questions.

Before I started to research my family history, I had an unclear and incorrect attitude that the past is gone – it was 'long ago' – and has little to do with the present. This, I discovered, was an unconsciously inherited attitude that the European side of my family imbued me with in their attempt to cope with the horrors of the Holocaust: block out, block off the past. Having gone through the process of research which I relate in the following pages, I know now that the past is always with us. It is not 'gone' – it influences us day in and day out, in our outlook on life, in relationships, in our attitude to the society we live in and in the work we do.

Family research, as challenging as it can sometimes be, can also be profoundly enriching and can help us to connect with long-gone relatives. That enables sense-making of the present on a personal, societal and global level. It facilitates understanding who we are and why we are as we are. May the following narrative inspire you to research your family's past and gain access to your personal history.

A note on place names, German words, abbreviations and citations

The ghetto Theresienstadt and Terezín are the same place, as are Troppau and Opava, the town where my relatives came from. I use the Czech and German names interchangeably in the following because I think my family did that. *Holocaust* and *Shoah* are another two words with the same meaning. *Holocaust* means 'consumed by fire' and is the name given to the genocide of European Jews by the Nazis. *Shoah* or *Sho'ah* is Hebrew and a widely used term: it means 'catastrophe'. I have used only the Polish name of Łódź for the Łódź ghetto and not the German name: the Nazis attempted to Germanise the town in 1940 after they invaded Poland, by calling it Litzmannstadt. This was later than the name changes associated with the founding of Czechoslovakia in 1918 and the use of official Czech name places.

Some words are best left in German, for example, *Reichskristallnacht* and *Anschluss*. *Reichskristallnacht* refers to the 'night of broken glass', echoing what happened during the pogrom which took place on 9–10 November 1938. It is, however, a term stemming from the Nazis, readers should be aware of this. *Anschluss* means 'alignment', 'connection', and 'link-up'. It well describes what happened when the Nazis annexed Austria in 1939, which was an invasion but one for which most Austrians cheered.

Nazis were those people who sympathised with, followed and supported Hitler's fascist regime and his party, the NSDAP. NSDAP stands for Nationalsozialistische Deutsche Arbeiterpartei, the National Socialist German Worker's Party, and the party's success led to Hitler being named (by democratic means) Chancellor on 30 January 1933. SS stands for Schutzstaffel, which was Hitler's major paramilitary protection squadron. *Gestapo* is an abbreviation of Geheime Staatspolizei, the Secret Service Police. I have explained other German words which are used in the following when they turn up.

A list of books I read to help me to write *The Unspeakable* is provided at the end of the book. Short quotes used in the text where I have not read the whole book are noted in footnotes. While I have aimed for accuracy regarding historical facts and an expert of the period has checked my work, I nevertheless take full responsibility for any mistakes, should there be any. Some first names of living people have been altered to protect identity.

FOREWORD BY PETER RICHARD PINARD

"The unspeakable" – a historian's view from Prague

'I'm wondering if others in this group have experienced the hushed side of the Holocaust in their families?'

Nicola Hanefeld posted this question on the Facebook Jewish Genealogy Forum in October 2022. As I hesitated to answer, my mind flashed back to a family get-together in America from the 1960s.

I was perhaps five years old at the time, and grandparents, aunts, uncles, and cousins were all dressed in their finest, as was I myself. As we sat down to the abundant holiday feast, one very elegant, older aunty removed her long gloves. Above her milky-white pianist's hands, an ugly, dark-blueish script appeared, tattooed on her forearm. Middle-class ladies from Long Island, New York, did not have tattoos in the 1960s. I had only ever consciously noticed one tattoo at that point – on my Little League coach, who had been in the Navy. If Aunty also had a tattoo, she was clearly very different from the other ladies I knew and very special. Had she also been in the Navy?

I was entranced and stared directly at her arm. Just as I wanted to ask her about it, Father whisked me away from the table to a bathroom far off at the back of the house, muttering: 'Oh, someone needs to wash his hands ...' Once there, Father stood me up against the wall, squatted down to my height, extended his index finger in front of my face, and said: 'You will not stare at Aunty's arm. You will not even look at Aunty's arm. And you will not ask any questions about Aunty's arm.' He said the words through slightly gritted teeth in a calm yet utterly menacing tone, which I knew from experience promised a serious spanking for disobedience. Only later, in adulthood, did I learn that Aunty had been married before World War II and had lost her first husband and children in the extermination camps.

During post-graduate studies at Prague's Charles University, I slipped into the topic of local Holocaust history. A lovely, older researcher at the Czech National Archives had pointed out the existence of archived police files on Holocaust victims. The files were full of details of life in the late 1930s and 1940s Prague. At times fascinating, at times comical, but often also harrowing. In my free time, I started helping people with archival research who were writing family histories. Others just wanted to understand the worlds of their missing aunts and uncles, cousins and grandparents. In one happy case, I was able to bring together a pair of friends – one Gentile, one Jewish – for the first time since the Jewish woman's deportation in 1942. It was heartwarming. I learned a lot and made new friendships. This type of research is its own blessing and reward.

But a family taboo? Most families have taboos, of course: the cousin who looks distinctly like a neighbor, the uncle with a drinking problem, etc. Such situations can and do regularly blight lives. However, they generally only affect a few individuals at once. What type of family taboo might be connected directly to the Holocaust? Taboos on the perpetrators' side are obvious and understandable. One can imagine family reunions in Germany and Austria after

World War II spent desperately trying to avoid the topic of what Dad had been doing out in the forests of Ukraine or Cousin Horst at some camp with an unpronounceable name in Poland.

But how can the victims and survivors have taboos around the subject?

Back in the present, Nicola's question on the forum had brought back an unpleasant memory; I realised her reason for asking was not likely to be uplifting either. But something seemed to radiate from that simple question. Perhaps I sensed that, like Aunty's tattoo, a bigger story existed behind it.

And so, I responded, saying yes, I did know something about families that hushed up the Holocaust. Nicola eventually sent me chapters from her manuscript with interesting and incisive questions. Her research covered several complex personalities from her extended family, whose memories she had clawed back from oblivion – an oblivion caused in part by her own relatives' silence on the topic. Over months, as I read, a rich and intricate tapestry of intertwining survival strategies, of losses and triumphs, played out across several European countries and against ever-worsening odds. *The Unspeakable* is essentially the gripping tale of a successful, highly assimilated, German-speaking Jewish family from Czechoslovakia who are suddenly confronted with the very real and – although they did not always know it at the time – potentially lethal threat of Nazism to their lives.

What should they do? How do they escape? Do they escape at all? Based on an extensive collection of surviving family documents and archived primary-source materials, Nicola takes the reader on a thoughtful journey through several countries and sets of more or less perilous historic circumstances. Some stops include the so-called Protectorate of Bohemia and Moravia (that is, Nazi-occupied Czechia), Austria, Vichy France, Switzerland, and the United Kingdom – all of which forced family members to jump through numerous hoops as they sought to save their very lives. And those lives are far from simple black and white, good and bad. Here are complex characters facing extraordinary circumstances. Even as someone who has researched and written about the Holocaust for decades, I found new and unique material and insights in *The Unspeakable*.

However, this book is not simply a distant review of exotic and rare historical sources. On the contrary, the author takes the reader along on her own very personal journey of discovery about what taboos do to a family and its members – to those too affected by painful events to speak about them and to those born into the deafening silence thereafter. Any reader looking for an uncommon and refreshingly different approach to the Holocaust and families caught up in it will find *The Unspeakable* a very good read.

– Peter Richard Pinard, PhD, Prague, September 2024

PROLOGUE

It was a drab spring day in 2004 when the door to the past suddenly flew open. On a visit, my son had told my father that he was studying the Third Reich in history lessons. My father must have felt it was time to share some facts about his family that had, until then, never been spoken of. I was forty-six at the time; my son was fifteen and my father was seventy-eight. He had terminal cancer, and he would die a year later, in May 2005. After the visit, my father sent us his aunt's passport; her name was Margarete Lanzer, born in 1884. I stood there, transfixed, holding the document, issued on 4 March 1935. It smelled a little musty, but it was otherwise in good condition. My father had written on the left inside cover of the passport:

> *This was my father's (BRUNO) sister who was murdered with her husband in a concentration camp. So was the other sister and husband FEDERMANN mother of Hanne and Susi (Hanne married X[1] and they went to Australia, daughter Y,*

---

1. My father added names here which I respectfully omit at the request of the people I eventually found.

son Z). MOTHER'S MOTHER THERESA *also murdered in* THERESIENSTADT C.C.

My father's message was disturbing and confusing. There were no further explanations; he had not sent a letter with the passport. I grasped that he was telling me that my grandfather had had two sisters (whom I'd never heard of), and that they and my father's maternal grandmother had all been killed in concentration camps. I had never heard anything of my father's grandmother. As his life was coming to an end, my father seemed to be unloading unspoken traumatic facts about his family history to succeeding generations. I turned the pages of the passport hesitantly, expecting further surprises. There were none, but Margarete, known as Grete, had travelled widely, as I could see from the official stamps in her passport. I studied her date of birth; she had been a year older than my grandfather; they had grown up together. I searched the photo of my grandfather's big sister and found eerie family resemblances.

While growing up in south-east England in the 1960s and 1970s, I was unaware of my family's Jewish roots. I knew that my father originally came from a place that he carefully pronounced called *Czech-o-slo-vakia*, a strange word to my young ears. Troppau, another place, was equally strange, but my father also sometimes called it Opava. Why would a place have two different names? Occasionally, my father mentioned a large house that had been left behind, and there was some mysterious connection to a mammoth. When I was little, I often wondered why my paternal grandparents didn't speak English with each other when they thought they were alone. I never asked them. We were, as a family, not good at talking. I no longer recall how, but around the age of eighteen, I realised my father and his family were German-speaking Czech Jews who had fled the Nazis to England before the start of the Second World War.

My paternal grandfather, Bruno, had died in England aged ninety-four in 1979, when I was twenty-two. We had been close: I was his first grandchild. He had never spoken of sisters who were victims of the Holocaust, or indeed anything else about his past. Neither had Marianne, his wife, my paternal grandmother, spoken of her mother or other family members. Therese, whom my father had noted in the passport, was Marianne's mother. As I stood there digesting the new, sad facts that my father had shared through sending this passport, questions arose in my mind. How had the passport survived the war and got to England? Above all, why had no one ever spoken about these lost family members?

Growing up in the British Isles meant for me that the country ended at the coast; it had clear, unconfusing borders. At school, history lessons ended abruptly with Queen Victoria's death in 1901; we had not done the history of twentieth-century continental Europe. Later in life, I started to understand the complex history of European states and how national borders had frequently changed through violence and war. Vladimir Putin's war on Ukraine, which began on 24 February 2022, is part of this pattern. Czechoslovakia had been founded in 1918 after the First World War; its territory had previously been within the multi-ethnic Austro-Hungarian Empire. Until 1918, my grandparents had lived in the Habsburg province of Silesia. My grandparents spoke German with one another when they thought they were alone (as a child I didn't know that the language was German) because Troppau, where they had made their family home, was a predominantly German-speaking city. Troppau later became Opava, the designation in the new official state language, Czech, with the formation of the First Czechoslovak Republic. Troppau, the town's German name, was the minority-language designation.

I have been living in Germany for over forty years as I write this account. I made my home in Freiburg, in the south-west of Germany, in 1981, and the reason I live in Germany is part of this family story. Being fluent in German meant I was able to read numerous documents in their original language as I slowly unravelled my family's continental past. The German language is known for compound nouns such as *Zeitgeist*, *Weltschmerz* or *Kindergarten*, which the English language has adopted (usually without a capital) due to a lack of appropriate equivalents. The word *Erinnerungskultur* has not been adopted in English in this way, but it is important in the context of my story. It refers to the societal custom of remembering the past, especially the Holocaust. Although it is about much more than remembrance, when used in English within a European context 'culture of remembrance' comes close to capturing the meaning. Having lived in Germany for nearly two-thirds of my life, my way of looking at the past has been shaped by *Erinnerungskultur* in a way that would not have evolved had I stayed in England.

In the following, I share my experiences of being drawn into the fate of the paternal side of my family and its way of dealing with loss and trauma through forgetting, denying and suppressing. It's also a story of identity, remembrance and memories that bring the past into the present. In the first chapters, I write about the relatives I knew; I share my memories without introspection. These childish impressions are like the tip of an iceberg, with the true stories invisible under the surface. In the sea, out of sight, lay the lives of these relatives, hidden from my childhood perspective. I unveil how I found out about their lives in fateful historical contexts and discovered how little I knew about my ancestors' full biographies.

My emphasis throughout the following, and especially in the analyses of the wartime writings of my relatives, is on lived experience. Lived experience focuses on how people live through and respond to what they experience in everyday life occurrences. Self-awareness plays a role in reports (and interpretations) of lived experience, as it concentrates on ordinary, everyday events, the language used to relate them, and a person's search for meaning and attempts to make sense of things.

I saw in my family's history the destructiveness of humankind towards its own and other species and our planet, Earth. The Holocaust seems to me humankind's most destructive, atrocious and horrendous undertaking upon itself, with its mechanised, industrialised, state-organised genocide. I tell the story so that we never forget what war, hatred and racism can lead to. And I tell the story because I wanted to find the never-mentioned relatives and cherish them in my heart.

The main people in this book

Hans-Peter Vogel, my father

Marianne Vogel, née Wilhelm, Hans-Peter's mother, my paternal grandmother

Bruno Vogel, Hans-Peter's father, my paternal grandfather

Eva Waring (née Vogel), my father's sister, my aunt

Julia, Eva's daughter, my cousin

Grete, Else and Irma, Bruno's sisters

Therese, Marianne's mother

Heinz Gütermann, Bruno's best friend

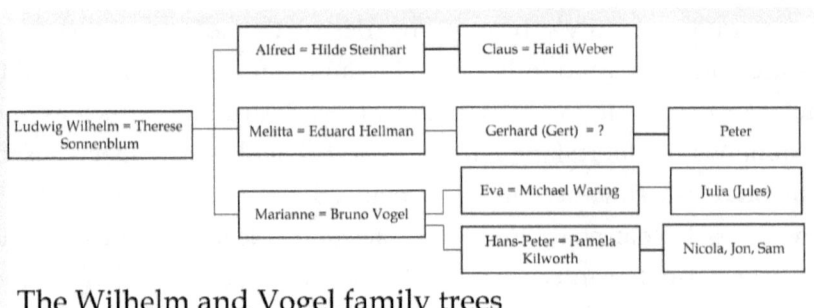

The Wilhelm and Vogel family trees

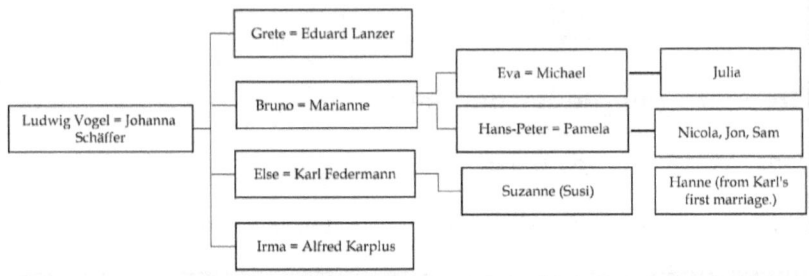

1 DAWN

The more I read and puzzle about historical connections, the more I have become convinced that history is a vital clue to understanding lives.

Susan Groag Bell[1]

A memory snippet: a thin woman who is always cleaning. She is wearing a blue overall. Her perpetual busyness – sweeping, polishing, scrubbing. Her face is shockingly wrinkled. I can see her through my eyes: I am small, she is big and stoops towards me as we speak, so I know it is not a photo as I am looking up at her from below. This was my great-grandmother, Minnie Gertrude Jones, née Gallifant, my mother's grandmother, who died when I was three.

Dancing and twisting *under* the table to 'She Loves You' by the Beatles. Summer 1963. The music filled the air; the radio was always on, the Beatles were part of life, and their specialness filled the

---

1. Susan Groag Bell, *Between Worlds. In Czechoslovakia, England and America: A Memoir*, p. 225 (hereafter Groag Bell).

household. I picked up that they were part of making things different, but what did they have to do with talk of a pill? I knew pills were medicine, something to take if you were ill. A pill, yes, but *the* pill? Why was one type of pill talked about more than other pills, and what illness was it for? Words puzzled me. How can people travel to a place called the same as when you really need something to eat? Or a place called the same as the huge bird roasted and eaten at Christmas? What was JFK and Dallas? That was all over the front page of the *Daily Express* in huge letters one autumn. I heard grown-ups speaking about Jews and Germans, words loaded with horror, but different types of horror. What were Jews anyway, and were Germans connected to germs that you could catch, that made you ill? There was the threat of an iron lung where you spent your life trapped if you got some illness, and did that have anything to do with the Iron Curtain? I knew iron was a metal, but how could something made of iron be drawn closed at night? I didn't ask. What did *playing bridge* mean? Bridges were things that went over a river or a road. My grandmother, Marianne, played bridge.

Marianne and Bruno were Granny and Grandpa, two very old people in my life. Grandpa was tall, straight and slim and he called his wife 'Mi'anne'. I called my paternal grandfather 'Dada Bruno', and I used this name I gave him as a toddler well into my teens. He called me 'Nicolina'. We – my mother, father, two brothers and I – saw them regularly, usually at the weekend when we visited their house in Ealing, London. If the weather was good, we went around the garden with my grandfather when we arrived. He showed us what was in flower in the rock garden and said things about the plants and how insects visited them. We always walked around the garden if it was not raining, and we listened quietly to Grandpa, who could talk a lot. Once, he pointed out a ring of stickiness on the stalk of a carnation, which he said caught unwanted insects and stopped them from climbing up to the flower. I said, 'But lots of insects could fly straight to the flower, they don't have to climb up the stalk', and he thought that was clever. He often wanted to explain something carefully to me, in not-very-good English, and I felt trapped. I never said anything, and he did not notice that I was fidgety. He spoke and spoke about stamps (he had a big collection) or plants, depending on the weather and if we were indoors or out. I sensed my grandfather's love for me as his first grandchild: I grew up feeling special to him. Half of the middle finger of his right hand was missing. I often reached out to touch the stump, drawn by the wrongness of the absent half-digit. I would make contact with his hand and feel the warm, soft, dry, old skin of his hand, but he would pull away suddenly. I never asked what had happened to his finger, and he never explained.

Granny was small, round and smiling. Her dresses were a bit too tight for her. She loved her grandchildren very much; she had four: me, my two younger brothers, Jon and Sam, and my cousin Julia, Eva's daughter. Eva was my father's sister. When Julia and I stayed the night at our grandparents' place in Ealing, Granny had the habit of asking during breakfast if we had already had a 'bowel motion'. I started to associate honey, on the table at breakfast, with going to the toilet. That made me feel uneasy, and I stopped eating honey. I was shocked one morning to watch Granny attach a false bun on top of her own hair, which was strange, straggly and thin. She always wore a bun at the nape of her neck, but her bun was not real. When lunch or dinner was ready, Granny would go to the lounge door, which made creaking sounds when she opened it, and shriek into the big garden in a surprisingly loud voice, from low to high, 'Bruuuuuniiiiii!'.

Bruno was always out in the garden unless it was raining. There was a large shed with tools on the wall at the back of the garden. Each tool had a silhouette drawn around it. I recognised this as his way of keeping order. No one would ever put a shovel on the nail with the outline of a pitchfork below it. There were bookshelves in the lounge, and I would look at them quietly, scanning strange words I couldn't read. Granny kept children's books in large type on one of the lower shelves; it was a special shelf. One was a story about a poor cobbler who magically cobbled golden footsteps and got out of poverty. I read it again and again when I visited; it excited me. There was a television in the corner of the lounge, but it was never on when I was visiting.

Grandpa's birthdays in the summer were special days. He drew the letters *NIJUJOSA* in chalk in large letters and bold colours on the patio slabs in front of the sitting room with the creaky door. As the years passed, I saw that NIJUJOSA stood for the first two letters of the names of his grandchildren. There were presents for us, which I didn't understand, as I thought the person whose birthday it was got presents. He'd do a high-jump competition with us, which I always won because I was the oldest and tallest. When the youngest, Sam, jumped, Grandpa would lower the string as Sam ran up, so he'd get over, and then he put it back up after a successful jump. I thought my brother must have noticed, but he never said anything.

Christmas was celebrated on Christmas Eve, not Christmas Day, at my grandparents' place. We'd sometimes wait over an hour for Eva and Julia to arrive; people got annoyed with Auntie Eva, who was always late. When they came at last, we were allowed into the sitting room, where the huge Christmas tree reached the ceiling and was alight with dozens of real candles and sparklers: it was a wonder. The tree at our home had only electric fairy lights. Granny sang 'Silent Night' in a high voice, we listened, and it was special. Then the doorbell would ring, and we rushed to see who was there, but no one was there, only presents on the ground. We collected everything, carried the presents inside, and opened them excitedly. Grandpa quietly watched us open our presents, and he only started opening his presents after everyone else had opened theirs. So then we watched him open his presents.

Grandpa often used his camera when we visited; it was a Rolleiflex with a hood and screen. He always let me look down onto the dark, mysterious scenes inside the hood; it was a secretive upside-down world that I saw, and that gave me surges of excitement.

His study had a big desk that took up most of the room. The wall opposite where we sat behind the big desk was covered with lots and lots of pictures. If I painted something for him, he'd put it on the wall, which gave me a nice feeling. His desk had drawers on the right where paper clips, very sharp pencils, coloured rubber bands, glue and scissors were perfectly ordered. When you sat at the desk, at eye level on the wall opposite was a black-and-white photo of an old woman with a big smile and a big gap between her front teeth. I stared at the photo and thought it was Aunt Irma, Grandpa's sister.

While I was growing up, Aunt Irma and Uncle Alfred lived on Argyle Road, Ealing, not far away from my grandparents, in a narrow, dark house with a garden full of flowers. The house had a strange mothball smell because hundreds of tapestries and wool were stored there. Tapestries were their business. They had a Siamese cat called Bimi who would slink around silently. Bimi sometimes let me stroke her soft, beige fur; her tail would twitch and I knew she didn't really like me stroking her: she was putting up with me. Uncle Alfred wore a beret to cover his baldness or to keep his head warm, I wasn't sure which. 'Night and Day' was a delicious dessert that Aunt Irma served when we had lunch at their place: tinned pears with whipped cream and melted dark chocolate. It was one of the reasons I looked forward to visiting them.

Several fires occurred as I was growing up: the factory fire, the kitchen fire and a fire in the caravan. But before those fires, Uncle Alfred died in a fire in 1965 when I was seven. A fire had broken out in an upstairs room at Alfred and Irma's place, caused by an electric heater. He'd tried to rescue the tapestries, got trapped and died. That fire left a shadow of dark sadness over the family. I felt it – but I didn't understand it, and no one spoke to me about it. Irma died about six months after Alfred's death, and I missed them and the visits to their place.

Another aunt was Aunt Martha, sometimes called Great-Aunt Martha, but she lived far away in another country and I never met her. She sent me a beautiful string of tiny pearls when I was twelve years old, and I treasured it. My grandfather couldn't say 'th' – he called her 'Marta'.

A scene: I must have been about thirteen or fourteen years old, and Bruno was well into his eighties. I had driven somewhere with him. His driving was awful, and going anywhere with him in the car was frightening. He used the clutch as a brake, and the motor screeched loudly in protest and stuttered violently when he abruptly slowed down using this strategy. When we arrived at his house, he drove the car up the short, steep hill, which was the driveway of their home at 13 Castlebar Hill, and parked it in front of the garage. As we got out of the car and shut the doors, the car started slowly rolling down the hill. He'd not put the handbrake on and not left the car in gear. We both stood shocked and silent, rooted to the spot, watching as the car silently rolled faster and faster down and away, across the road, crashing into the wall of the old people's home on the other side. Luckily, no cars were on the street at the time, and no one was outside sitting on the bench at the home where the car crashed. Bruno surrendered his driving licence; he was getting very old.

As I grew older and my grandparents did too, there was less contact between us; the frequent visits to their place stopped. But when they celebrated their golden wedding anniversary in 1972, we all went out for a meal. Granny got a little tipsy, and at the end of the meal whistled loudly with four fingers in her mouth to the waiter for the bill. A little old woman, our grandmother, loudly and inappropriately *whistling*! The adults at the table cringed; her grandchildren beamed with awe and delight.

These memories of my grandparents are the backdrop to the following narrative. I further set the scene and then move on to tell how I discovered the tragic lives of relatives I had never heard about and how I came to write this book.

2 THE BLACK FOREST

Whatever power the Germans may have over the persons and property of the Czechs, they have little influence over their souls.

George Kennan[1]

My father was managing director of Perivale Gütermann Sewing Silks Ltd, the fourth-largest manufacturer of sewing threads in the UK at the end of the 1970s.[2] It was a German sewing thread company, and he had taken over the position from his father, Bruno. Various corners of our house were stacked with a range of bright, beautifully coloured sewing thread. I was attracted to the colours but hated sewing; I couldn't sit quietly long enough to sew.

International European business colleagues employed by the Gütermann Company organised summer exchanges of their children

---

1. Quoted in Madeleine Albright, *Prague Winter: A Personal Story of Remembrance and War, 1937–1948* (hereafter Albright), pos. 2047 (chapter 10, paragraph 13).
2. T.A.J. Nicholson, 'Producing a Product Range: Perivale Gütermann Threads', in *Managing Manufacturing Operations: A Casebook.*

and, starting when I was twelve, I was regularly sent around Europe as part of these swaps. Looking back, it was strange because no conversation took place as to whether I wanted to undertake such visits. And when a daughter from somewhere came to stay with us in England in due course, it was awkward. I had to be friendly with someone I didn't know, and whom I couldn't understand. Learning a language was doubtless the good intention behind these exchanges, but it would have been nice to have been asked. During my summer holidays in 1975 I was sent to one of the many Gütermann families in Gutach, a little village in south-west Germany. I started to get to know various relatives of the extended Gütermann family. As I came to understand, many descendants of the company's founder, Max and his wife Sophie, still lived in Gutach, where their predecessor had set up the sewing thread company in the mid-nineteenth century. Gutach nestled in a quiet valley of the Black Forest. But it was confusing: there were so many different branches of the Gütermann family. I didn't know who was related to whom; they probably didn't know how they were related either. Alexandra Gütermann was one of the many children I met during those long-ago summers, and I remember her as younger than me and very quiet. Dozens of years later, Alexandra helped me sort out relationships through her family history books.[3] I also learned about the business and private relationships between my grandfather Bruno and her family through these books and gained the insight that my family had been saved by the business connection and strong bonds between the two families.

The Gütermann story and my family's association with them is at the root of why I left England and moved to the city of Freiburg, south-

---

3. Alexandra Gütermann, *Die Gütermanns: Eine Familiengeschichte. Band 1: Max, Sophie und Ihre Kinder (Die erste und die zweite Generation)*, and *Die Gütermanns: Eine Familiengeschichte. Band 2: Die dritte Generation Teil I: Stämme Fanny-Carl-Julius* (*The Gütermanns. A Family Story. Volume 1: Max, Sophie and Their Children* and *Volume 2: The First and Second Generation*, hereafter Gütermann II).

west Germany, as a young adult, 113 years after Max Gütermann moved his company from Vienna to Gutach, near Freiburg. It is why my children have German nationality and not British, although they can apply for British nationality because I am English. (But after Brexit, who wants that anyway?) As the Gütermann family history is intimately connected with my paternal family's history, I cannot tell my story without including theirs. In the following, I sketch one Gütermann family branch up to the third generation, piecing it together from two of Alexandra's books. It was this family and business connection that led to my leaving England forever when I was twenty-three.

The Gütermann family

Max Gütermann was born in 1828 to a Jewish family near the town of Bamberg in Bavaria, Germany. As a young man, Max left Bamberg to join his older cousin as an apprentice working in the textile industry in Vienna, and he became an Austro-Hungarian national. In 1866, Max founded a silk manufacturing company and searched for a better production place than Vienna. He then moved with the company and his family to Gutach in 1868. The idyllic village, 25 kilometres from Freiburg, had soft and clean river water flowing through it, a critical necessity for making silk in those days.

Disconcertingly from our present-day perspective, Max married his first cousin, Sophie, in 1854. They had their first child, Carl, in 1856 while still in Vienna, and then had eight more children within eleven years while living in Gutach. The couple must have been wary of antisemitism: they christened their children, who became Catholics. In 1870 Sophie died, aged thirty-seven, leaving Max a widower. Probably to avoid being involved in the various wars that were looming, Max applied for Swiss nationality, which was granted to him and his family in 1876, although he remained in Gutach.

Max and Sophie's children grew up, married and started families. All five sons joined their father's expanding and already successful sewing thread company. Carl, the oldest son, must have felt a connection to his birth city because when he joined his father's company, he moved back to Vienna and set up the Gütermann sewing thread factory in the street called Phorusgasse at house number 2. The company successfully supplied the vast Austro-Hungarian state with silk, almost achieving a market monopoly.

Carl married Anne Scheyer in 1885. She was the daughter of a well-to-do Jewish family from Bad Kreuznach in Germany. Assimilation seems to have been taking place, and we can assume that the Jewishness of the Gütermann families in the second and third generations was already, in some cases, less connected with religion. Carl and Anne had four children. Their oldest son, Heinrich, who was known as Heinz, was born in 1888 in Perosa Argentina in northern Italy, where Carl had set up a Gütermann branch and lived with his family. Carl died in 1912 at the age of fifty-six.

A few years before Carl died, Heinz had begun his studies at the university in Mittweida, in one of the eastern German states, Saxony. The University of Applied Sciences in Mittweida still exists; at the end of the nineteenth century, it was a leading private educational institution for training machine-building engineers. Heinz completed his studies in the same year that his father Carl died. While at the university, Heinz met Bruno, my grandfather, who was studying mechanical engineering. A deep and lasting friendship grew between them, even though Heinz was three years younger than Bruno. It was through this friendship and the business connection they later developed that my father's family was able to flee to England and escape the Nazis in 1938/1939. Heinz is the main non-family member who is a key figure in this book, and he played an important role during the Second World War with Marianne's brother's family.

Heinz was twenty-four when his father died. Having completed his studies, he took over the Austrian branch of the company in Vienna in 1912. He belonged to the third generation of the Gütermann family to have a Swiss passport, and he was called up to the Swiss army during the First World War (1914–1918), while Bruno became a lieutenant for the Austro-Hungarian army.

After the war, the state boundaries of Europe were rapidly redefined, and plans to found a Gütermann branch in the new state of Czechoslovakia, in Troppau, developed. Bruno became the manager of this branch, called Gütermannovo Šicí Hedvábí (Gütermann Sewing Thread).[4] Bruno was successful in his work in Troppau, and this branch became known as a 'jewel' within the Gütermann Company. Branches set up in Yugoslavia, Hungary, Bulgaria and Greece were less successful.

Heinz married Erica Brause in 1912, which was ten years before Bruno and Marianne married. As the couples had children, the families became close, spending time together in the summer at Heinz's holiday house, built in 1925, at Attersee, in western Austria. A photo album exists from the summer of 1933 showing the two families holidaying there during that fateful year when Hitler came to power. The photos show seemingly untroubled adults and children spontaneously interacting, but the mood in the background of the adults' minds and the content of evening conversation when the children were in bed must have been full of concern. Politically, dark clouds were gathering on the horizon, and increasingly, fear must have infused everyday life. In May 1933, student groups across Germany carried out public burnings of tens of thousands of books that they and leading Nazis regarded as 'un-German in spirit'. Joseph Goebbels, the propaganda minister, announced that 'Jewish intellectualism is dead' and supported the students 'cleaning up the

---

4. Obituary, *Das Schachbrett* (*The Chess Board*; internal company newsletter), 151 (April 1980), p. 24.

debris of the past'.⁵ It was an early taste of severe state censorship and of darker things to come.

Heinz had been christened, like his father, but he was still counted as a Jew according to the Nazi's Nuremberg Decrees issued in 1935. On 12 March 1938, when the Nazis annexed Austria (the Anschluss), Heinz knew it was time to leave Vienna. His Swiss nationality meant that he could relocate to the Swiss Gütermann branch in Zurich. Ultimately, both Heinz and Bruno lost all their property and possessions to the Nazis. In Nazi jargon, it was 'dispossession on racial grounds', as noted on the copy of a document I found in the unsorted family archive in an old suitcase at my mother's house. The Nazis confiscated the Attersee house from Heinz and his family in 1943.

In February 1944, Heinz became very ill and had to go to hospital, as Alexandra's books document. I don't possess any of the original letters and have relied on her books to piece this part of the story together. Erica wrote graphically that 'Worry and fear have moved in with us'. She reported that Heinz had been ill with sepsis since 1 February, and he had been in hospital since 11 February. The bacteria's entry place was unknown, and he was 'terribly ill and weak and only weighs 57 kg' (8.9 stone). He was stable at that point, but they were expecting another outbreak to happen at any time.⁶ Heinz was allowed to go home at the beginning of June and had two relatively quiet months with his family. Then he had to go back to hospital because his state had worsened, despite injections and an operation. At the end of August 1944, via the Swiss consulate, Bruno managed to get the new antibiotic penicillin to his friend. Marianne was a pharmacist, and she was probably able to get hold of it. Either it was too late or the amount of penicillin was not enough: during the

---

5. www.ushmm.org/collections/bibliography/1933-book-burnings
6. Gütermann II, p. 57

night of 2 September, Heinz died. Bruno wrote in German (I have translated) heart-wrenchingly a few days later to Erica:

> *The world is now empty and has lost virtue, interest, and joy – which I so happily shared with Heinz even though in recent last years I have been so far away from him. For almost 40 years I have not experienced anything of significance without thinking 'that would make Heinz happy' and 'what would he say to that?' or asking myself 'how would he do that?'*[7]

On 8 February 1945, Bruno wrote a letter in German to Anna, Heinz's mother. This is my translation:

> *Heinz was the only one I could call a friend. My life was so much better through him, more beautiful – and richer. Being with him made me content, it gave me self-confidence and made me happy. Heinz was my ideal person, he was exemplary as a husband, father and as a son. He was only hard on himself and in this respect good, dear Erica helped him. I would be so happy to know that she is settled. Through his own self-discipline Heinz calmed everybody and was an example to all. I could weep to make my heart feel lighter but self-discipline as a medicine best helps me now and all others around me too.*[8]

I cannot read these words without tears coming to my eyes. Bruno's anguish and grief about Heinz's death is palpable. Possibly the whole tension of the war, leaving his home, and the uncertain fates of his sisters and mother-in-law flowed into his mourning. It was stunning to see such emotive words from my grandfather in a family history

---

7. Ibid.
8. Ibid., p. 60

book of someone else's family and to discover his friendship with someone I'd never heard of.

In her second book, Alexandra quotes Ernst, Heinz's son, as saying that Bruno was his father's only and best friend and that Bruno was 'an excellent man'. When I discovered quotes from my grandfather in this book, I contacted Alexandra in Gutach to ask if she had the original letters. I introduced myself, and she remembered me from my long-ago summer holidays in the village. She could not say where the original letters were, which disappointed me, but she suggested I contact Christoph Gütermann, one of her many cousins and Heinz's grandson. Christoph lives in Vienna, where Carl, his great-grandfather, had set up the Gütermann Company all those years ago.

Alexandra gave me Christoph's email address and I reached out. He answered immediately. Touchingly, he said he remembered me as a child from fifty years (!) earlier in the 1960s in Ealing, playing in the garden one afternoon at my grandparents' house. We met via Skype. Christoph, I learned, was born in 1947, just three years after his grandfather Heinz died, and saw in Bruno a kind of ersatz grandfather, and that moved me. I could imagine how Bruno offered that kind of relationship to Heinz's grandson to ease the personal pain of having lost his friend. In November 2019 I was giving a course in Vienna, and I planned to visit Christoph. Although we didn't know one another, when we eventually met at his house, we clicked and talked like long-lost friends. Our grandfathers' friendship reached down to us through the years, and it carried us as we talked, getting to know one another.

Having explained some of the Gütermann family history as it relates to my family, I now briefly relate how it came about that I left England. Summer visits with one branch of this family during my late teenage years changed the course of my life. When I was seventeen, my father sent me to Gutach to stay with them. I fitted in easily, and my unconscious continental roots started to flourish. I fell in love with the Black Forest, and a farmer (and the farmer's way of life), and started living between two worlds. My 'home' was England, where my family lived and where I completed my schooling and went to university to study botany and zoology. But each summer for five years, and once in winter, I visited the Black Forest for several weeks. I learned German surprisingly quickly, and I felt strongly drawn to the continent. As Marianne and Bruno's lives were coming to an end, as the 1970s decade was closing, I was transitioning to leaving England for Germany for good.

In July 1980, instead of visiting the Black Forest, I drove alone across the continent in my little car to business friends of my father who lived near Munich. I left England and my childhood behind me and explored new fields in Germany. During that summer holiday near Munich, at the start of a new decade, I met someone from Freiburg and left England forever, driving over to him in the summer of 1981 for a 'holiday'. I had taken the plunge: I moved to Germany and settled there; I never went back to England apart from visits. I set up a new life in Freiburg, the 900-year-old city in the valley surrounded protectively by the hills and mountains of the Black Forest.

Lady Diana and Prince Charles got married that summer, and I watched with an uneasy feeling, knowing it would not work out well.

It was, therefore, because of my family's long-standing connection with the Gütermann family that I moved to Germany. A connecting thread (pun intended) with the Gütermann family lives on in my family. In 2022, one of my brothers found some old wooden golf clubs in my mother's garage and asked who they belonged to. My mother answered 'Gert Gütermann'. He had worked in the family business in England before being interned as an enemy alien during the war and then sent to Canada, only to die when the British ship the SS *Arandora Star* was sunk by a German U-boat in 1940. My grandfather inherited the clubs after Gert's death. When Bruno died in 1979, the golf clubs were passed on to my father, and after my father died in 2005, they became my mother's when in 2006 she packed them with her other possessions and moved house. She has honoured the Gütermann connection by keeping them.

3 THE PERSON WHO WROTE THIS BOOK

This sunlight linked me through the ages to that past consciousness.

Richard Jefferies[1]

In the Prologue, I wrote about how Great-Aunt Grete's passport fell into my life and prompted my researching my paternal family and writing this book. I have shared fond memories of my paternal grandparents and a little about myself and told the tale of how it came about that I left England for Germany in 1981. I now jump forwards thirty years to 2011 to continue the story of how I became motivated to find out more about my family members who had never been spoken about, and their fates. There were intense experiences as I discovered the host of tragedies that befell my family, and I write about that. But first, a rough outline of my life in Freiburg.

After moving to Freiburg in 1981, I found a flat, made friends, got married in 1986, and had three children in 1987, 1989 and 1994.

---

1. Richard Jefferies (1848–1887), English nature writer. www.allgreatquotes.com/quote-382393.

Family life was intense, and I loved being a mum, with all its discoveries and challenges. I learned to speak German fluently and felt at home speaking it, although I never mastered writing it because I have no patience with its grammar. My father regularly visited the Gütermann HQ in Gutach as managing director of the factory in the UK, and we met in Freiburg and spoke German together. He retired and therefore stopped travelling to Germany in the 1990s, but I visited England and stayed in contact with my family. The Berlin Wall fell in 1989 and the two Germanys reunified. In 2000, I acquired German citizenship while keeping the British; that felt right.

I trained in Freiburg from 1986 to 1989 in the Alexander Technique, a holistic mind-body method. This professional training gave me some skills to tackle this family history project that unconsciously started when Grete's passport entered my life. These are not the skills of a historian but personal resources involving observing, simply seeing what is going on. The Alexander Technique is a practical, hands-on self-management method, based on awareness, for addressing unconscious habits that limit wellbeing. The Alexander Technique teacher cultivates non-judgemental observation when working with a client, and that played into how I dealt with the information that my research brought to light. It also affected how I looked after myself during the research and how I wrote about my subject matter. There was a lot to observe as I researched and drafted this book, and I recount my emotional journey in some of the following chapters as I uncovered and reconstructed my family's past.

I began by researching Bruno's older sister, Grete, in 2004, the year my father had sent her passport to us. It was disturbingly easy to find details of her fate, although the Nazis had tried to cover up their persecution and murdering of Jews, Romani and Sinti, homosexuals, disabled people, communists and other political opponents, Jehovah's witnesses, and people who protected the persecuted. In 2004, though, I was not ready to delve deeper.

In 2011, thirty years after leaving England and six years after my father died, I found, as I will explain in the next chapter, a cache of letters in the attic at my mother's new house, which she had moved to a year after my father died. This find meant a big step forward in uncovering my paternal family's unspoken past, and the letters became the backbone of this book.

After finding my father's letters and discovering what had happened to Grete during the war, I started to experience sudden mood changes – something that was new to me. I felt drawn to go deeper into my family's past but was surprised by how the subject of the Holocaust emotionally exhausted me. Out of the blue, huge waves of sorrow might overcome me. I'd be happily driving along somewhere, and everything was fine; I was feeling good, the sky was clear – and a surge of sorrow would suddenly gush over me. Tears stung my eyes. It could abruptly overwhelm me, and in time, I came to associate it with the Shoah. I started thinking that it was not my sorrow but a collective sorrow from *then*, as if I, for a few seconds, was tapping into the tragic consciousnesses of millions of persecuted people that was somehow, somewhere, still out there and accessible. In my mind, I came to call it 'the Great Sadness', and it had an intensity that was utterly exhausting. Researching this book meant shouldering a new emotional burden – that is, a new conscious emotional burden: I now think that the burden was there during my childhood, but not consciously.

I also observed changing states of awareness while researching the subject, and sometimes I went down what I called a 'Shoah time tunnel'. I first entered this tunnel in 2001 – some three years before seeing Grete's passport and starting to sense my Jewish heritage – when I met Buddy Elias (1925–2015), Anne Frank's cousin. Buddy, chairman of the Anne Frank Foundation in Basel, was seventeen years older than Anne and he had known her. I was then chairwoman of the parent-teacher association of the Anne Frank Primary School in Freiburg, where my daughters went to school. The association invited Buddy, who lived in Basel, Switzerland, 60 kilometres to the south of Freiburg, to an event at the school. Four girls who were around Anne's age while she was in hiding read their favourite excerpts from her famous diary. We asked Buddy to engage in an exchange after the readings and speak and answer questions about his cousin.

I picked Buddy up at Freiburg's main train station, and I remember briefly observing him before he spotted me. He was a small, wide-awake, charismatic and athletic seventy year old. From the very first moment that I was with him and we spoke, I had the uncanny experience of perceiving the darkness of that time, as if a parallel awareness opened alongside my everyday consciousness, and I could see and feel the Great Sadness and black despair from *then*. Later, during the event, tears stung my eyes while the girls read from Anne's diary, and it was the first time that I consciously opened to the strong emotions connected to the Holocaust. Over a hundred people attended, and my eldest daughter was one of the three girls who read diary passages. In the following years, I stayed in contact with Buddy, and I visited him in Basel. A friendship grew.

Once I started delving into my family history, this parallel awareness, the dark Shoah time tunnel, could also spontaneously open if I spent (too much) time researching old records, whether looking online or at the documents I owned. I did not think this strange, as I believe that different states of awareness are available to humankind, only we don't often access them. But it was exhausting and emotionally demanding, and my ability to master my everyday life – work and being a mother – was weakened if I stayed in that zone too long.

My marriage, which had had cracks in it for a long time, finally fell apart in 2003, a year before the fateful day when my father sent Grete's passport. By 2011, my youngest had left home (the older two children had already left) and that set emotional capacity free: when the next surprise struck, I had both time and inclination to delve deeper into the past of the paternal side of my family.

4 LETTERS

The settlement of the Czechoslovakian problem which has now been achieved is, in my view, only the prelude to a larger settlement in which Europe may find peace.

Neville Chamberlain[1]

After my father's death in 2005, I continued to travel to England once or twice a year. I visited my mother, who lived in the south-east part of the country, and met up with my youngest brother and my cousin Julia, in London. Once, during a visit to my mother's place in 2011, my mother, one of my brothers and I were talking about the continental side of the family's past. We remembered the black-and-white photos of the family house in Opava that my father had passed around after lunch when Julia was visiting one Saturday, many years

---

1. British Prime Minister Neville Chamberlin on 30 September 1938. He was wrong. The 'problem' was that Hitler wanted part of Czechoslovakia, the German-speaking Sudetenland, in exchange for peace. The Munich Agreement with Hitler allowed this but led to the dissolution of the first Czechoslovakian state. However, the agreement strengthened Hitler and only put the war off for a year.

ago. The interior of the house looked beautiful. I remember experiencing my father's unfamiliar enthusiasm and chattiness as he explained the photos to us as we sat around the table. There was an aliveness about him that contrasted with the otherwise frequently withdrawn and sleepy father I was familiar with.

We decided to go up to the attic and search for the photos. So, up the ladder we went, one by one, and we explored in the gloom under the roof, rummaging in boxes lying on the dusty floor. While we didn't find the photos, I did find something else: a box full of hundreds of letters my father had written to his parents during the war. As I opened the box and the mustiness of old paper wafted up to me, I realised what I had found. A thrill of excitement zapped through me: the door to the past flew open again.

Downstairs, out of the dark and narrow attic, I hurriedly looked through the letters; although they were over seventy years old, they were in excellent condition. Skimming through the oldest, I realised that my father had learned English quickly, and I was fascinated. The first letters he wrote were addressed to his parents in London, and the building they stayed in at Lancaster Gate still exists (as I later discovered), although it is no longer the hotel named on the envelope. At first he wrote in German, but within a few months he was mixing the languages, and by mid-1940 the letters were in reasonable English. He was thirteen and a half when he had been sent to Cliftonville Boarding School in Kent upon arrival in England in March 1939. He had written regularly to his parents, Marianne and Bruno, above all to his mother, in careful, adolescent script which quickly matured to the handwriting I was familiar with.

The content of these letters excited me, and I recognised them as well written; they promised to shed light on the blank era of family history that my father had hardly spoken of, which his parents, my grandparents, had never mentioned. I counted over 240 letters as well as dozens of postcards. I randomly divided the letters into three piles, one for each of his children. The ones in my pile were written between early 1939 and the 1950s. Although the letters slowly filled family history gaps as I read them during the following months, they also opened new gaps. Some questions were answered but more arose in my mind. The biggest of these new questions was: why had no one ever spoken about the past that I now had access to, documented and captured in the letters?

Back in Freiburg, I started studying my father's letters more closely and ordered them chronologically. One letter, which I share in full below, particularly gripped me, and I read and reread it. To give some context, my father returned as a twenty year old to Opava, the place he'd left as a thirteen year old. It was now September 1945 and he reported in detail to his parents about his trip. In this letter, his loyalty to England comes across, his respect for his parents and his loving relationship with them. Furthermore, he writes graphically about Czechoslovakia in its post-war chaos and about how the Russians behaved. There are cryptic mentions of family members murdered by the Nazis and reports of happy reunions. The letter is understandably full of references to people my grandparents knew. Milos (Schafranek) was married to Joyce; he had been my father's pilot while he'd been in the Czech division of the RAF. Dr S. and Mr and Mrs Chalupas were family friends, and the Sykoras were people who had worked for Bruno and Marianne in house and garden. My father reports about them all and what happened to them during the war. From the letter, I understood for the first time that Bruno's sisters, Grete and Irma – my father's aunts – had lived near my father's family in Opava. I discovered that Marianne's sister had also lived close by. Her name was Melitta. My father reports meeting up with Tante Litta's husband, Onkel Edi.

There is a mention of the mammoth ('elephant') that I had heard of in my childhood. He wrote that it winked at him as he walked past, and in writing that, my father sparked it into life in my mind. I didn't (yet) understand this part of the letter – that came five years later.

During this visit, one of my father's main tasks was to find out the post-war state and status of the family's house. He took on responsibility for decisions about investing in repairs and who should inhabit it. He wrote cautiously, shielding his parents from the whole truth about how damaged it was. The letter's main language is English, but he peppered it with Czech and German, even a bit of Polish and Russian. Although by this time he was fluent in English, his first language was German, and he sometimes thought in German but used an English word, and meanings are obscured for these reasons. My knowledge of both languages helped me to understand these parts of the letter. The most vivid section is his description of returning to the house where he'd grown up, and here he switched to German.

He wrote the letter on the Czech squadrons' RAF writing paper. Wearing his uniform gave him a certain standing during his trip back to Czechoslovakia, and he shared that this made him feel proud and grateful. Throughout the letter, he wove in comments suggesting that his parents would return to Opava. They never did. Cigarettes seem to have been important presents (or units of currency) during his return and he had taken many with him, although he remained a life-long non-smoker. He also thought aloud in the letter about his uncertain future. He wanted to study agriculture in Brno in Czechoslovakia. Like hundreds of thousands of people after the war, he had to pick up the pieces and find his way, and that was an arduous process of weighing things up, considering and making decisions.

The letter is twenty pages long and carefully written. It must have taken a long time to write it, and towards the end, he concluded with a numbered summary of the points relevant for his parents. What a cocktail and whirlpool of emotions he must have experienced during his return, and he may have been using the process of writing to digest things and create some order in his mind. There must have been a lot swirling under the surface, yet he wrote clearly, coherently and with self-confidence. He was only twenty, still a quite tender age to digest everything and deal with the extreme situation he was confronted with. He seems, in a way, almost to stand above the incomprehensible, nonsensical evil inflicted upon Jews and members of his family. However, this may already be the manifestation of the family habit of not dealing with *the unspeakable*. To a certain extent, how my father documented happenings and interpersonal relationships in this letter reflects the bigger political picture of the upheaval that Czechoslovakia had gone through – and was still going through. The broad strokes of the larger political picture played out on the interpersonal level, and vice versa. He mentions, for example, a jump from twenty-six to one hundred and twenty-six first-degree 'half-Jews' in town. Here people were 'transitioning' from trying to protect themselves from danger and persecution by hiding their Jewishness, to seeking the safety of post-war protection through 'utilising' their status as Jewish.

I have left my father's English uncorrected – as I do when transcribing all of his letters and citations in the following pages. As my father had not had schooling in Czech since he'd left as a thirteen year old, it's understandable that he left off the diacritics (marks on letters indicating how a word is pronounced) and made some mistakes in Czech. These have been corrected in the footnotes. There are many footnotes in the following transcription, but this preserves the flow of my father's writing better than if I had inserted brackets where explanation is needed.

DEL KASARNY[2]
PRAHA–RUZYNE
7th IX' 45

---

2. Presumably written from the *Dělostřelecké kasárny*, artillery barracks, which is in Prague-Ruzyně. It was an SS barracks during the war. The same complex houses the present-day Czech Central Military Archives.

My dear Parents,

Well, what shall I head this, 'Mission to OPAVA' or Home again?' Anyway, here is all my news, although I have had no letters from you at all as yet. I hope there will be a <u>long</u> letter with all the news from lovely England in the parcel Joyce has for me. (Don't let the adjective in front of England give you any ideas, but without a doubt England is a more civilised country that the Č.S.R.)

So here I go, I will try to give you as fair a picture of my 14 days leave as I can. Obviously, I have small prejudices e.g. I know England, dislike the Russians but otherwise my observations might be near enough true, I hope. My plan was to go [to the house in Opava] and make a brief inspection, report to Dr. S. and then come on to England. Dr. S. expected difficulties and wanted Father [Bruno] to write all his stuff, house etc. in my name in England. With that, he wanted to dive into reclaiming the house. I left at 4.15 pm. There I might say I made my first contact with 'my people'. For Praha [Prague] is really very normal; except that people rush at trams and shout and quite a few dogs have Maulkorbs[3] *it might be an English town. Nearly – almost – but never.*

Well, here comes my first hearty dig at the Russians. They are pigs, totally primitive, uneducated beings. The ones that are here, anyway. But they all have revolvers and use them for all purposes. If they want a watch, a bike or even a place in a train they wave that thing about and that way usually get what they want. Thank God there are few of them now only left but I think I can fairly say that in places like Brno, Opava etc. everything the Germans did not take the Russians did. One thing they did by coming and staying, made certain that

---

3. *Maulkorb*, German, 'muzzle'. He has anglicised the plural with an 's'; the German plural is *Maulkörbe*.

Kommunism hasn't the slightest chance, for everyone has well and truly seen what it means in Russia. For a Russian to stop a lonely bicycle rider with a 'davoj masinko'[4] *is an everyday occurrence. If such a case gets reported, true enough, the thief gets at once shot but that isn't a remedy and just as appalling in a way.*

All the westerly forces greet each other with 'at sije zaped'[5] *and we stick very well together. Trains are at the moment very crowded and, as our people don't know what sorry means and in what way it must be accepted, there is usually a lot of shouting and swearing. Poor conductor. He has to beg everyone for the fair and they shout at him when he slips on someone's toes! The people are all OK but it is the education*[6] *that is bad. For they are terrible egoists and not in the least trained to be members of a human society. If you see what I mean. As the Russians turned out to be Liberators not only from the Germans but also most people's property, the people on the whole are very disappointed. At the moment I feel there is a lot of discontent and the courage to rebuild will not return as long as the Russians are amongst us. But you will hear all the Russian horror stories when you come, so I won't bother you.*

It is evening now, and I am back from a 2 hour ride, from a visit to Mr and Mrs. Sufanek. They live at the other end of town. I found them in a rather miserable mood but am glad to report, left them much happier. As for the parcel and letter it goes without saying thank you very much for both especially the coko.[7] *Your reward ought to be to see the shiny eyes it*

---

4. *Davoj masinko*, Czech-Russian, 'give me that' – literally 'hand over the machine'.
5. *Ať žije západ*, Czech, 'long live the West'.
6. 'Education' is probably translated from *Erziehung* in German, 'upbringing' in English.
7. *Čokoláda*, Czech, 'chocolate', *čoko* for short.

causes when offered to children who know it only by name but if under 6 have never tasted it.

By the way Father, I must tell you: I took some flowers to greet Joyce to Č.S.R. A pot of cyclamen. It worked wonders. I am only telling you because this was one of the many things I remember you used [to] and do, do. I only hope I shall be able to remember all the good habits both my parents have. Really I mean it! I realized on seeing Milos (who is a civilian already) that I left out a bit in my letter. I was supposed to see him on Wednesday outside the university [in Brno] for the interview with the Dean. (Wed. 22 Sep.) but I waited an hour, and he did not turn up. So, with beating heart I went alone and as expected, he did not take me till the next zapis.[8] I didn't like him much, he was rather ruff and explained that they had already more than 6 thousand Zuhörer[9] too many on the list. So I started my leave [from the RAF] with a rather defeated heart.

Our train arrived [in Brno] instead of at 9 p.m. (RYCHLIK[10]) at 1.30 am so I spent the first night in a hotel although it cost 85 Kr.[11] I was glad, for I had a bath and arrived well shaved and clean at about 11 am on 31 Hav. Ul.. Mrs Chalupas – rather wearily I thought – opened the door. As I had written she wasn't very surprised, not even enthusiastic. Brno is very damaged, and things aren't as they should be after the war – the Russians stole most clothes and silver etc. etc. from the Chalupas. So they, the old ones, are rather tired. But she is a very efficient woman and they are on the road again. As for

---

8. *Zápis*, Czech, 'admission'.
9. *Zuhörer*, German, 'enrolled students'.
10. RYCHLIK, express trains in Czechoslovakia (correctly: Rychlík, from *rychlý*, 'speed').
11. Kr.: *Kronen*, Czech currency. The situation with currency was chaotic after the war. The correct abbreviation of the Czechoslovak currency *koruna* was K.

food, all through the war her 'tuchtigkeit'[12] *kept them well supplied. He, and the sons and most members of the [?] relations had been in prison. concent.c., Mr. Chalupas 2 years I believe. To that she did wonders by sending parcels to lots of people, most of them Jews. She really is a very fine woman; you'll hear it all yourself no doubt. But I'll try to show how it was for me. I myself was annoyed at the state the town was in. No-one had even cleared the roads. And I realized for the first time what this Russian occupation meant to the Č.S.R.: 10 years back at least! We had very nice chats with Mrs Chalupas and we even got to know each other. I like Mrs. Chal. very much now, she is a very generous, kind, intelligent woman. I left at 11.15 pm to Ceska Trebova*[13] *changed then Okres Olomouc*[14] *to Svinov [near Ostrava]. Changed. To arrive in OPAVA at 11 a.m ...*

So here I was, I said to myself while thoughtfully climbing past Tante Grete's house. The garden showed about a year's unattention. In the house itself was a Public Kitchen. On past the missing BOZENA NEMCOVA.[15] *Past posts of Haltestelle.*[16] *Obviously there was a bus running up to us. Most of the houses showed hard signs of fighting. The few people I met obviously did not know my uniform and looked at it very doubtfully. Now I was in Karpluses*[17] *garden, I only just managed to get in through all the overgrown and uncontrolled bushes and vines. The little house with its cellar was a sad sight. Full of rubbish, everything torn down, but the*

---

12. *Tüchtigkeit*, German, 'diligence', 'hard work'.
13. Česká Třebová, Böhmisch Trübau in German.
14. Olmütz in German.
15. Božena Němcová, probably a memorial for the female Czech writer of the final phase of the Czech National Revival movement.
16. *Haltestelle*, German, 'bus stop'.
17. Irma and Alfred Karplus. Irma was Bruno's youngest sister, who also emigrated to England.

walls stand. That's the main thing. Even the sunwatch[18] *has lost its telling handle. I bet some Russian has it in his pocket, hoping to get 'casy'*[19] *from it. Yes, and there opposite was our house, our garden. A red rag was waving from the blitzableiter*[20] *near the chimney.*

The key I had did not fit so I wandered up to try the garage. Closed too, a mist-haufen[21] *inside it. Next door I hear a soothing voice. At once I recognized the younger one of our neighbour's daughters. She was pushing her baby up and down. 'Chcete neco?'*[22] *and then she recognized me and I answered their questions about 'Evika'*[23] *etc. That Evika was 'no vojne'*[24] *had always and everywhere a very marked effect. Over a schnaps we recalled Easter eggs and decided that our children shall have to carry on that habit. This time on my way past the elephant I managed to give him a hearty smile. I am sure he winked with one eye at me.*

As Chalupas had given me a letter of introduction to her brother the stavitel[25] *I made there then [a decision] as I expected I'd have to spend the night there. They, when they knew who I was were very sweet to me. They lent me a bike and I went straight to the NARODNY VYBOR.*[26] *Now here a word to the present organisation of things here: All Germans (T. Irma's Friedl*[27] *at the moment too) wear a big 'N' and are*

---

18. *Sonnenuhr* in German, literally 'sun' plus 'watch', meaning 'sundial'.
19. *Casy*, Russian-Czech, 'time' in the sense of clockwork.
20. *Blitzableiter*, German, 'lightening conductor'.
21. *Misthaufen*, German, 'rubbish pile'.
22. *Chcete něco*, Czech, 'Do you want something?' or 'What do you want?'
23. Evika, diminutive for Eva, my father's sister.
24. *No vojně*, Czech, 'in the war'/'in the military'.
25. *Stavitel*, Czech, 'builder'.
26. Národní výbor, the state administrative body in Czechoslovakia, 1945–1990.
27. Friedl, Irma's German friend.

on Jewish rations.²⁸ *A terrible revenge on them really. Are in camps and under restrictions. In charge of everything in each place are these NAR. V. a few good Czechs being its members. They, quite unqualified people, run their own villages. The whole thing is Russian and on very communistic lines.*

*Well, it was about 2 when I got there. 'May I speak with the President please?' 'Not here yet'. After an hour he came. 'I ... I used to live in Kylesovice 474' I stammered. He looked at me bluntly then: 'Oh, you mean what we call 'VOGEL VILLA!' You must be Mr. VOGEL'S son. Really glad to see you!!' And he shook my hand until it nearly dropped. When everyone had finished this so reassuring process and asked 'and when are they all coming?' etc. I managed to get my breath back. 'I knew the Vogels would be coming', said the secretary. The president agreed. 'So I let the roof be recovered', he said. 'Shame to let such a nice house be spoiled'. Before I knew it, one of them was with me on our way to inspect the house. Here and now I must once more take my hat off to both of you. Wherever I went Parents, I was very heartily and above all, sincerely, I think, greeted. Which made my whole job very easy. You are very obviously very popular amongst the people. Pravda vitezi!!*²⁹ *Doesn't it! You must be very good people which I didn't realise. I often thought that my welcome might be something like, 'When it looked bad you left, now that we are on top again, you come back'. But amongst all people who knew us it was, 'How right you were to leave, these swines would have killed you all, you are coming back, aren't you?! Doesn't matter if your father doesn't speak Czech, he'll manage!' And so he will.*

---

28. N stood for *Němec*, Czech, 'German'.
29. *Pravda vítězí*, Czech, 'truth prevails'. National motto of the Czech Republic, previously Czechoslovakia.

And so I looked over our house. I had to get in over our neighbours garden. Im 'Guck-ins-Land'[30] sind Schützenegraben,[31] die Tannen sind gefällt[32] and the 'Grube'[33] is (not quite) filled with a lot of rubbish. How very funny, I was startled with the smallness of everything I so well remembered. I used to take 3 steps, now one. I found the same in all our rooms, everything was so small. But the plums tasted the same, damn good. Now the less said about the state the house and garden are in the better. The walls stand, the rest can be put right again. From our things nothing is left, the Russians searched the house and made a very thorough job of it. The library room is least damaged of all. They obviously lived in the house to judge by all the nails everywhere in the wood, and walls where they hung up their things. Glass there is very little in the windows.

As for the garden ... The people who were the last domarcas[34] (the fourth in all, as Herr Thomas was not only a good but sehr[35] exact person) are perfect pigs. Their geese, goats and chickens run wild in the garden in our Wiese[36] they put in one row of potatoes; altogether the garden really needn't have been in a state it was in. So, very annoyed, the first thing I did was tell them to get out, very quickly. She mumbled something about she was going anyway, that a Sykora had already told them to go but she didn't listen to him. 'Sykora' I asked?? Sykora!!! Where are they? Birmanova 21. I left the man from the N.V. behind me and truly 'wie ein Blitz'[37] was there. An

---

30. *Guck-ins-Land*, German, 'lookout point'.
31. *Schützengraben*, German, 'trench'.
32. *Die Tannen sind gefällt*, German, 'the pine trees have been cut down'.
33. *Grube*, German, 'pit'.
34. Czech, meaning unclear – possibly *pan domácí*, 'landlord'.
35. *Sehr*, German, 'very'.
36. *Wiese*, German, 'field'/'garden'.
37. *Wie ein Blitz*, German, 'like lightening'.

unknown face shouted 'Honze je tuc'.[38] *And then Mr Sykora was embracing me and Mrs nearly kissed me. Dear, sweet loyal Sykoras. They had not forgotten us!! If I were their son, they couldn't have greeted one more heartily. I couldn't answer quickly enough. Buchty,*[39] *so good ones! And koffy appeared from nowhere. But it is impossible to explain in 100 such pages what they did for me. Kindness radiated from them. 'Your father did so much for us too and Mutti, is she still so pretty, pretty? pretty?' Yes, I answered them!! About 6 we had quietened down and just grinned at each other. Mr. Sykora was so very proud of me, he kept saying he knew I'd be in the forces, he stroked me, just like a father. And he said he feels like one to me. How very nice people you must be Mother and Father!! The Sykoras, just think, wanted to move into our house as before again, only the bastards didn't let them in. Said they had no authority.*[40] *Poor Mr Sykora. He was supposed to be executed. 7 days before the date, he was liberated by the Americans. He was in a C.C. for over 2 years. Oh, what a good man he is. I never met the goodness of a person before.*

In my eagerness, I left straight away, well, after being filled with all the best they could offer to see Uncle Edi.[41] *Well, while all the news was being told Mr. Hellmann soon appeared. He looks very thin, mager,*[42] *old. He didn't recognise me. But then he too embraced me. His spirits are very high. I am amazed at his cheerfulness. He needs nothing he told me and seems to be really happy. The sooner Tante Litta*[43] *comes the better! At the moment he has no disadvantage as the Czechs are very decent. He is being tolerated. His*

---

38. *Honze je tuc*, Czech, 'Hans is here' (correctly: *Honza je tu*).
39. *Buchty*, Czech, small cakes.
40. Authority, probably from *Authorität*, German, 'permission'.
41. Eduard Hellmann, a German, husband of Melitta.
42. *Mager*, German, 'gaunt'.
43. Melitta Hellmann, née Wilhelm, another of my father's aunts; Marianne's sister.

disadvantage is that he has half tickets [rations] for food. All Jews are now being accepted by the Czechs as Czechs. Before they made differences between Germans and Czech Jews but now this has been changed. He lives in a bottom Wohnung[44] *but it is not at all bad. He has some sort of a woman who looks (and did so all the war it seems) after him. I left him soon. Just think!! He DOES NOT SMOKE!!*

Back to Sykoras and my first night in under a real 'Federbett.[45] *The afternoon with Mrs. Chalupas [and] relatives for tea and another visit to our neighbours who loaded me with apples for you, which at the time I had hoped to deliver. Monday morning I left. Mr. S. insisted on my taking 500 Kr.*[46] *Mrs. S. gave me food and two lovely huge pears to bring to you.*

The Jelinek boy, although only a half Jew is in charge of the Kultusgemeinde[47] *there. Poor chap. During German occupation in OPAVA there were over 26 registered half Jews. Now his register shows 126, all people who are now Jews in order to be saved from internment. His mother is a very depressing person; the only nice thing she said was that IVO*[48] *was much too great a firm to be a concurrence*[49] *for her.*

Arrived Tuesday in Praha. Reported to Dr. Sob. He was content but still wanted Father to write over all property. As I intended to see you, I thought I'd talk it over with you anyway. Left Tuesday afternoon for England. So I thought then, I regret I did a very stupid thing. Instead of waiting for a plane straight to England, I took a plane to Paris where I thought it

---

44. *Wohnung*, German, 'flat'/'apartment'.
45. *Federbett*, German, 'duvet'.
46. *Krone*, legal tender, *koruna*; Kč, abbreviation from 1919 to 1938.
47. *Kultusgemeinde*, German, Jewish religious community.
48. IVO Tapestries was the company Bruno's mother Johanna founded; Irma inherited IVO in 1931.
49. Concurrence, from *Konkurrenz*, German, 'competition'.

ought to be easy to get to London. When I got to Paris they wanted to look me up. Panic everywhere. Frenchmen, their hands flying all over the place discussing everything. Not at all approving of their ideas and finally seeing I'll never get onto a London plane from there, I came back to Praha. This was on Friday morning. On arrival I heard that the Meteorolok [50] report was bad for three days. These three days I didn't want to lose so off once more to Brno.

My own personal problem is this. Should I study or should I take over a big farm of 70 hectares or even one of 150 hectares which they would have given me. Given. All near OPAVA, one in Litultovice. They would have even given me its previous German owner to work for and under me. Just think. In OPAVA that, then on to the Agric. School. I found that they will have a 5 month course every winter for 2 years. Making a complete course in 2 years. All I would need I thought was a motor bike to get there and back and all would be ok. But I also thought 1) You'd be cross 2) that to have a title which a university offers is perhaps better if I did not want to stay for ever on a farm. So I left that to let myself be definitely registered in Brno at the University for Agriculture there. There they are not overfilled and were very sweet and helpful.

Going to Chalupas was like going home this time, I really like them. He was charming and insisted that if I do get my discharge [from the RAF] and come studying to Brno I must live in their house. That would help a lot in the money way, although it will have its drawbacks. The biggest plus will be their social life. I think Vlaso [their son] will be able to introduce me to lots of nice chaps etc. So I think I am decided to go all out to study in Brno. They might let me have a year

---

50. *Meteorologická předpověď*, Czech, 'weather forecast'.

which would mean that in 1948 I'd be an Ing.⁵¹ – if I pass the exams!! The studious atmosphere of their home should help. Otherwise of Jewish friends only Marianne Müller was living she said.

Off to OPAVA again, this time I found Gert⁵² + wife. My 100 cig gift didn't even provoke a thank you. He looks well, has no doubt suffered, but is the sort of kind of what to me now is an unsympathetic, all-knowing person. He is very charming really but just not my type. The sort of man who thrives – and did thrive – on the black market. As for his wife, she too is a half Jewess and definitely his type, far from being my and Father's type though.

Gert was all for my taking some sort of a factory with him. Now here is another problem, one which really needs a chat. In Opava and all around are factories. Places which belonged to the Germans, they all are crying out for managers. If Father were to come for a visit to OPAVA he could come and choose. Then I as a returning fighter could claim it and get it!! Hand it to Father and that would be that. Really, that's how simple it appears to be. Mendek for example has already a huge shop next to the Krone.⁵³ Amongst other people, he came to me and asked when Father would return to Opava. (Herr Leduer is at the moment busy repairing locks everywhere, they say he was a beast.) He obviously wanted to work for Father, so does Mr. Gansmann, and he told me that in Wagenstadt⁵⁴ there was an undestroyed factory for Kunst-seide⁵⁵ standing idle. How about it, Father? Really, right now lots of things are to be had

---

51. *Ing.*: *Ingenieur*, German, 'engineer'.
52. Gerhard (Gert) Hellmann, Melitta and Eduard Hellmann's son, a cousin of my father.
53. *Krone*, German, 'crown'. The Crown was a pub in Opava.
54. He may have meant Wagstadt, now Bílovec, about 30km south of Opava.
55. *Kunstseide*, German, synthetic sewing thread.

for the asking. As for your factory, it must have been burned by pouring petrol on it. I don't understand such things but I think it is a total loss. The only thing I did there was to tear down the big swastika that had withstood all fire.

So personally, why not try to get here and have a look around yourself. Sykoras would be delighted to feed you!

Re. house. Gert will live there now, as soon as we get some furniture from the Narod. Vybor. I handed the whole house over to him officially for the time being. They did it all at the N.V. in Kylesvice for me. Wrote out my application to be possessor of the house till Father comes and hand it over to Gert during my absence. Really most helpful people. Cigarettes no doubt played a major role in most of my actions. And I still have 3 hundert. If I were to sell them 3000 Kc.

Ran into Mr. Köppler who, how he doesn't know lived through it all in Theresienstadt. He has all the information. Tells of T. Grete's terrific 'Tüchtigkeit'. She had, in camp, the whole organisation for the Laundry for 46,000 people under her. Just think! But even that did not help her, she and T. Else[56] finally left for Poland. He [Mr Köppler] took me to see Friedl. He says she saved his life and did wonders.

Yes, a deep bow to Friedl; one of the finest, most unselfish women I ever met. She is although now persecuted as a German (she had to join the Partei[57] to keep the shop of KOPPLERS) is so cheerful and only wanted to know how the Karpluses are, what they are doing etc. etc. etc. She, good soul, thinks Tante Grete might live because last autumn she quite unexpectedly received a postcard from her. I wonder. It was

---

56. Else Federmann, another of my father's aunts, Bruno's younger sister who did not flee.
57. *Partei*, German, political party, NSDAP (Nazi party).

her who told me that T. Martha is well and fit. Together they regularly sent parcels and really risked their necks. Friedl is a darling, a national hero! But very unrecognised at the moment. I was glad to be able to help them with coffee and powdered egg. etc.

On returning to Praha I applied for Demobilisation. As it is I hope to be a fully fashioned civilian in 5 days. Now you must admit, it couldn't be better, could it?

Now let me try and sum up.

1. There is a great deal of disorder here.

2. The people are, in comparison uneducated in the social line.

3. The people are very democratic, I am sure, it is part of their very life.

4. All Jews are now being accepted as Czechs.

5. German speaking people are obviously unpopular but not a bit fanatic about it. In Opava people are tolerant.

6. As far as I see, nothing is officially in the way if you wish to return.

7. Mr. Sykora says definitely YES, come by all means.

8. OPAVA is 80% burnt out (by the Germans). If you come it would obviously mean a step down on the social sphere.

9. There is still a certain uncertainty here in respect of the Russians, the Poles and there is frequent talk of a third war.

10. In my opinion if you really still want to come back, now is the time. The sooner the better. People will get easier used to you, while things are still unsettled and jobs still free. And here is my opinion: The first year will be hard, there might not

be much coal etc. but come soon if you don't fear hard work. If you do come, prosperity will be your reward.

Re. house. If I get my discharge, I shall have a month in civis before starting school [university]. I will spend that time getting everything as ship-shape as possible. Germans are to be had for such work daily. So we ought to make the house liveable before you return. What worries me is money. Should I borrow 50000 from Mrs. Chalupa? She offered. The house will need a stavitel[58] you know, as it is a bit knocked about from that explosion, when the bridge went up.

At the moment there ought to be enough money for my discharge for a start, anyway. As for your reply, well? Everything depends on it. I don't think letters are censored anymore but write carefully anyway. Kommunists are stupid and have lost all hopes they ever had, but they are still active.

Well, I hope I did not miss out any major issue. If I did, I'll write again. Eva – tell her that ČSR is at her knees, really waiting for her to come back. There will not be the slightest difficulty. Even if she is in civilian when she comes, she must wear her uniform. It not only is a big plus but everyone here is wearing one. Tell her to come soon, English lessons are waiting for her in OPAVA.

I'd better start another page, I remembered I didn't answer your letter as yet. Before I do so here is something for you only Mother. Onkel Edi says T. Litta should come as soon as possible. So she should. There is NO obstacle in her way. She would have the peace she so much longs for and deserves. But, judging from Gert's remarks it would appear that this woman who works for O. Edi is on quite intimate terms with him. So I don't know?? But O. Edi definitely wants T. Litta to come, the

---

58. *Stavitel*, Czech, 'builder'.

sooner the better! Anything like shirts etc., will be welcomed by Gert and O. Edi.

By the by, our house stands in Ul. Jos. Stalina!!![59] *Well, have to rename that. Good old Winnie*[60] *ought to be remembered too I think!*

About university, it's a good idea. As there is very little written work for a start, I am not terribly worried. My Czech has improved already and I don't find reading in Czech so tiring anymore. Czech matura[61] *would be much harder, even impossible within a year.*

For myself, I am on top of my ladder, perfectly happy, very content. Things couldn't be better. At the end of this month, I will know if the university really will take me, but I am 99% sure they will. By the way, on finishing my studies here I STILL will have my choice whether here or anywhere in the world. See, OK?

By the way, I am convinced that in all Europe the Czechs (except Switzerland) are by far the most advanced in the world already. Here there is really a democratic people.

Well, that would seem all. News about Dr. Sob., demob. and final acceptance at Univer. etc. will follow by post (Air mail) from now on, Love to you all, hope your spirits are as high as mine!! Yours HPV.

In the months after finding the letter in 2011, I read it again and again. I typed it up and translated the phrases and words that were not in English. I became familiar with and 'worked' with the letter. It

---

59. *Ul. Jos. Stalina*, Czech, 'Joseph Stalin Road'.
60. Winnie: Winston Churchill (1874–1965), British Prime Minister during the Second World War.
61. *Matura*, Czech, university entrance exams.

stood out from the dozens of other letters because of how my father, as a young man, vividly described the situations and people he encountered during his return to Opava. He tried to capture and relate everything in detail to his parents. A sense of honesty and a tone of urgency and excitement permeate the letter, and there is a dash of youthful naivete too. His writing that everything in the house seemed so small (because he was now bigger) especially touched me. He captured the coming together of his thirteen-year-old self with his twenty-year-old self and experienced, on a physical level, the difference between them. He literally shared having perceived how he had grown during the previous six years. Possibly, at that moment, he also touched within himself all that had happened in those six years. The plums from the garden still tasted good, and he seems to be touching base with their (past) house and home. It's as if he was sending reassurance through consistency to his parents: 'So much can happen and be destroyed but the fruit in our garden is still damn good'.

He wove in the different languages with ease, making me feel that my father was a European. He had had a sense of trepidation regarding how he'd be received upon returning to Opava after the war. He was relieved at the warmth with which people of his childhood responded to him upon this return. His mention of a *Federbett*, a duvet, is touching because one of the few things I know about his boarding school experience when he came to England is that sheets and blankets were not something he adapted easily to; he felt trapped when he was tucked in. He would loosen the sheets and blankets because he was used to sleeping under a *Federbett*.

The letter also depicts his resourcefulness in travelling around Europe – to Prague, to Opava, to Brno, to Paris, to Opava again and then back to London in the aftermath of the war, the continent in ruins. This demonstrates his courage, self-confidence and tenacity. It is surprising that the trains were even running, illustrating that relatively little of Czechoslovakia was damaged during the war, compared with other countries. He mentions visiting the ruins of Bruno's Gütermann factory and removing a swastika. This is a small, disturbing fact that he shared with his parents, symbolic and poignant.

He signed the letter *HPV* for Hans-Peter Vogel (or Hanuš, the Czech version of his name). Using initials to sign off when writing to one's parents seemed strange to me. Through studying his letters, I sensed my father had an identity issue, and his signature using initials (and how he referred to himself with different names) was a manifestation of that. He wrote with a bit of pride about his aunt, having heard that Grete was responsible for organising the laundry in Theresienstadt. This is something that I have not been able to verify, but Friedl, a family friend had received a postcard from her the year before, 1944 (after she had been transported from Theresienstadt to Auschwitz in December 1943, as I later discovered). Reading my father write that Grete and Else finally 'had to leave for Poland' was heartrending for me; it was his very roundabout way of saying the Nazis murdered them. Two months later, on 19 November 1945, my father wrote to his parents with news of Marianne's mother (his maternal grandmother) following a visit to someone called Marianne Feuerstein:

> *I might as well tell you that our Grossmama* [Therese] *was with them in T.* [Theresienstadt] *She even lived with them for some time – until she was sent to Poland. I am sorry to have to put this so bluntly, but I must tell you that Marianne says she was, while with them, really cheerful and strong all the time, almost thriving she said.*

That someone was 'almost thriving' in Theresienstadt seems highly doubtful, and he is tactfully glossing over things for his mother to avoid anguishing her. But 'strong' and 'cheerful' sound plausible, and this was possibly part of Therese's natural resilience. The use of these figures of speech – 'leave for Poland', 'sent to Poland' – suggests that the phrases were already used in the family. The horrendous truth about concentration camps and gas chambers was still emerging, and, as the family must have had no word for a long time from Grete, her husband Eduard, Else, her husband Karl or Therese, they must have talked about the likelihood that none had survived. In one letter, my father wrote about his family then corrected himself to 'what is left of it'. As I was to learn later, Bruno and Marianne were able to confirm the truth about the fate of their family members only thirty years later, in the mid-1970s.

The following chapters are devoted to the lives of family members I knew and those unspoken relatives I drew out of history, and how I learned more about them and their fate through studying my father's letters. I draw on their own accounts which have survived the years. My cousin Julia, Eva's daughter, contributed notably. I researched in various archives and books to reconstruct the lives of the family members I had never heard of. While I have tried to embed the narrative within correct and factual historical context, my emphasis is on what these people lived through before, during and after the war (if they survived). I wanted to come close to their lived experience. My main research and writing began in summer 2021.

5 BRUNO
1885–1979

We who have been torn loose from all roots that held us, we, always beginning anew ...

Stefan Zweig[1]

One dreary winter's morning in 2021, while the fourth Covid wave had Germany in its grip, I woke up realising that I'd only known Bruno for a fragment of his life. I worked it out: it was around 23 per cent – the other 77 per cent was unknown to me. And my 23 per cent was hardly a very conscious wedge of relationship; I was a child for most of that time. But while he was alive, I'd known him 100 per cent of my life. Writing this book feels like mining the remaining 77 per cent, respecting that I cannot do someone else's life full justice, especially when they are not there to ask and had lived for an amazingly long ninety-four years. While he was alive, I was too

---

1. Stefan Zweig, *The World of Yesterday: An Autobiography*, p. 43. Bruno and Zweig were distant cousins and their families stemmed from the same area in Moravia. Austro-Jewish author Stefan Zweig lived from 1881 to 1942; his great despair about the war led to his suicide when he was 61 years old.

young to think in this way or to ask. My guess is that Bruno would have been evasive and avoided answering anyway. When I look back at our communication and interactions, my grandparents, Marianne and Bruno, were like people without pasts.

Over time and as I grew familiar with my father's letters to his parents, long-dead relationships within the family and the unspoken past re-emerged. I glimpsed how the nuclear family – Marianne, Bruno, Eva, Hans-Peter – was before I had known them. Bruno, who had been close and gentle to me as a grandfather, was forty when his wife Marianne gave birth to my father in June 1925. As I studied my father's letters, Bruno appeared as a strict and distant father to his growing son. In contrast, it was clear that mother and son had a close and warm relationship. In the following, I have reconstructed the first part of Bruno's life from what I found in the old suitcase at my mother's house.

Born in Jägerndorf (now Krnov), 16 July 1885, into the 'World of Yesterday', Bruno had a unique position within his family as he was the only son of Johanna and Ludwig Vogel's four children. He came after Grete but before Else and Irma. This Jewish family may already have been assimilated and no longer observant – possibly meaning they had stopped going to the synagogue and celebrating Jewish holidays or keeping the Sabbath.

Bruno was good at school, as a copy of an 1891 primary school report shows. His sisters almost certainly had no opportunity to go away to continue their studies after leaving school, but Bruno did. He went to the Technikum Mittweida[2] in the central German state of Saxony to study mechanical engineering. There he met Heinz Gütermann. When he was twenty-two years old, his parents divorced – something rare in those days. As the family story goes, Ludwig, Bruno's father, mistreated Johanna, which was the reason for their separating. I

---

2. Mittweida is now in eastern Germany.

found a photo of Ludwig looking uneasily into the camera. He was in the sewing and material trade: a cloth manufacturer, born on 2 November 1854. I don't know the date of his death; he has slipped from family history, shunned for being violent to Johanna, but his line is the one connected to Zweig.

Johanna set up her company, IVO Tapestries,[3] after the divorce, and IVO became successful. The black-and-white photo of a smiling woman in Bruno's study that I'd stared at as a child was Johanna, not Irma, but mother and daughter looked alike in old age. I found the original photo in the suitcase full of jumbled family documents and mementos at my mother's house when I started my research. It surprises me that this one image from my grandfather's study in Ealing has stayed in my mind through the years, as there were dozens of pictures on the wall of his study, opposite the large desk. This one image has stuck; the photo of his mother was a visual, silent link to Bruno's unspoken past, and I now imagine Bruno looked at it frequently. Perhaps I picked that up as a child during the many hours we spent together in his study on rainy days during visits.

There are numerous possessions of Bruno's which are still with me, like a web of invisible, minute umbilical cords to him and days gone by. They sit there quietly as if I am still connected to him and he is still here, looking after me, giving me input and talking to me at length, showing me things he thinks I should know. I have his Rolleiflex camera and his British Isles stamp collection, and my son owns his 1920s Leitz binoculars, which my father gave him (Leitz later became part of the well-known Leica group). Bruno's slide rule from his studies at university before the First World War is still around, as is a medal he was given during that war for bravery, and a pair of gold cufflinks that may have been given to him as a retirement present. Besides these objects, I own dozens of documents, letters,

---

3. IVO is a corruption of Johanna Vogel. The 'J' became an 'I' followed by VO, the first two letters of her surname.

official papers, drawings and watercolours – Bruno was an accomplished artist. Some of these things were in the suitcase at my mother's house, some I'd inherited during my childhood and had kept. While initially working through everything, starting with the task of reconstructing family history, I suddenly had the strange feeling that all of these things had been patiently incubating in the dark through the years. As if they had been waiting for me to puzzle everything together and write about my paternal family.

A remarkable document was a letter Bruno wrote as a thirty-year-old lieutenant of the Austro-Hungarian army during the First World War, dated 30 December 1915, which has survived in excellent condition. The illustration he sent to the people he was writing to demonstrates his drawing skills and eye for detail. It is a sketch of his underground home, and he writes about what they had to eat. He seems quite content with his situation. His handwriting, which became dear and familiar to me, is clear and flowing.

Another object that Bruno left was an unpublished book. It tells the story of his time as a prisoner of war in Siberia during the First World War. As far as I know, it was written in the 1960s with his English teacher to practise his English (which was necessary), around forty-five years after he had been freed from the camp in 1919. The narrative often sounds (as Julia once said) as if he had a jolly good time. While it is a fascinating document, revealing how enterprising Bruno was, it is stilted in style. The fort-five-page book does not seem to be Bruno's true voice, and the author's soul doesn't come across. I believe Bruno never really found his voice in English during his forty years in England. (He'd say 'cheerio', meaning goodbye, instead of 'cheers' when toasting someone, which made people smile. He'd probably been told what was correct by Marianne, but the mistake stuck.) As I had read numerous letters in German that Bruno wrote, I was familiar with his written voice: courteous but to the point and with a meticulous use of words. That quality does not come over in his book *Behind the Scenes in a Siberian War Prisoner Camp*. His daughter Eva illustrated the book; she had inherited his artistic skills. His four years in Siberia must have profoundly influenced him, but being a prisoner of war was an experience that Bruno never spoke of. At least there is a written record of it.

Susan Groag Bell (1926–2015), a Jewish Czech-American historian specialising in women's studies, was born in Troppau in the same decade as my father. She wrote about what happened to her father during the First World War. Possibly, her father and Bruno were in the same camp in Siberia. Her father was also a soldier in the Austrian army, was captured by the Russians and was interned in Siberia. After the end of the First World War, he 'returned to Europe with a shipload of other captured Austrian officers via China, San Francisco, and the Panama Canal because of the Russian revolution. He spoke seldom of this period.'[4] My mother recalls that Bruno mentioned returning from Siberia via the Panama Canal, and the closing sentences in his book are:

> *when I learned the next Czech draft would be leaving Tomsk to return home via Vladivostock* [coastal city, Russian Pacific Ocean] *at the end of September, my name was one of the first on the list, and I spent the last few days straightening my affairs and putting my house in order generally. Little did I know my journey* [home] *was to take me all around the world and that it would be another whole year before I saw my relatives and friends again.*[5]

The soldiers returned to an entirely different country. In their absence, the Czechoslovak Republic had been created in the wake of the collapse of the Habsburg Empire after the First World War. Troppau, the town's German name, became its second name. In

---

4. Groag Bell, p. 12.
5. Bruno Vogel, *Behind the Scenes in a Siberian War Prisoner Camp* (unpublished, ca. 1965), p. 44.

Czech it was now Opava; Czech had become the official language. Groag Bell explains why my father (born 1925) spoke both German and Czech while Bruno only spoke German. Troppau, she notes, then had a population of 40,000 inhabitants and most spoke an Austrian variety of German, while the rural population in the surrounding countryside spoke Czech. This was a centuries-old pattern, established during the old multi-ethnic Habsburg Empire. The Austrian minority had ruled over its far-flung subjects, which included Czechs, Slovaks and Hungarians, and Serbs, among others. After the First World War, the town became part of the new Czechoslovak Republic under president Tomáš Garrigue Masaryk. Czech was decreed the official language and Prague became the national capital. The Czechoslovak government aimed to make Czech the dominant language, and hence Troppau became Opava. However, the new Republic's tolerance meant that children could attend either Czech or German schools that coexisted. German-speaking children had to learn to speak and write Czech in school, and both languages were freely used. My father probably spoke German at home and Czech at school.

The First Czechoslovak Republic existed only twenty short years (1918–1938) before it got caught up in the run-up to the Second World War. My grandfather set up the Gütermann factory in Troppau/Opava soon after his return from Russia, and by 1929 he had built a large house for his family. The family's area of the Czechoslovak Republic was sacrificed in March 1938 to Hitler in the Münchener Abkommen,[6] the Munich Agreement (widely referred to simply as 'Munich' as the agreement was signed there) in which Britain, Italy and France had decided, without consulting the Czechoslovak government, to relinquish the German-speaking part of the country called the Sudetenland for the sake of keeping the peace. Madeleine Albright (who was born in Prague and became US

---

6. www.youtube.com/watch?v=7-sByElE9a4: a short video explaining the development of the crisis.

secretary of state from 1997 to 2001) notes in her book: 'In the end, Munich had three losers: Czechoslovakia, England, and France; it had two winners: Hitler and Stalin. That's a fair one-sentence summary of a historic disaster.'[7]

I imagine that Bruno and Marianne were acutely aware of political developments and of danger because they were Jewish, even if they were non-observant and had christened their children out of fear of antisemitism. The Nazi's antisemitic Nuremberg Laws had increased the tension since 1935. I own the little notebook in which Bruno did his accounting and see that he ceased his bookkeeping in the summer of 1938. I think that by then, they had already decided to leave; their involuntary emigration to England seems to have been carefully planned. I imagined the many hushed evening discussions before they left. With his sister Grete and her husband Eduard. With Melitta, Marianne's sister. And with his youngest sister Irma and her husband, Alfred. Likewise with Therese, Marianne's mother, who lived nearby; it was a close-knit family. Therese must have known of their plans and possibly encouraged them to flee with their children – her grandchildren. Bruno's other sister, Else, and her husband, Karl, lived 35 kilometres away from Troppau in Ostrau; they may not have been as close regarding the planning. Bruno seems to have had no illusions that his service in the Austro-Hungarian army during the First World War would protect him, and I sense Marianne's pragmatic stance regarding the decision to emigrate. The German army began crossing into the Sudetenland on 1 October 1938 and occupied the area without firearms being used. On 5 October, the Jewish Day of Atonement, President Beneš of Czechoslovakia resigned from his office under Nazi pressure and sought political asylum in France. A third of Czechoslovak territory and population was ceded. A day after Reichskristalnacht, 9-10 November, the synagogue in Troppau had been burned down. It was not 'just' one

---

7. Albright, pos. 175 (chapter 8, paragraph 20).

night, though; between 7 and 13 November 1938, more than 1,400 synagogues and thousands of shops, homes and cemeteries of Jewish people were destroyed. About 30,000 Jews were arrested and sent to concentration camps. Hundreds took their own lives.[8]

These happenings obliterated twenty years of Czech independence, and the areas called Bohemia and Moravia were soon incorporated into the German Empire and became the so-called 'Protectorate' on 16 March 1939 after the invasion the day before.

One of the most gripping pieces of Bruno's surviving writing is from late 1938, not long after the November pogrom and after he and Marianne had left Troppau but had not yet reached a safe haven. He was fifty-three at the time, a difficult age to start anew. Bruno called the following document his curriculum vitae, and he seems to be taking stock of himself and his life. This is different from the modern format of a CV as we understand it today; curriculum vitae content has changed through time. I am not sure who this CV was intended for, because the plan was to work for the English Gütermann branch in Ealing near London, and they wouldn't have needed such a document because the company already knew him well. Perhaps he wrote it to reassure himself of his abilities on the cusp of a transition to a new life in a country whose language he did not speak. Or maybe he was not sure that working for the Gütermanns – which was, after all, a German company – would work out, and he'd have to present himself to another employer. In the upper right-hand corner of the CV he wrote the place – 'Prag'. 'Zollikon' has been crossed out. He must have started the document before leaving Opava and written where he thought he would be writing it – Zollikon, Switzerland – before later replacing the location with 'Prag'. He was not as far away from home when he began to write as he'd expected to be. Bruno crossed out some parts of this document; they were slightly more emotive passages. He was trying to be concise about what he had

---

8. https://de.wikipedia.org/wiki/Novemberpogrome_1938.

already accomplished in life, but he also seemed to be defining himself as a person. I have translated from German.

Prag ~~Zollikon~~, 30. Nov. 1938

Bruno Vogel curriculum vitae.

I was born in Jägerndorf [Krnov], *then Austrian monarchy, on July 16, 1885. My father was a cloth manufacturer. After graduating from secondary school, I worked as a trainee for one and a half years in a machine factory of the Guttsmann brothers in Breslau. Then I fulfilled my military duty and became a reserve officer. Then I studied technology with great success and received a mechanical and electrical engineer certificate. I immediately got a job at Maschinenbau A.G. Balcke in Bochum* [Germany], *where I worked in the design office as an assembly and materials testing engineer, and finally in the Berlin branch as an acquisition engineer. During this time, I also represented the branch managers of our plants in Vienna and Katowice on a case-by-case basis. In 1916, I was taken prisoner of war in Siberia. I took the first opportunity to create a production of sealing varnish, ink and other products lacking there, which I had to do with the most primitive means, without any capital, from scratch, mainly by reinventing the production path. Soon I managed to supply all the critical stores in Tomsk and to create excellent living conditions for* [myself and] *many others. The chemical factory 'Orion', Tomsk, my competitor, contacted me to hire me as the head of their factory. I accepted this offer. Not knowing the Russian language, I nevertheless succeeded in reorganising the primitive factory and making it exceptionally productive, considering the conditions there.*

After my journey home in 1920, which took me around the world, I received an order from Gütermann & Co. to start a

> *new factory in Czechoslovakia. Gütermann and Co. commissioned me to build a sewing silk factory in the Czechoslovak Republic, of which I am a citizen. I was entrusted with the entire production, starting with the acquisition of the land for the factory, through the elaboration of the construction plans, the appropriate installation of the whole plant, the training of an utterly untrained workforce, as well as the organization of the purchasing and sales apparatus.*

This document gave me a good summary of Bruno's professional life, but I missed the personal information: he was married and the father of two children. He states that he is a citizen of the Czechoslovak Republic, and he does this almost pointedly. Unsurprisingly, Bruno emphasises this because he was a German speaker, and the country he was heading to was trying to appease Germany to avoid war. Bruno's identity beyond any official documents was, however, Austrian. He felt himself to be a citizen of an empire that no longer existed; maybe he felt he was Czech by 'historical accident'.

Getting into England was an uncertain affair. Louise London, herself a daughter of two Jewish immigrants and author of a book on these difficult times, notes, 'To escape from the Nazis, resourcefulness and money and support from family, friends and strangers were necessary, but rarely sufficient'.[9] While Jewish organisations played a significant role in supporting emigration, raising money and approaching the government to increase the numbers granted asylum, leaders of such organisations were also cautious because of their fears of antisemitism. London concludes in her book that the plight of Jews ranked low on the British government's priorities list, with letting Jews into the country assessed against national self-interest. Irma's account in Chapter 7 is first-hand testimony of these politics. Britain, therefore, took a stance like other countries,

---

9. Louise London, *Whitehall and the Jews, 1938–1958: British Immigration Policy, Jewish Refugees and the Holocaust*, p. 6.

including France, the Netherlands and Belgium, of offering temporary refuge but not settlement, even in the face of unprecedented atrocities. London suggests that the British government's stance was more 'what to do with the Jews' rather than setting a precedent for saving them.

It must have been a tense and unsure few months of listening to the news on the radio and studying the papers before they left Switzerland to arrive in London in spring 1939. After they left Opava, it is unclear how long my father's family stayed in Prague and later in Zollikon, a municipality of Zurich, Switzerland, close to Heinz Gütermann's family, late in 1938. A letter shows that they had arrived in England from Switzerland by March 1939. Several different sources lead me to believe that the phase after leaving Opava and arriving in England was five months.

Bruno and Marianne were christened during this time in Switzerland, as an attempt, so my mother told me, to make it easier to 'get into England' (although the UK did not have regard to such things). Marianne's notes on one of my father's letters suggest that he went to grammar school in Prague for at least a month.

In Bruno's obituary in the internal Gütermann newsletter,[10] the following passage was published:

> *Bruno Vogel was given only 15 years for his work on setting up the company in Troppau. New war clouds were gathering on the horizon. When our troops occupied the Sudetenland in 1938 – in peacetime – Bruno Vogel moved the headquarters of the Czech Gütermann branch to Prague. But even there, he found no peace, and moved on to Heinz Gütermann in Zurich and then on to Gert Gütermann, the brother of Kurt [Gütermann] in England. The year was 1939, and right at the*

---

10. *Das Schachbrett*, 151 (April 1980).

beginning of the war Gert Gütermann was interned in England as a German. When Gert Gütermann wanted to sail to Canada, his ship was torpedoed by a German submarine. Gert Gütermann is buried on one of the Scottish islands.

Three phrases in this short passage need looking at more closely. 'He found no peace' is evasive. Writing 'Bruno was Jewish, the Nazis were antisemitic, and he had to flee his country to save himself and his family' would have been more accurate. The Gütermann family also has Jewish roots, but family members I know are vague or evasive about this. In the same vein, to say 'he moved on' circumvents the issue: Bruno and his family emigrated because they were Jewish. 'Moving on' does not come even close to describing the uprooting of the family. A further inaccuracy concerns Gert Gütermann, one of Heinz's thirty cousins, and also explains why it was so important for Bruno to begin working in England. Writing that Gert 'wanted to sail to Canada' misrepresents the fact that during the Second World War, German, Austrian and Italian civilians who were believed to be a potential threat to Britain's war effort were interned and likewise subjected to involuntary emigration.

Alexandra Gütermann's second family history book states that this was indeed Gert's fate and that he was made to sail on the *Arandora Star* in 1940. A German submarine torpedoed it on 2 July 1940, killing eight hundred people. The sinking of the *Arandora Star*, which was on its way to Canada with internees, is well documented. Shortly before 7am, the ship was struck, and thirty-five minutes after impact it sank. A month afterwards, bodies washed up on the Irish coast and Scottish shores; many could be identified as passengers from the *Arandora Star*.[11] Gert Gütermann had been the technical manager of the English branch, Gütermann Sewing Silks Ltd, since 1925. He'd studied in America and spoke perfect English. Gert's

---

11. https://de.wikipedia.org/wiki/Versenkung_der_Arandora_Star.

tragic death at the hands of fellow countrymen meant that Bruno was more urgently needed at the English Gütermann site to compensate for the loss of Gert's expertise.

Bruno and Marianne, Eva and Hans flew by plane from Switzerland to England, as my mother told me. Initially, Bruno and Marianne lived in a boarding house called Hotel Averard at Lancaster Gate, and their children were immediately sent to boarding school. How was this financially possible? Perhaps they had taken money with them to Switzerland or had sent money to England in good time as they prepared to leave?

By summer 1939, Bruno and Marianne had moved west from central London to 15 Freeland Road, Ealing Common, as a letter written by Bruno on 7 July 1939 to Frank Muller-Steffens shows. Muller-Steffens was a German-speaking colleague in the Gütermann Company, possibly of Swiss nationality but working in Paris. Bruno wrote with great relief that he'd been granted a work permit for a year just that day. In the copy of the letter, Bruno mentions that 'Herr Richard' [Gütermann] had just left London. Richard Gütermann (1892–1979), another cousin of Heinz, had been helping Bruno find his feet in the London branch, which was renamed Sewing Silks Ltd and ran under the Swiss company Interfina. Muller-Steffens' original typed answer to Bruno has also survived the years, dated 10 July 1939. He confirms having received Bruno's letter of 7 July and is delighted about Bruno's work permit news. He adds that the permit will give Bruno and his family 'inner peace', and encouragingly suggests that getting an extension to the permit will almost certainly pose no problem. Muller-Steffens wrote from Paris, and expresses hope that a war will not happen. But in that eventuality, he reckoned with German people working at the English Gütermann branch being interned, as happened with Gerd Gütermann.

Bruno kept a handwritten letter from Muller-Steffens, written after war had broken out. Muller-Steffens reports that he had relocated to Davos Dorf in Switzerland and was living in the Derby Hotel. The letter is dated 27 December 1939 and is addressed to Bruno, who was now living with his wife Marianne at 62 Hanger Lane, Ealing.[12]

Father-son relationship

While settling into England and finding his feet at work, family issues were also on Bruno's mind, and I gained insight into his relationship with his son – my father. My father had not done brilliantly at school, having only been in the country for a few years. He had unsurprisingly failed the English language part of his School Certificate exam,[13] which meant it was uncertain how his education would continue. The tone in which Bruno writes about his son in a letter to Loughborough College School is harsh and judgemental, even given that someone had helped him write the letter. It is dated 8 September 1942, and he was searching for a new school for his son to attend while my father was trying again to pass his School Certificate exams:

> *The reason for my wishing to have someone to take an interest in my son's movements out of school hours is the fact that up to the present, he has shown too much enthusiasm for sport and outdoor life, but I am sure that if he has suitable guiding, he will take the right interest in his studies.*

Something else about the relationship between Bruno and his son

---

12. Google Earth shows that the houses at two addresses where Bruno and Marianne lived after leaving the boarding house in central London are typical Victorian houses. The one in Hanger Lane looks larger and was possibly in a better state than the one in Freeland Road. At the end of the war, their address was Oaklands, 30 Argyle Road. Marianne and Bruno moved to 13 Castlebar Hill in 1954; it was their final home in England.

13. The School Certificate exam was usually taken at age sixteen, and each subject was graded. Pupils had to pass maths and English plus four other subjects to be awarded a certificate. This system was replaced by GCE O-levels in 1951 and by GCSEs in 1987.

emerged from the cache of my father's letters: there seem to be only a few instances where Bruno wrote to his son. For instance, I found little evidence that Bruno wrote about how best to deal with the family house in Troppau when he returned there after the war. I found no letters from father to son on this topic, at least among the letters in my possession and the ones that Sam has (I haven't seen the letters Jon owns). In contrast, my father often wrote to both of his parents. It seems to have been almost exclusively Marianne's task to answer. In a letter from 5 March 1946, writing during his post-war stay in Czechoslovakia, my father says of the family house in Opava: 'Father, Mother writes you do not want me to spend my savings on the house. That's rubbish of course if I may say so'. To write 'rubbish' was my father's way of quashing Bruno, and I sense that power issues existed between them. My father seemed to be taking on a pragmatic and generous stance to righting the wrongs of the war. He wrote vividly of the need for glass in the windows at the family's abandoned house: following a snowstorm, about 30 centimetres of snow had drifted into most rooms, even though paper was stuck up at the windows. It seems strange that Bruno did not directly offer input on how to repair the family's house or finance improvements. It is easy to find excuses and say that, Bruno, in 1946, already sixty-one years old, was tied up in his work, and 'had no time' to write. It is probably more honest to suggest that Bruno was an emotionally remote and inaccessible father with high expectations that his son struggled to fulfil.

After the war

During the war, Bruno was cut off from the headquarters of the Gütermann Company in Gutach and had to go it alone. Correspondence with Muller-Steffens after the war reveals the tension, worries about the future, and the exhaustion he and his business colleagues were experiencing. This echoes what millions of people were dealing with: relief that the war was over but deep uncertainty about the future. The war's horror, tension and trauma started to recede as the second half of the 1940s progressed, but it became clear that a return to Opava was out of the question. Germans were brutally expelled from Czechoslovakia, and while Bruno and Marianne were not German, they were German speakers. My father reported to his parents in a letter of 3 March 1946 the exact number of Germans expelled: 2,143,167. He wrote further in this letter:

> Re. your not returning, I myself wanted to write to you [and] even [Irma and Alfred] Karplus [to] perhaps get used to the idea of staying in England. There are various things I don't like here. They don't in any way affect me, but they might never let you 'feel at home' in the CSR. The political situation is rather bad I feel, but not a glimmer of war, I am sure. Here, the 'All-share' idea with the big 3, Stalin, Beneš[14] and Tito are being mentioned; a very dangerous thought I feel. Eastern 'Block' etc. which I don't much like.

On 26 May 1946, the Communist Party of Czechoslovakia won a victory in the general election and became part of a coalition government. In the years following, communism grew in the country and Czechoslovakia became, from an English viewpoint, obscured behind the Iron Curtain. This was not the liberal democracy in which Bruno's family, and the factory in Troppau, had flourished. I imagine that the thought of returning became increasingly remote, although the ownership of his house remained unresolved. Slowly but surely, it must have become painfully clear to Bruno that his house and factory would be lost forever.[15]

---

14. This seems to have been a misconception on my father's part but may well have been the narrative in the press at the time regarding Beneš and my father adopted it. Beneš aligned as a left-leaning nationalist with Stalin and Tito, but he wasn't a communist.

15. I learned that in the mid-1970s, Bruno received about £2,000 compensation for

In 1960, aged seventy-five, Bruno retired, but he remained chairman of the English Gütermann branch for several years. He now had time to devote himself to gardening and stamp collecting. In 1970 a fire devastated the factory, but it was rebuilt within a year. Queen Elizabeth, the Queen Mother, came to the opening ceremony of the new factory. A photo of the occasion says it all. Bruno's delight at being introduced to her by my father, who is stretching his hand towards him, is unmistakable. He is literally taken aback with pleasure at meeting the Queen Mother. His huge smile lights up his whole person. It must have been one of the highlights of his long life, and the image stokes an inkling that he was reconciled with the past. Marianne is at his side, smiling broadly from under her large hat.

It was only in 1974/1975, when he was approaching his ninetieth birthday, that Bruno officially confirmed and acknowledged the death of his sisters Grete and Else at the hands of the Nazis. He must have known for the thirty years that had passed since the end of the Second World War that he would never hear anything from them again. By any standard, thirty years is a long time to wait before doing that. Bruno's and Marianne's lives included a string of tragedies, and, as a couple, they were affected by each other's losses. I believe leaving the house he had so lovingly built for his family and the destruction of the factory he'd founded caused Bruno great sorrow and pain. These losses also affected Marianne, but I sense in a different way.

Family, friends and some Gütermann business friends came over from Gutach to celebrate Bruno's ninetieth birthday on 16 July 1975. I was seventeen at the time. I remember the birthday cake with ninety candles that were quickly blown out because the heat threatened to instantly melt the cake. Short snippets of the party at Eva's house, captured on Super 8 film and later digitised, give an impression of the celebration. In the film I see my lively, happy,

---

the family house. That seems little by today's standards, but it was worth about £18,000 in those days.

healthy grandfather enjoying being in the middle of things and having his nearest and dearest around him. There are glimpses of Eva, my mother, Marianne, my brothers and Julia. Julia and I stayed close to one another. My father was behind the camera, and I remember hating the harsh, bright light directed at the people he wanted to film. It was needed in those days to get proper film exposure, and many people in the film shielded their eyes from the light. But what a valuable piece it appears to me now, and I am grateful that we have this record.

The company gave Bruno the book *Der ewige Brunnen*, a collection of over 1,600 poems in German from throughout eight centuries.[16] *Ewig* means everlasting and *Brunnen* is a fountain. The dedication read:

> *Dynamik war's und Fröhlichkeit*
> *Genauigkeit vor allem –*
> *Die Treue war's ein Leben lang,*
> *das hat uns stets gefallen.*
> *So gratuliert am heutigen Tag*
> *Mit besten Wünschen zugetan*
> *Und Dankbarkeit im Herzen*
> *Ihre Familie Gütermann.*

(Roughly translated: *Dynamic and cheerful, above all accurate – lifetime faithfulness, always appreciated. So congratulations on this day with best wishes and gratitude in our hearts, your family Gütermann.*)

Although Marianne is seen full of vitality in the birthday video, dementia developed after an operation, and eventually she moved into a care home; it must have been around 1977 or 1978. Bruno was living on his own for the first time in about sixty years. My mother

---
16. Ludvig Reiners (ed.) *Der ewige Brunnen* (*The Eternal Fountain*).

prepared a meal for him every day, and my father took the meal to Bruno on his way to work. Bruno stayed at his home in Ealing and never went into care. We often got phone calls from him and patiently explained to him how to make a boiled egg or how the kettle worked. At one point, he became weary and did not want to get up anymore. He was tired and so very old. By then, in 1979, I had lost contact with him, having become distant to my self and others and depressed. I was unable to reach out; the reason why is a different story. I deeply regret that I couldn't deal with his advanced old age and approaching death. I didn't say, 'Goodbye, I love you and thank you from the bottom of my heart for everything'. I remained far away at my first job, as a biology teacher at a comprehensive school in Wales, and I didn't contact him but left him alone as his life energy faded well into his ninety-fifth year. As I write that, self-reproach wells up inside me and remembering brings tears to my eyes. But my family didn't address challenging emotional situations; from afar, I see that as the cause of my behaviour. I had not learned to be there for someone who was struggling. Julia also regrets not visiting him before he died. It was a dark December evening when my mother rang me to tell me that Bruno had died. I became detached as I heard the news and wondered why my father had not rung.

I wrote in my diary in December 1979:

> *On December 8th, Saturday morning, at a quarter past eight, my grandfather died. 'Dada Bruno', as I had named him, is dead. At the funeral, I could not stop crying. A huge part of my childhood has vanished. The garden is overgrown; the study is bare, and my pictures that I'd drawn for him over the years have been taken down from the wall.*

Seeing the overgrown garden after the funeral particularly distressed me. Bruno had put so much love and care into tending every single plant, and now everything had run wild; it looked a dishevelled mess.

When I consider Bruno's biography, it becomes stunningly clear how important his four grandchildren must have become in helping him to accept his earlier losses. His grandchildren were born in 1958, 1959, 1961 and 1966. We must have played a role in his healing from the trauma of the murder of his sisters and mother-in-law, the loss of his house and factory, and in helping him settle in England and establish a new identity. I gave this chapter about her father-in-law to my mother to read, and on her eighty-eighth birthday (26 January 2022), she rang me and said, 'You know you were *made* for Bruno'. He had been gently nagging my parents after their marriage in 1955 to start a family, and, as he was 'so old', they did so a little earlier than planned. He was seventy-three when I was born in 1958, and Bruno lived to see me grow up and get a university degree in 1979. As a child and a teenager, I was certainly not remotely aware of the significance we grandchildren played in Bruno's life, nor of his past; neither was I aware that he even had a past. I perceive this lack of awareness as a shortcoming, but not only from my side. In a family with a highly developed inability to talk openly, it is not surprising that I didn't ask questions.

Interestingly, the only photo of a family member at 13 Castlebar Hill in Ealing, where my grandparents lived, was of Johanna, Bruno's mother, Marianne's mother-in-law. Her death when she was seventy-one years old in 1931 may have seemed natural and was probably not associated with trauma. Life expectancy has grown through the decades, and reaching seventy-one in those days was possibly akin to ninety these days. Johanna's photo on Bruno's study wall might have been a non-distressing reminder of the past.

As a child, I just saw Bruno as an old person. In no way did I understand, even when I was older, that he had experienced not one but two momentous, devastating world wars. While I have been writing this book, he has metamorphosed from 'just' being my much-loved grandfather to being Bruno, a courageous, innovative, intelligent person who experienced multiple losses during his long life but successfully navigated them with Marianne without becoming bitter.

6 MARIANNE
1896–1980

Silent, mournful, abandoned, broken, Czechoslovakia recedes into darkness.

William Manchester[1]

When I was little, I often asked my grandmother how old she was. With a twinkle in her eyes, she would answer: 'I'm as old as my tongue and a bit older than my teeth'. I needed years to understand what she meant. As a child, I never found out how old she was. I never asked Bruno how old he was, but I knew Granny and Grandpa were really old. Granny was gentle and warm, and she delighted in her grandchildren. When we arrived for a visit, she would make happy noises while we stood in the small, dark hall. She'd hug everyone and, for a few seconds, she pressed my face to her big, warm, soft bosom and her hug took my breath away.

Only years later did I understand that Marianne had a sharp mind

---

1. William Manchester, *Winston Spencer Churchill: The Last Lion, Volume 2: Alone, 1932–1940.*

alongside her warmth, and that she had studied pharmacy and perhaps worked as a pharmacist as a young woman before her marriage in 1922. She had qualified at university and had a title: *Magister, Pharmacie*; that was very unusual for those days – not that she used her title. During the war, Marianne retook her exams in English, passed, as a certificate from 1943 shows, and worked as a pharmacist in London. As avant-garde as she was, Marianne was conservative in how she did her hair: the bun pulled back to the nape of her neck never changed during her lifetime. After she died, I inherited her pharmacist's white coat. I used it in my darkroom, where I developed 35mm films and black-and-white photos in those chemical, pre-digital photography days. I wore it for years until it fell apart.

Marianne was born on 22 October 1896, the youngest of Therese's three children. As I discovered through reading my father's return to Opava letter, she had a sister, Melitta, and a brother, Alfred. Writing this book made me realise that Marianne had grown up without her father, Leopold. He had died young, aged thirty-seven, when Marianne was three years old – a tragedy for Therese and the young family to lose a husband and father. Therese must have had support from her parents, Marianne's maternal grandparents, Leopold and Regina Sonnenblum. They lived locally and ran the business S. Sonnenblum, Troppau, a textile company with a telephone and its bank headquarters in Prague, as a letterhead from the 1930s that I own shows.

Bruno and Marianne met and fell in love soon after Bruno's return from Siberia. I don't know how they met; it must have been in Opava, where Bruno was setting up the new Gütermann factory. Perhaps they met through Marianne's parents' business. They married on 16 May 1922, when Marianne was twenty-six years old – she was eleven years younger than Bruno. Their marriage certificate states their religion as *mosaisch*, meaning 'of Moses', i.e., Jewish. Marianne became pregnant almost immediately and gave birth to Eva on 22

April 1923. My father was born two and a half years later, on 12 June 1925; he was baptised and not circumcised. This suggests two things: that Marianne and Bruno were assimilated Jews with little affinity to custom, and that they were wary of antisemitism. They brought up Eva and my father as Catholics. This is something I heard not from him, but years later from Julia.

There is a family photo which might have been taken on Bruno's birthday one July, all that time ago before the family fled. In the photo, my father looks around five years old; perhaps it was Bruno's forty-fifth birthday in 1930. The lawnmower on the left of the picture was possibly Bruno's birthday present – why else would such a thing be in the lounge? There were summer flowers on the table and other things that might have been presents. My father is wearing shorts; it was warm weather. Bruno is looking approvingly towards his children, and Marianne is smiling radiantly in his direction.

Marianne was the linguist of the family, although she had not studied languages, and she most probably started learning English before leaving Czechoslovakia. I believe she came to feel at home in England and felt comfortable speaking English; I cannot remember her having an accent – in contrast to Bruno, who never became fluent and spoke with a heavy accent. Marianne's handwriting, usually in English, is to be found on many of my father's letters. She often noted how long the letter had taken to be delivered, and she highlighted bits that were important to her; she also corrected her son's spelling mistakes as he gradually transitioned from writing in German to English. This suggests that she was very sure of her English and was the parent taking the most interest in the letters. The following uncorrected letter of hers in English to my father is dated 4 October 1945, six months after the end of the Second World War. It gives a glimpse of the family and insight into Marianne's state of mind. She addresses her son as Hanus, the Czech version of Hans, which, correctly written, would be Hanuš, but she dropped the diacritic.

My dear Hanus, we have not heard from you since your letter written on Sunday morning September 16th, rec. Sept. 22nd. This is such a long time, and I was only glad to see your letter to Ravingdon [to Irma and Alfred Karplus] dated Sept. 22nd. Did you not write to us at all since September 16th? Or did a letter or two go astray? We don't know whether you received our various communications, meanwhile, I hope you did. Evicka [Eva] arrived last Friday night, very fit and brown. She has been busy since to find out whether she could find transportation for a visit home, but although everybody at our embassy has been extremely kind and helpful it does not seem possible to be certain to make it in time to be back before the end of her leave. Therefore, we all are hoping you will be able to come over here to meet her. She just went to see the dentist, but she sends you her best love and she will write to you one of these days, although she insists that you owe her a letter! We are most anxious to hear about your progress at Brno University, when does it start? It would be lovely to have both children here for my birthday. Did you see Aunt Martha? So sorry that Gert is feeling lonely in the [family] house, give them both our love. Litta was with us yesterday; she awaits her certificate from the Nar. Vybor, certifying her loyalty. She is most anxious to be repatriated as soon as possible. Now please write soon and do keep us up to date about your enrolment etc. Evicka has a lot to tell us, but she firmly refuses to tell me anything about any boyfriends!! Father and I would so much love to talk over your plans for study with you and everything. All our best wishes and lots of love.

The letter shows how fluent Marianne's English had become. Almost all of the letter is about her children, and she was trying to organise them. Her tension is tangible between the lines, and there is an inkling of the tension between her children which would later openly flare up. Marianne seemed aware of their problems; she was trying to bring them together by organising a meeting and encouraging Eva to write to her brother. Eva sidetracked that. Marianne mentioned her sister, Litta, who had also fled Troppau to England, and who had a clear wish to become repatriated and continue her marriage with Eduard Hellmann (my father mentions 'Onkel Edi' in his return to Opava letter) and be with Gert, who was, at the time, living in the family house in Opava. For Marianne, 'home' is still Opava.

Marianne openly shares that she'd been interviewing her daughter regarding relationships, and again, something intense comes over; she might not have been respecting boundaries. Marianne was hoping her children would be with her for her forty-ninth birthday on 22 October. The war was now over, both her children had been conscripted and Marianne's wish was to have the family together again. However, Eva was now twenty-two and Hans (or Hanus/Hanuš) was twenty; both were active and competent young adults spreading their wings in the aftermath of the war. I don't think they turned up for Marianne's birthday.

Little snippets of information giving clues about the past have filtered down to me through the years, often via my mother. When my mother met my father in 1953, she also met his parents. She told me that back then, she thought that the family had chosen to come to England – that their migration was due to political persecution of Jews remained unspoken. This suggests that little candid conversation was going on between my mother, my father and my mother's in-laws. Marianne shared a story with my mother which she passed on to me: when they arrived in England and lived in the Averard boarding house for the first few months, Marianne had told Bruno that she longed for her own place. Astonished, Bruno said to his wife: 'But who'll do the cooking?' His answer reveals several things: first, that they were well off enough in Opava to employ a cook. The comment also suggests that Bruno had not updated himself regarding their new life in Britain, but his resourceful wife had. When they did move, Marianne visited an Austrian 'living upstairs' (as my mother told me) and learned how to cook, taking lessons from this woman. She became a proficient cook and learned to run a household.

As a child, I thought it strange that Bruno and Marianne did not share a bedroom and sleep together in a double bed like my parents. However, Groag Bell, who also grew up in Troppau, sheds light on this aspect of their marriage. She noted that her parents thought plenty of privacy with little forced togetherness was the best path for marital happiness: 'as soon as space allowed, quite early in their marriage, they had separate bedrooms. In the same vein, they often had separate vacations.'[2]

Both of my grandparents smoked, and giving up the habit was not easy. As Marianne aged, she secretly smoked in the downstairs toilet but forgot to open the window afterwards. I remember noticing as a child that Bruno pretended he hadn't noticed.

My cousin Julia was close to Granny, and I was close to Grandpa; they divided their attention between their first two grandchildren. By the time my brothers arrived, they were older, and I don't think they had the emotional capacity to enter into the kind of intense relationships they had with Julia and me.

There is no doubt that Marianne and Bruno had a long, happy marriage. They experienced so much together and gave one another mutual support. I have put a forty-second snippet of one of the digitised Super 8 films my father shot in their garden, from their golden wedding anniversary in 1972, online.[3] Bruno was eighty-seven at the time and Marianne was seventy-six. They look happy and relaxed and the way they interact suggests their love for one another. There is no hint of any bitterness of old age. Marianne brushes her forehead, wondering if her 'horns' are visible. She had

---

2. Groag Bell, p. 21.
3. https://vimeo.com/674545921/35366df2c5.

developed two slight protrusions (calcifications) that she let her grandchildren touch. 'Granny's horns' were a bit of a joke among us. In the video, Bruno gesticulates laughingly and dismissively about something Marianne says. Their vitality is tangible despite their advanced age.

Although my grandmother Marianne was eleven years younger than my grandfather Bruno, she declined faster than he did. After an operation for a hernia and a postoperative stay in hospital, she started suffering from dementia. Once, Marianne and Bruno were at our place for lunch and she explained carefully that vegetarianism meant one did not eat bread. Bruno argued softly with her that it meant not eating meat. She was sure that one left off bread ... then she turned to my father and studied him closely, pausing. She asked who he was. He answered brightly, 'I'm Peter, your only son'.

'Oh, yes', Granny said solemnly, 'I thought your face looked familiar'. Her grandchildren roared with laughter, but of course, the situation was tragic. The scene must have been deeply painful for Bruno, who looked on with his astute, clear mind. Soon Granny was put in a care home; it must have been around 1977, when I was nineteen. She left the grounds once, hailed a taxi and sent the driver off over London. Upon arrival, the taxi driver wanted payment, but she had no money and did not know why she was at this address. I suppose the taxi driver drove her back to the home and someone gave him his money. Years later, I learned from Julia that the address she had asked the taxi driver to take her to was 13 Castlebar Hill – to Bruno.

Marianne outlived Bruno by six months and died on my father's birthday, 12 June 1980. They had been partners for nearly six decades. Strangely, I can't remember Granny's funeral, which I am sure I attended – but perhaps I was still numb from losing my grandfather six months earlier.

I don't think that Marianne or Bruno saw themselves as 'survivors' of the Holocaust. However, some academics define survivors more broadly than those who got through the concentration and death camps, enforced labour, or time in hiding.[4] Is early escape really 'survival'? I don't think so. My grandparents were people who fled Nazi persecution in time to save their lives and the lives of their children. 'Survivor' connotes danger to life and limb; but my paternal family were nevertheless victims because of the impact Nazism had on their lives. In a way, that has trickled down the generations as an invisible wall of silence. This was a wall that was not built with brick, but nevertheless, it was heavy and an unconscious burden.

Marianne must have agonised about her mother Therese's fate for the rest of her life. In my mind, I imagine Therese during what became the final farewell in late 1938. I picture her fearlessly encouraging the family to go, saying that things would work out, they would meet again soon, and that she was old and not frightened. But that's just my imagination; Marianne never spoke about that.

---

4. See Emanuella Grinberg, 'How the Definition of Holocaust Survivor Has Changed Since the End of World War II' (1 May 2019), www.smithsonianmag.com/history/what-and-who-defines-being-holocaust-survivor-180972076.

7 IRMA
1893–1965

This annihilation of the past is familiar to displaced people of all kinds.

Helen Epstein[1]

In 2011, after discovering my father's wartime letters to his parents, my interest in the past surged. Each time I went to England, I was drawn to the family archive in the old suitcase at my mother's home and started exploring its jumbled contents, trying to make sense of it all. Most written documents were in German; some were in Czech. There was an assortment of papers, official documents, passports, letters, photos and some objects. It was a suitcase of relics, and it was sometimes surprising what had been saved. Many people I had never heard of were mentioned in the documents; I felt a bit overwhelmed. I drew dozens of family trees through the following years to comprehend relationships and become familiar with these ghosts.

---

1. Helen Epstein, *Where She Came From: A Daughter's Search for Her Mother's History*.

The only people I knew were my father, Aunt Eva, my grandparents Bruno and Marianne, and my great-aunt Irma and her husband Alfred. I'd heard of Aunt Martha, also sometimes called great Aunt Martha, but I didn't know her. (Actually, she was a great-great-aunt of mine because she was my grandfather's aunt.) Slowly, I found out about others. My great-grandmother Johanna was Bruno's mother. I'd stared at her photo on the wall in my grandfather's study as a child, as mentioned. Next, I discovered Grete and Else, the women my father had noted in the passport he'd sent me in 2004. I found Therese, my father's maternal grandmother. And I learned a lot more. Of all the people in the family tree, I'd known (or heard of) only six of them: my grandparents, their children (my father and aunt), and Irma and Alfred. I slowly drew the others out of history through letters, documents and various online archives and started to understand a little of their lives.

Irma, Bruno's youngest sister, had also escaped the Nazis to England with her husband, Alfred. I tell her story now because a piece she wrote was one of the first original documents I found. Her account had lain in the suitcase at my mother's house for nearly eight decades. I share it, translated from German, in full. It gives details of the couple's first time in England, although she wrote it a few years after they had settled there. It helped me understand more about my paternal family at the start of my journey into the past. Exploring this piece of writing that documents Irma's wartime experiences honours her, and it allowed me to get to know Irma and part of her past that I'd never imagined had existed.

Irma's reflections

Irma wrote her account at the end of 1943 for her sister Else. Else had stayed in Czechoslovakia (as did Grete) with her husband Karl when Bruno and Irma had fled. I can say with certainty that Irma had not heard from her sister Else, nor her brother-in-law Karl, for over two years at the time of writing, because they had been transported to the Łódź ghetto in German-occupied Poland in October 1941, as I found out through my research. The sisters may have lost contact as early as March 1939, when Irma emigrated to England – the same time that Bruno and Marianne had arrived in the country.

Irma typed the piece, suggesting that it was important to her. She wrote on the last day of 1943, after over four years of war. She was looking back over what had happened after her nieces Hanne (affectionately called 'Hannerl') and Susi, Else's daughters, joined her in England. I was familiar with their names, as my father had noted them in Grete's passport. I later discovered that Hanne was Else's stepdaughter but have not been able to find out when Hanne made it to England. Nevertheless, Hanne and Susi were both my father's cousins, and they became real people in my mind as I read and re-read Irma's account.

Irma records the day that Susi arrived in England and vividly reports the difficulties and anxieties of getting into the country to escape the Nazis. The text seems steeped in pent-up emotion. She seems compelled to create a record for her sister and brother-in-law. In writing for her sister (and not to her as in a letter), Irma seems to sense how far away they are; perhaps in her heart she already knew they were no longer alive. Irma's writing also appears to be an attempt to justify supporting Susi's flight to England.

'Ravingdon'
Pitchcombe, near Stroud
Glos. [Gloucestershire] *31.12.1943*

I have to write down for Else and Karl what I know about Susi. We arrived on the 12.2.1939 in London. We left Prague on the 8.2. and at the start were in Amsterdam. Immediately we rang Hannerl, and I can't say how happy I was when I heard her voice; one no longer felt so forlorn. Hannerl's only thought was: the parents must also get out, Susi must get out,

Franz must get out. I had been so unhappy that I'd been going on and on at Alfred to end it all. For what and why should we bother? We're too old and dispirited to start anew. But, above all, why and for whom?

Anyway, I could not convince Karl and Else to come to England. But for young people, it was different. That is why I supported Hannerl in her efforts to get Susi over. We were so happy when we received the news that she would come. It must have been the middle of March; I no longer know which day, but it was shortly before her birthday and about 14 days before Hittler [sic] came to Prague. She was expected to arrive in the evening, and Alfred, Hannerl and I went to the station full of happy anticipation. We walked up and down for a long time; the train was late. Then Mr Winner came up to us, breathless. He came in his car to tell us that Susi had rung from – where was it? That they are not letting her on land. By 10 o'clock in the morning one had to find an English person who would vouch for her, otherwise she would have to return on the same ship on the following day at 10 o'clock. How come and why, we didn't know and we were of course, totally shocked. Mr Winner was incredibly helpful and good. He said straight away that only Bloomsbury House[2] could help. He would go there straight away tomorrow, early. He would vouch for her personally. If it would all work out, he naturally did not know. Bl. H. only opens after 10, so he found it doubtful. Anyway, he did it. He was there early next day and rang from there – or an official, credible person from there did, and it arrived a few moments before the ship left. How Mr W. did

---

2. Bloomsbury House was the headquarters of many of the main refugee agencies: the German Jewish Aid Committee (later the Jewish Refugee Committee), the German Emergency Committee (Quakers), the Church of England Committee for Non-Aryan Christians and many others; www.ukholocaustmap.org.uk/map/records/bloomsbury-house.

this, I don't know, as I have been there myself and know how one sits around for hours and must wait before it is one's turn. Later, when we repeatedly thanked Mr W. for his helpfulness in that situation, he always said: I wish it hadn't worked out and Susi would have to have returned, then perhaps it would have turned out differently. So, another one of us cursed themselves for helping bring her here. But he had such endlessly good intentions.

Susi was expected to arrive in the afternoon. The three of us were at the station again. She did not arrive with the train that one had told us from the ship that she would come with. We asked around and waited for other trains to arrive. As she didn't arrive, Alfred and I went to our hotel, and Hannerl went to Winners, where she was working. When we arrived at the hotel, we were told that Susi had already arrived and had gone to her room to sleep. There was such happiness in seeing each other again. So, then she told us everything that had happened to her. First all her jewellery had been taken from her at the German border. She had been given a deposit slip and told that her parents would get it back when they sent in the slip. When she had wanted to leave the ship, the English officer had questioned her. He had done this with us too but let us go straight away when we could show him several invitational letters from our English customers [of IVO Tapestries]. He was suspicious of Susi; we couldn't understand why. Above all, he asked to whom she was coming. She said the name of the people she would be staying with; she also had a letter from them which she showed. She was asked if she knew these people, and truthfully, she said no. So why is she going to them? What is she going to do there? The poor child naturally could not say much in response. Mr Winner often told us later how surprised he was when he saw the shy child later for the first time. He'd imagined her to be completely different because the officer on the telephone at

Bloomsbury House said that he didn't know what to do with her; she's full of cheek and a liar. The poor child was nothing other than clueless; I can't understand why the Englishman, even if he couldn't understand her well, didn't realise that. The English, whether police or officials, are otherwise so exceptionally humane, and we admired that always when we had anything to do with them, we were astonished. However, later we often heard that terrible scenes often happened when people landed and that many were sent back. One never knew who was allowed in and who was not. There was no visa, but they simply didn't let some in if there was any sort of reason not to. No one really knew what was necessary to get in. We had already noticed this in Prague: no one could give information either in the Engl. Consulate or in a travel agency.

Shortly after arriving, Susi asked me: do you think I'll be able to go home in a few weeks? I don't want to stay here; I want to finish my Matura. So, I said of course you can go back, whenever you want. Take a look at things here then you'll see what you want to do. I didn't believe she could go back as I was sure that the gate would soon close; however, I never thought that would happen as quickly as it did. But it calmed her down; she didn't have quite so much homesickness if she thought she could and would go back. That's what I thought, anyway.

Soon she went to the people who had invited her. I think they were called King und lived near London. I knew the couple, I'd met them before Susi came. They were a very young married people. They were not much older than Hannerl, modest but generous, simple folk. Her husband was an architect, and also very young. I thought it was a good place for Susi, to be with young people. Susi didn't have any particular work to do there. (Remaining page(s) missing.)

In writing this short, memoir-like reflective piece, Irma was trying to make sense of events while she documented her memories of Susi for Else. Irma brought her thoughts and feelings of anguish to paper; however, she did not write directly about her emotions, which was probably too painful. In the following, I'm inferring most of them.

Hanne spoke with urgency during a first call with Irma about the need for her parents, her sister and Franz to also 'get out'. (Franz was Hanne's future husband; he later changed his name to Frank.) The unimaginably high tension and uncertainty in the months before Britain declared war on Germany comes over. Irma then switches her writing stance to recall her own state of mind while deciding to flee; remembering that first telephone call with Hanne triggered her memory. Irma's decision to leave Czechoslovakia was associated with hopelessness and despair, suggesting that she had experienced depression. She had thought of suicide. Irma struggled with her decision to flee and start anew aged forty-six, which involved experiencing strong negative emotions. Irma had no children. That might have played into her desperate state of mind; she had asked herself who she should bother to continue living for.

She had not been able to convince her sister, Else, and brother-in-law, Karl, to leave the country. This suggests that Else and Karl had told Irma that they felt too old to start anew, or perhaps this was Irma's interpretation of their hesitancy regarding the threat of the Nazis and deciding to emigrate. Possibly they didn't have the financial options needed to facilitate emigration as Bruno and Irma had, although I later discovered that Else was also a co-owner of the flourishing IVO Tapestries. A chill breath of resignation to their fate seems to come across in Irma's piece regarding Else and Karl. As people, they remain remote in her writing; it is as if they are already not there.

Irma then takes up her report again for her sister and writes that she and Hanne were delighted when they heard the news that Susi would also come to England. Her happiness suggests understandable relief. Hitler marched into Prague on 15 March 1939, and for Irma this was the striking event, the cut in time that changed everything. She says that Susi arrived about two weeks beforehand. Irma mentions Susi's birthday; she was eighteen when she fled Czechoslovakia and joined her stepsister and aunt in England.

The next part of Irma's writing details Susi's arrival, and she returns to her original intention of writing everything she knew about Susi for Else and Karl. As I later discovered, tragically, Susi killed herself on 7 May 1940. Irma's account, written after Susi's death, seems like an attempt to capture a small ray of light in the darkness, the hopeful new beginnings associated with Susi's arrival, although her niece had been dead for three and a half years at the time of writing.

Waiting for Susi at the train station, Irma's mood fluctuated and instantly changed from happy anticipation to shocked incomprehension upon hearing that Susi might not be allowed on land. Safety and survival ('in') or the threat of persecution ('out') existed side by side; the switches between them were not under Irma's control.

The most tragic part of Irma's writing then follows, but years passed until I understood it as my research progressed. She wrote that she had repeatedly thanked Mr Winner for his help and endless good intentions, but he always said he wished he'd failed, and that things would have turned out differently if he had. This seems to be indirectly referring to Susi's suicide, but as I only found Susi's death certificate years later, this passage remained cryptic until I discovered Susi's fate and re-read Irma's piece. Irma seems to have felt responsible for Susi's fate; she is harsh and judgemental towards herself and possibly experienced guilt alongside painful regret. She may have been using the process of writing to address her conscience and report on Susi's arrival for Else, to explain exactly how things had happened and openly share her thoughts and motivation. It is notable and tragic that Irma was writing for her sister and brother-in-law, although they were, at the time of writing, no longer alive.

The details that Susi shared with her aunt give testimony about trying to enter England and are harrowing. Irma documented her shock at hearing about dramatic scenes when people landed but were not admitted to Britain and were sent back to their almost certain death. Irma's recollections document fatal harshness and a lack of clarity about who was allowed into the UK.

Susi arrived in England on 11 March 1939 at the port of Harwich, as a document issued by the British Committee for Refugees from Czechoslovakia states. It seems likely that Irma's memory was not accurate on all the facts: although she writes that Susi made it to England shortly before her birthday (which I discovered was 24 March) and about fourteen days before 'Hitler came to Prague' (15 March 1939), Irma's latter estimation is incorrect: Susi arrived only four days before Hitler invaded. The story about Susi's jewellery throws up questions. Susi reported that her jewellery had been confiscated. She must have departed from Czechoslovakia by train, and the Germans confiscated her jewellery around 10 March 1939 at the border. They may have confiscated it because she was a minor without a letter stating that she had the right to take the property out of the country; perhaps that was the excuse they used. Her Czechoslovak passport would not have identified Susi as a Jew and a German customs official could therefore not have pin-pointed her as such, but it may be that they realised she was Jewish and did not want to allow someone to escape with valuables that they intended confiscate soon anyway.

The last surviving page of this document ends with Irma repeating the heartrending question that Susi asked her aunt regarding her return in a few weeks, almost on the eve of the Second World War, with the Holocaust looming on the horizon. Irma consoled her niece, but in her heart she did not believe that this return would be possible. I have often wondered what Irma wrote on the lost pages. Perhaps she even wrote about Susi's death. Years after finding Irma's document, I learned of Susi's suicide in England in 1940. Her parents were transported in October 1941 to the Łódź ghetto, and I have wondered whether Irma (or Bruno) had informed Else and Karl of the tragic news. The way Irma wrote makes me think that she didn't (or couldn't) notify them; there was little possibility of sending letters in German at that stage of the war from England to Czechoslovakia.

More recently, my mother handed me another snippet of information she had heard from my father. Susi might have been pregnant when she took her own life. The details on her death certificate from May 1940 read: 'Arsenical poisoning, self-administered, there being no evidence to show the state of her mind at the time'. Under occupation is stated, 'Spinster. Gardeners' assistant. Daughter of Karl Federmann, a Professor.' I recoil at the word *spinster*, which seems harsh to describe a nineteen-year-old when *unmarried* or *single* would have done, but the connotations may have changed through the years. Susi appears to me to have been an indirect victim of the Nazis, and my heart went out to her spirit when I discovered her fate. It was as if I had touched her through the decades; I sensed the desperation that led to her decision to kill herself.

Irma and Alfred's first years in England

Irma and Alfred lived at the house called Ravingdon from 29 February 1939 to 6 May 1947, as they recorded in a photo album in my possession. John and Hazel Wigham inhabited the house and perhaps owned it. My mother suggested they were Quakers, like the King family to which Susi went – again a snippet of information she had heard from my father. Irma and Alfred were employed by the Wighams as housekeepers, although the company IVO Tapestries was being built up in England and Wales simultaneously; their business needed time to grow. Details of this time comes from Alfred Karplus, Irma's husband, in a document he wrote in English entitled, 'SHORT History of My Life from School-Age Onwards':

I married in December 1920. I joined shortly afterwards my wife's business. That business was a foundation of my mother-in-law, Mrs Vogel. This business was dealing with all kinds of Art Needlework. My wife and myself started to build up the manufacture of TAPESTRIES. We succeeded in exporting this article on a big scale. When leaving our native town in autumn 1938, we employed more than 150 permanent clerical and manual workers in our workshops and about 500 out-workers. My wife and I decided, fortunately, to leave my native town [Troppau] *in the middle of September 1938, just a fortnight before Munich. We had to leave behind practically everything. Houses, properties, and personal belongings apart from business. First, we went to Prague, where we lived in our office for about four months. We left Prague for England at the beginning of February 1939 and arrived in London on February 9. I want to mention that after the first world war I became a Czechoslovakian citizen. We applied for permission to manufacture work in this country. This was granted by the Home Office about end of June 1939.*

Irma noted 12 February as the date of their arrival in England. The significance of being Czechoslovakian is clear; being a German-speaking refugee must have been a source of tension while living in England, which was at war with Germany.

When Irma's husband, Alfred, died in the fire at their house in Argyle Road on 1965, I was coming up to my seventh birthday. I remember the sense of shock and the darkness of that time. Irma's death six months later is in my mind too, but it is less associated with shock. Only memory fragments of Irma remain with me. The seven-year-old me remembers her as softly spoken, quiet and gentle. That is all is there is; it is not much. I can't remember anyone ever speaking about Irma or Alfred after their deaths, nor were there any photos that Bruno or Marianne pointed to at 13 Castlebar Hill, where my grandparents lived.

In 2011, I heard for the first time from my mother that Irma's death in September 1965 was suicide. Sadness filled me – I hadn't known. After the fire at her house and Alfred's death, my parents had invited Irma over sometimes at weekends; she hardly spoke – she was deep in depression and blamed herself for Alfred's death. She had opened the front door to shout for help and the incoming air had fanned the fire. My mother recalled those times: 'Irma sat with her hand on her head full of sadness'. She had had suicidal thoughts before when deciding to leave Czechoslovakia. Now, without Alfred, life was no longer worth living. Irma died in her kitchen by turning on the oven's gas and breathing it in. The disturbing, horrific ironies jumped out at me. Alfred died in a fire; Irma gassed herself: the cremation of Jews in ovens in concentration camps after their murder comes to my mind.

I wanted to find evidence that John and Hazel Wigham had been Quakers. I entered 'Hazel Wigham Quakers' into an online search engine, and a document entitled 'Forty Years of Quaker Life in Nailsworth' came up. It was the digitised minutes of Quaker meetings from 1914 to 1954, put online in 2017. And there on page eight was the name Hazel Wigham, mentioned in a meeting from March 1938. I searched for the village of Nailsworth; it lies only a few miles south of Stroud. That seemed evidence indeed that Quakers had taken in Irma and Alfred.

8 GRETE
1884–1944 (?)

... goods wagons closed from the outside, with men, women and children pressed together without pity, like cheap merchandise, for a journey towards nothingness. A journey down there, towards the bottom.

Primo Levi[1]

Researching the Holocaust

This and the chapter about Else and Therese were so hard to write – and complicated. Although the chapter is titled 'Grete', the historical context has meaning for all my relatives who were killed during the Holocaust. I know little about Grete's life – I know more about her death – but she was the oldest of the four siblings. She and her husband Eduard possibly did not have the financial means to leave Troppau as Irma and Bruno did. Grete's sister, Else, also did not

---

1. Primo Levi, *If This Is a Man.*

leave, although Irma, the youngest of the four, had encouraged Else and her husband Karl to do so.

To write this book, I had to read about Terezín (Theresienstadt), the Łódź ghetto,[2] Treblinka, Kulmhof (Chełmno) and Auschwitz. I felt the need to go deeper than the superficial facts I knew about the Nazis' industrialised, state-led murder, and I struggled to intensify my research. These places, the machinery of genocide, and the unspeakable things the Nazis subjected people to there, are abhorrent and difficult to address. But a compulsion to understand Grete's fate, Else's fate and Therese's fate had grown in me. I was searching for the full, unspoken truth, so I could know and bridge the silent gap I'd inherited from my father and grandparents. I felt I had to engage and at least try to fathom how it was to live and die in these places. By *die*, I mean be murdered. And for *live*, *exist* is the more correct word. I wanted to pay tribute by remembering Grete, Else and Therese and writing about their fates. But I started from almost nothing; I had to reconstruct history from shreds of data.

I regularly planned time out to read so that I could write this chapter on Grete, which was the first I tackled about my relatives' persecution. She was the first never-mentioned relative I'd encountered when my father sent her passport, so I started my research with her. But instead of doing the research, I found myself doing my bookkeeping, housework or shopping – anything but what I had intended. Initially, I found it almost impossible to sustain my attention when reading the literature on the Holocaust and the concentration camps and ghettos. It was not just that the topic was difficult to grapple with. Increasingly, as time passed while I was trying to research this chapter, starting with Theresienstadt, I sensed a subtle wall within me, a bodily felt sense of resistance.

---

2. Łódź is pronounced 'lodge'. In Polish, it's pronounced like 'lwodge' – with a soft 'l'. The Nazis changed the ghetto's name to Litzmannstadt, after the Prussian general and politician Karl Litzmann (1850–1936).

When I woke one morning in autumn 2021, it suddenly dawned on me that this was the passed-on stance of my family not having addressed what had taken place in the ghettos and concentration camps. The wall was a sheet or a veil in me, and it safeguarded me from pain and horror. It was a curtain that deleted the past by blocking it out. It meant that I kept looking forward, not looking back; it was the silent, hidden, non-narrative buffer against the past. I was, without realising it, paradoxically touching the handed-down culture of not looking closely at where and how family members had been killed while concurrently trying to understand more. But until that morning, I hadn't realised that that was what I was doing. That was part of my struggle dealing with the topic.

It took some weeks to dissolve the wall, but by becoming aware of it and its profound meanings and functions, and with support from friends who knew what I was writing about, it gradually wasted away. I felt how my acquired blindness was replaced with being prepared to learn in detail about the Holocaust; a new consciousness settled on me. Being able to understand more felt honest, and my new perspective had an air of earnestness that felt appropriate. I now felt fully prepared to research the unspoken family stories of the people my father had noted in Grete's passport. But there was also humility in me; I knew that I could never really understand what it had been like in the Nazi concentration camps and ghettos. Only the people who were there could really know; I was writing from only an intellectual understanding. While we humans use language to symbolise experience, I was uncomfortably aware of not even coming close to what my relatives had truly gone through.

Grete: Fate intertwined with history

When Great Britain declared war on 3 September 1939 after Hitler had invaded Poland on 1 September, two of the four Vogel siblings were refugees/émigrés in England and two had remained in Czechoslovakia. To recap: Bruno and Irma had already fled; Grete and Else had not. Bruno and Irma had business connections to England, which enabled their involuntary emigration, but Grete and Else seemed to have no such connections or financial possibilities. Or perhaps they didn't have the impulse to flee. Therese, my father's maternal grandmother, Marianne's mother, had also not flown; emigration was almost impossible for older people. It is unclear how family members stayed in contact at the start of the war, or even if they stayed in touch; there were possibilities via the Red Cross, but they were minimal and I have no idea if they were realised. All were German speakers, and any post coming into England was probably censored; no letters have been found in the suitcase at my mother's house or elsewhere. The immense strain and worry that infused those days at the start of the Second World War are challenging to reconstruct, and any description or attempt I make to capture the mood is inadequate.

I initially used three data banks to search for Grete: Yad Vashem, the Terezín data bank Holocaust.cz and the Czech National Archives. I found a document that had been issued on 29 February 1940 which recorded Grete as a Jew and registered some of her details. It was an application for an ID card. *Zidovske* means 'Jewish'. There are two *J* stamps (for *Jude*, Jew) on this document. Originally, the stamps must have been blood red; time has faded them. The address in Prague was Jindrisska 32a, where Grete had moved from Troppau with her husband, Eduard Lanzer. They had married in Jägerndorf in 1911, where Bruno's family had lived; they had no children.

I found Grete's ID application document back in 2004 in the early days of my research; there is a lot of information about her in it, and it is laden with history, documenting the tortuous bureaucratic struggles of those times.[3] According to the Munich Agreement between Hitler's Reich and the Czechoslovak Republic, non-German citizens living on the territories ceded to Germany (that is, those who

---

3. This and other family documents can be found on my website, www.speek.de.

'became' German because of Munich) could opt for Czechoslovak citizenship by 29 March 1939.[4] The act of taking this option was called *optování* in Czech. And that's what Grete apparently did, as proven with an *opční osvědčení*, an option certificate, confirmed by the Czech Interior Ministry on 31 October 1938 and noted in hand on the above-mentioned document. Furthermore, in the lowest section of this document (the *Vojenský doklad* section, meaning 'military document'), it is noted that Grete, whose official status was therefore German, became a citizen of the Protectorate of Bohemia and Moravia by choosing Czech state citizenship. I sense that Grete didn't feel herself to be a German, although the family spoke German; like Bruno, her felt identity was probably Austrian – a citizen of the collapsed Austro-Hungarian Empire.

Someone had crossed out the Czech version of her name on the above document. 'Marketa' was replaced with her German name, Margarete. Also crossed out was 'Jana', and 'Johana', with a single *n*, had been written for her mother's name. Who made the corrections? I thought (perhaps somewhat naively) that Grete had made them to signal her affinity to the German language and not Czech. The more correct interpretation was suggested later by a historian who supported my research. The two languages existing side by side (what that meant and how it worked) was one of the big factual things I found confusing while writing this book. In time, I realised that language is only the surface expression of different people ('ethnicities', Slavic and Germanic) sharing the same geographical space. In this context, it had a long history and involved often antagonistic, hostile encounters. Jews were a minority in the thick of it. The culmination of these disputes was the expulsion of Germans from Czechoslovakia after the war.

Why had Grete, Else and Therese never been spoken of, and why had their fates never been mentioned? These questions hung over

---

4. Czecho-Slovak Law No. 300/1938, of 20 November 1938, § 3.

everything I researched. Grete looked so much like Bruno, and I imagined how close they must have been growing up together. They had been born only a year apart towards the end of the nineteenth century. That Grete was a victim of the Nazis was abstract knowledge that my father gave me when he sent her passport in 2004. Finding documents online about Grete made that knowledge close and real and plunged me into days of sadness alternating with numbness. Yet, strangely, it felt as if not all that sadness was mine. It was a sadness that not only I experienced; in spontaneous shifts of consciousness, I somehow logged in to the tragic collective past consciousnesses of millions of people for fleeting seconds while doing the research. An endless, silent, dark and solemn place of immeasurable grief, anguish and hopelessness. I would be in that realm for only a few moments, but it was real. I felt it. I experienced it.

I still know little of Grete, but I think of her as resourceful and having strength and energy. She survived for two years in Terezín, which meant that she had resilience in the face of immense challenges. My father noted in his letter to his parents that he had heard from someone that she had a role in the laundry service; as mentioned, I have not been able to confirm that.

On 9–10 November 1938, Reichskristallnacht, the synagogue in Troppau had been burned down; in May and June 1939, some synagogues had been burned in the remaining part of Bohemia and Moravia in the First Czech Republic, which was now called the Protectorate. Konstantin von Neurath had been named 'Protector'. I use inverted commas as there was nothing protective about what was happening.

An official Nazi document[5] published by the Central Office for Jewish Emigration in Prague dated 2 October 1941 summarised the

---

5. Susanne Heim and Maria Wilke (eds), *Die Verfolgung und Ermordung der europäischen Juden durch das nationalsozialistische Deutschland 1933–1945* (The

development of the situation for Jews in the so-called Protectorate. The period considered runs from 15 March 1939, when Hitler 'came to Prague', until 1 October 1941. The author was Hans Günther (1910–1945), an NSDAP (Nazi party) member since 1929. He was a Hauptsturmführer,[6] a military rank in the SS, like a captain in a regular army. The document confirms the development towards a policy of exclusion of Jews from ordinary life. The account states that Jews had already been removed from public life, politics, press, radio and education, as a 'natural result' of changes starting from 15 March 1939. Furthermore, the document confirms that two (racist) paths were being taken to exclude Jews from commerce and industry.

First, Jewish professionals – lawyers, solicitors, patent attorneys, doctors, vets, dental technicians and engineers – were banned from working, and likewise Jewish employees in public and private enterprises. Gradually, the Nazis liquidated Jewish retail and wholesale trade. As of 17 May 1939, Jews were no longer allowed management positions within industry. Bruno left with his family in autumn 1938, months before he could be excluded from his company. Günter's document confirms that apart from occasional exceptions, so-called 'economic necessities', Jews no longer had a working life. These newly unemployed Jews were increasingly assigned to work in building construction, civil and underground engineering, rail engineering, agriculture and forestry. In Prague, Jews had to work clearing snow in winter and at similar tasks the year round.

The second racist path the Nazis took concerned Jewish assets. Günther's document records that without special permission, Jews were forbidden to possess private or business property. As of October 1939, the Nazis blocked their assets and Jews could only withdraw

---

Persecution and Murder of the European Jews by Nazi Germany 1933–1945; hereafter *VEJ*), vol. 6, pp. 651–653, document 242.
6. *Hauptsturmführer* literally means 'head storm leader'.

150 Reichsmarks a month (converted to 2024 value, about £677). They were not allowed to rent their flats out. The various regulations meant that Jewish property and assets had to be registered. Jews suffered other degrading limitations. From August 1939, hospitals had to treat Jewish patients in separate wards and later in different hospitals. Jews were prohibited from renting cars or owning radios and were excluded from clubs and registered societies. They were not allowed to move house without permission or unless on orders. When Jewish institutions and organisations closed, their financial assets were paid into a fund to finance deportations. Any Jews who emigrated had to contribute according to how much they owned financially. The document summarised matter-of-factly that 'after two and a half years of the Protectorate, the Jewish economy was almost completely destroyed and Jewish life was restricted in all respects'. An overview was attached to this document with statistics, whereby the Jewish population's decline is apparent, primarily due to emigration.

Furthermore, there were multiple limitations in societal life. The police decree on identifying Jews (requiring them to wear a yellow star in public) began on 1 September 1941 and was enforced for Jews over six years of age. This was one of the Nazis' most drastic measures. Jews had already been forbidden from visiting entertainment and sporting venues, parks, public baths and from using certain roads, theatres and libraries. In Prague, Jews were only allowed to go shopping between 3 and 5 pm. They had to visit banks between 8 and 9am. Jews could only do business at specific post offices, eventually only at one on Ostrovní Street, a building that today houses the Václav Havel Library. In Prague, starting from September 1941, Jews had to travel in the last tram carriage. The sheer pettiness of the antisemitic measures is stunning. Sometimes, Jews living in scattered rural communities were relocated and concentrated in larger towns before deportation. In Prague, they were progressively concentrated in *Judenhäuser*. Jewish communities outside Prague remained in their towns until deportation.

These laws emboldened those with a racist agenda within the Czech fascist association called Vlajka, who had been nationalists during the First Czech Republic. Their far-right position meant that they were also anti-German, which theoretically positioned them against the Nazis and was a source of tension. However, the Nazis used members of Vlajka as informants and collaborators, and while the Vlajka could abuse Jews with impunity, ultimately it was the Nazis who decided who took over confiscated Jewish businesses.

The racial laws and these dehumanising changes must have deeply affected Grete, Else and Therese's sense of self – to say nothing of the constant uncertainty and fear that continued to infuse daily life, as it had increasingly done in the previous years as Nazi terror spread through Europe.

One of the most cold-blooded Nazis, Reinhard Heydrich, took over Neurath's 'Protector' position after scheming against him, arriving in Prague on 27 September 1941. In July 1941, Herman Göring had given Heydrich the task of dealing with the 'final solution of European Jews', the *Endlösung*, and he was the person who decided to establish Theresienstadt. Because of his brutality, Heydrich became known as the Butcher of Prague. The Czech resistance was alive, though, and two agents (as part of Operation Anthropoid) trained by the exiled Czechoslovak government in London under Eduard Beneš resolved to kill him. Heydrich died nine days after an assassination attempt on 27 May 1942. The cause of his death has been the subject of speculation.[7] Joanie Holzer Schirm suggests that the Czech medical team at the Bulovka Hospital intentionally gave him blood from the wrong blood group during a transfusion, to speed up his demise.[8] He was thirty-eight years old. After his death, the Nazi regime acted out horrific reprisals, including destroying the

---

7. Ray J. Defalque and Amos J. Wright, 'The Puzzling Death of Reinhard Heydrich'.
8. Joanie Holzer Schirm: *Adventures Against Their Will: Extraordinary World War II Stories of Survival, Escape, and Connection – Unlike Any Others*, pos. 3260.

village of Lidice in Bohemia. At least three hundred and forty people from Lidice were murdered, one hundred and ninety-two men, sixty women and eighty-eight children, because the Nazis falsely accused partisans there of having aided the attack on Heydrich.

Transport: to Terezín, to Auschwitz

> *If they are not supplied with water during the transport, they then try to get out of the train at every possible opportunity to get water or have water brought to them, despite that being forbidden.*[9]

I'd found Grete's card in Czech documenting her fate online soon after receiving her passport from my father back in 2004. I no longer recall in which data bank. Else and Grete's cards showed that they lived together in Prague with their husbands before they were deported to different destinations. That time together before transportation must have given them at least a little comfort as they speculated day in and day out on what was to come. I wonder how they occupied themselves and what they lived on while they waited in fearful anticipation. Possibly they lived from selling their possessions, although that would have put them at risk. Otherwise, they must have lived on their savings. Else and Karl received their order to report to the meeting point for their transportation in mid-October 1941, and Grete and Eduard at some point in mid-December 1941. Else and Karl were sent to the Łódź ghetto and Grete and Eduard to Terezín. When the sisters parted, they must have known that it would be forever.

Eva Mändl, who I discovered was on the same transport to Terezín as Grete, recorded how she experienced the nights before being transported. Mändl, later Roubickova (1921–2013), was a secretary

---

9. *VEJ*, vol. 6, p. 244, document 59.

and translator. After the war, she met her fiancé Robert Roubicek, and they married and had two children. The following is from her handwritten diary entry, dated 17 December 1941, Theresienstadt. Mändl's diary entry allows a glimpse of what Grete most likely experienced. Jews were sent to so-called 'transit centres' before being deported with others who had also been singled out. Eva added details about the journey and arrival in Terezín. I have translated from German:

> *Up early at six o'clock. Sleeping is terrible; all the time people going back and forth, people constantly coughing. Mutti has slept terribly badly; I [slept] better the last two nights. All the men had their hair cut, but not the women. At nine o'clock, we were led to the train station, guarded by terribly heavily armed German soldiers with loaded weapons. Put into sealed wagons and only left at one o'clock in the direction of Theresienstadt. Terribly cramped in the wagons with all the luggage. All this is so strange that one simply does not understand it. Thank God, because if you understood everything, you'd go crazy. In the afternoon at two o'clock in Theresienstadt. There I was immediately received by the 'Hilfsdienst'.*[10] *The boys all look pretty bad, little to eat, and unshaven, but the frame of mind is not too bad.*[11]

A sense of being stunned by the happenings comes over in Eva's comment that everything was so strange it was incomprehensible. That incomprehensibility somehow shielded her; otherwise, she felt, she would have gone insane.

Professor Anna Hájková's book *The Last Ghetto: An Everyday History of Theresienstadt*, published in 2020, helped me to

---

10. *Hilfsdienst* means 'help service'; Terezín was self-administered by the people who were kept prisoner there.
11. *VEJ*, vol. 6, pp. 688–689, document 257.

understand more about this ghetto-cum-concentration camp. Upon arrival, there was no selection process as there was, for example, in Auschwitz, but people were searched, and women experienced crude overstepping of boundaries as they were intimately probed. Some new arrivals attempted suicide, and the health service department, aware of the shock that the newly arrived experienced, established a 'welcoming committee', offering psychological help for those in danger of taking their own lives. Inmates were not forced to wear prisoners' uniforms.

Helen Epstein, in her book *Where She Came From: A Daughter's Search for Her Mother's History,* describes Theresienstadt as an enormous waiting room of a train station where thousands of people died before their train drew in; it was a transit ghetto before the inhabitants were sent to the death camps. By September of 1942, the population included about 58,500 Jews, many of them too old, too young or too sick to work. The star-shaped garrison town, founded towards the end of the eighteenth century, had previously supported around three to four thousand people. Therefore, overcrowding was inescapable, and oppressive; people were never alone. There was no privacy in bathrooms or bedrooms, adding to the psychological pressure of imprisonment.

The following is a report about Theresienstadt by Wolfgang Salus, translated from German:

> *Czech Jews, German Jews, amphibians,[12] internationalists, Slovaks, Magyars, Poles. They are all imprisoned by the hundreds in the barracks. Women and men separated. Families torn apart. Father here, son there, mother somewhere else, children somewhere else. Meetings of family members are*

---

12. 'Amphibians' were those who spoke two or more languages, to whom it was difficult to assign a distinct nationality. Prof. Elisabeth Harvey suggests that typical 'amphibians' were speakers of Czech and German (personal correspondence, 7 November 2022).

very complicated; meetings of whole families are impossible. If an irritable policeman or even a German official notices a kiss between mother and son, husband and wife, or father and daughter, there will be 25 lashes on the bare back. And the wounds are bad. The victim can neither sit nor lie on his back for several days. All over that lies a grey cloud of boredom and hunger. Young, healthy men arbitrarily herded together 60 to 350 persons per room on straw sacks or on a mattress in 2- to 3-story beds or on the concrete floor.[13]

Theresienstadt was not a labour ghetto, and Hájková suggests in her book that it had the most refined organisation of all ghettos and concentration or death camps. It developed into a complex society in which Czech, German, Austrian, Dutch, Danish, Slovak and Hungarian Jews with different cultural backgrounds, speaking different languages, were thrown together and had to somehow navigate their new and perilous living situation. People from such diverse backgrounds encountered one another on the streets, at work, while queueing for their food and in their scant living quarters – and had to get on with one another.

Therese, my father's maternal grandmother, was transported to Terezín on 20 June 1942, six months after Grete and her husband arrived. They each would have experienced illness, which was rife, and hunger as well as the lack of privacy. Hájková states that the overwhelming majority of the thirty-four thousand deaths in Terezín were from starvation. Everyone who could work had to do so for ten hours a day. Saturday afternoon was free. This was presumably the first time Grete had worked outside her home; she had been a housewife. When I found documents about Grete online, I also discovered documents about Grete's husband, Eduard. He died in

---

13. Wolfgang Vaclav Salus (1909–1953). *VEJ*, vol. 6, pp. 716–717, document 272.

Terezín, and I do not attempt to describe the anguish and sorrow that his death must have caused her.

On Eduard's application for an ID card in Czech, his parents were noted: Zigmund Lanzer and Charlotta, whose maiden name was Bellakova. The German version of the street name of his residence in Prague was Heinrichgasse, and so it was noted on his death certificate. Someone had gone over the top with the five red *J* stamps on his document. Years later, I can sense the spite and hatred in the person's movements behind those five *J* markings as he stamped them.

There are many details on Eduard's death certificate, which was filled out with chilling efficiency. The cause of his death on 7 August 1942 was recorded as pneumonia and cardiac insufficiency. Like most people interned in Theresienstadt, he was emaciated and suffered malnutrition. His wife's name was typed in its German form, reflecting German SS presence in addition to the Jewish-Czech self-administration. The official language of the ghetto was German so that the SS could understand everything. Other relatives were noted as Hermine Reicher, Regine Liebschütz and Dr Adolf Lanzer, who might have been his (married) sisters and a brother. Eduard's profession was stated as tradesman. Dr Julius Elkan confirmed his death. (He must be the Dr Elkan who was transported in summer 1942 to Theresienstadt with his wife and mother-in-law. He and his wife Nelly survived.[14])

Hájková describes Terezín as a place of intense human suffering. She writes that of all the jeopardies and hardships inmates faced, they must have most feared the transports to the East. Between 26 October 1942 and 28 October 1944, the Germans deported 46,750 Jews from Theresienstadt to Auschwitz in twenty-seven transports. The first twelve transports, involving between 20,168 and 20,204

---

14. www.geni.com/people/Julius-Elkan/6000000029625669115.

people, arrived at Auschwitz between 26 October 1942 and 20 March 1944.[15] Is it possible to imagine what people experienced when they knew they were to be transported to the East, supposedly to a labour camp but with deep uncertainty and fear of worse things? Hájková writes that some people's emotions changed to panic, but some became apathetic and gave up hope, unable to realise what was about to happen to them. Others stayed calm and said goodbye. The Jewish self-administrators organised departure transports and faced the immense psychological pressure of selecting people to be included in the transport. Jewish administrative functionaries tried to do their best, sending away families with food and in good shape with a chance of surviving the upcoming immense strain and stress. The deportees had to go to a building before their departure. The self-administration usually emptied one of the barracks or part of it for this function and had the usual inhabitants moved elsewhere until the transport had left. Deportees were registered and waited for the transport, as did those on the standby list. The SS oversaw the transport's departure.

The name *Oświęcim*, the Polish name for Auschwitz, is on the lower right of Grete's card. That place embodies the most unspeakable, atrocious acts of Nazi evil: only Treblinka harbours even greater unspeakable evils. Grete lived in Terezín from 17 December 1941 until she was transported to Auschwitz two years later. She travelled to her final destination for two days, starting that journey in mid-December 1943. I can't begin to imagine a journey imbued with such overwhelming fear, cold, hunger, exhaustion, inadequate ventilation (the wagons were sealed), and disgust at her own and others' excrement. There were no toilets in the wagons, usually just a bucket in the corner, which quickly became full. How degrading; how dehumanising.

---

15. https://encyclopedia.ushmm.org/content/en/article/theresienstadt-concentrationtransit-camp-for-german-and-austrian-jews.

Ruth Klüger (1931–2020) was thirteen years old when she was transported to Auschwitz from Terezín in September 1943; she described the appalling journey and how she saw an old woman gradually losing her mind. The woman first wept and moaned, then sat on Ruth's mother's lap and urinated.[16]

How cramped Grete's wagon was, I do not know. Sometimes so many people were herded into the transports that sitting down was impossible, and people suffocated; some died during the journey, of dehydration or starvation. Altogether, over eighty-seven thousand people were deported from Terezín to the East. About four thousand survived.

Auschwitz

The Auschwitz concentration camp consisted of three main camps: Auschwitz I (Stammlager), the main camp; Auschwitz II (Birkenau), a concentration and extermination camp; and Auschwitz III (Monowitz), a labour camp. Birkenau was further subdivided into nine sections separated by electrified barbed-wire fences. It had the largest prisoner population, and its extermination centre included four gas chambers and crematoria. During its existence, 1.3 million people were sent to Auschwitz.[17] The people arriving in Auschwitz on transports from Theresienstadt and destined for the 'family camp' (so called because children were also incarcerated there) were not gassed upon arrival, as thousands of other Jews were. Klüger writes about her arrival at Auschwitz: how she was momentarily relieved at the prospect of fresh air and no longer being in the cramped cattle car. But once off the train, the air she breathed was not fresh: 'sie roch

---

16. Ruth Klüger, *Weiter Leben Eine Jugend* (published in English as *Still Alive: A Holocaust Girlhood Remembered*; hereafter Klüger).
17. www.history.com/news/auschwitz-concentration-camp-numbers.

wie sonst nichts auf dieser Welt' ('it smelled like nothing else in this world').[18] The stench was from the crematoria's burning bodies.

Grete – like Ruth Klüger, in an earlier transport – was sent to one of the nine subsections, the Theresienstadt 'family camp'. Men and boys lived in odd-numbered barracks, woman and girls in even-numbered. As part of Auschwitz-Birkenau, it was officially called BIIb; in her book Klüger calls it B2B. The reason the Nazis set up this particular camp, which was distinct from other parts of Auschwitz, has remained unclear. It has been suggested that its function was to (potentially) deceive the outer world, like the Red Cross's visit in June 1944 to Theresienstadt.[19] However, prisoners' survival was short-lived. These people were unaware that their fate had already been decided; they would be murdered after six months and receive what the Nazis, in their depravity, cynically called *Sonderbehandlung* – special treatment.

BIIb was an area of about 600 metres long and 130 metres wide, surrounded by barbed wire. Sectors BII b, c, d, and e each contained thirty-two residential barracks, six containing washrooms and toilets, and two kitchens. Of these thirty-two barracks, twenty-eight were residential blocks, two blocks were used as hospitals, one for weaving, and one was a combined school and kindergarten block.[20] The prisoners' sleeping quarters were dark wooden or brick barracks on either side of the road through the camp. Often these barracks did not have windows, and the people 'lived' in cold, dirty quarters with hundreds of others. Inside, wooden beds were attached to the walls, and several people slept – or tried to sleep – in one bed: along with the cramping and lack of space, lice were everywhere. There were washrooms for quick bathing, with limited amounts of water. Toilets were holes in long raised planks that many prisoners used

---

18. Klüger, p. 112.
19. https://encyclopedia.ushmm.org/content/en/article/theresienstadt-red-cross-visit.
20. www.auschwitz.org/en/history/auschwitz-ii/the-construction-of-the-camp.

simultaneously. Klüger writes of the suffering especially of old women using mass latrines in public.

The new arrivals destined for the family camp were tattooed on their lower left arm, but their heads were not shorn as was common in other parts of the camps. Although prisoners in all three sections of Auschwitz were forced to work, and SS guards and their dogs patrolled each area, these BIIb prisoners had the 'privileges' of not wearing prison clothes and being allowed to wash their hair, write (censored) letters and receive packages. However, much of the incoming mail, especially if it contained food, was stolen before delivery.

After being woken before dawn, the prisoners had thirty minutes to wash, dress and clear up their living quarters before the long morning roll call. Prisoners, constantly malnourished, had to do strenuous physical labour and work on completing this part of the camp or on road or water canal construction. Others worked in delousing and potato peeling Kommandos. Kommandos were prisoner work gangs, and Kapos were SS-assigned prisoner functionaries in charge of the Kommandos, who belonged to the organisational management of a concentration camp. Many Kapos were criminals, chosen for their brutality; this gave the SS the advantages of having less direct involvement in keeping things going and fewer costs. Kapos were selected from among the prisoners and earned privileges such as more food rations. The long day ended with another roll call. Sundays were not workdays, but prisoners had to tidy their personal space and take their weekly showers.[21]

Inadequate clothing meant the prisoners were cold most of the time, and lack of food meant they were always hungry. The daily soup was salty and the prisoners suffered from continual thirst, as Klüger recorded. When they became ill, there was no adequate treatment.

---

21. https://en.wikipedia.org/wiki/Auschwitz_concentration_camp.

Klüger wrote vividly and hauntingly about her experiences in the BIIb camp, and I bow out of trying to describe further what Grete (and the thousands of others) went through. In the end, there is no way I can imagine and know what she suffered. Ruth Franklin describes the dead, dying, thinnest, weakest, sickest: 'The bones piled up like sticks in mass graves, the empty faces peering out from the bunks after liberation – in short, the ultimate symbol of the Nazis' depravity.'[22]

As I record these facts and cite authors on the subject, I see Grete in my mind, emaciated and desperate, a tragic shadow of herself. Perhaps she worked in the weaving mill, making belts for machine guns from leftover material. She must have also seen what Klüger described: heaps of intertwined naked corpses on lorries, the swarms of flies on them, the corpses' tangled hair and scant pubic hair. I do not know how long Grete survived; it was a maximum of six months after arriving at Auschwitz from Theresienstadt. Maybe she died of starvation, illness, fear, hopelessness and anguish before the older people on her transport were sent to the gas chambers when the six months were up. Younger people had a chance of not being selected and surviving, but as Grete was now sixty, she would have had no chance of not being sent to the gas chambers, if indeed she was still alive when the six months were up.

Over 10,000 prisoners were sent to the gas chambers between March and July of 1944. The people were told they had to bathe, be disinfected and undress. The Sonderkommando had to escort fellow Jews to the gas chambers. People were herded into the chamber, some dreading what was to come. The doors were locked, and pellets of Zyklon B, a poisonous cyanide-based pesticide, were thrown in. First, the people nearest the source of the toxic gas started struggling for breath, for their lives. Then, panic broke out as people surged to the

---

22. Ruth Franklin, *A Thousand Darknesses: Lies and Truths in Holocaust Fiction*, p. 52. Hereafter Franklin.

locked doors, trampling one another, while an SS doctor watched through a peephole. After the screams of the victims died away the chamber was opened, and the Sonderkommando prisoners dragged out the corpses, covered in excrement and vomit. They cut off the women's hair and removed metal dental work and jewellery. Bodies were incinerated and burned like refuse. Sonderkommando prisoners used wooden mallets to crush into powder any bones that were not fully burned.

Everything was loaded onto trucks and carried to the banks of the Vistula river, beyond the woods in Birkenau, where it was shovelled straight into the water. Human ashes were also dumped into the Soła river near the Auschwitz I camp, and into holes and depressions in the terrain. They were used as a base for building roads or reinforcing dikes and as an additive to the compost heaps used on the camp farms. Significant deposits of human ashes are extant in the vicinity of the crematoria.[23]

When my father returned to Opava in September 1945, he heard from a family friend, Friedl, that she had received a postcard from Grete about twelve months previously. The timing of Friedl's postcard suggests that Grete indeed horrifically survived some months in Auschwitz.

---

23. http://70.auschwitz.org/index.php?option=com_content&view=article&id=290&Itemid=179&lang=en.

PHOTOS

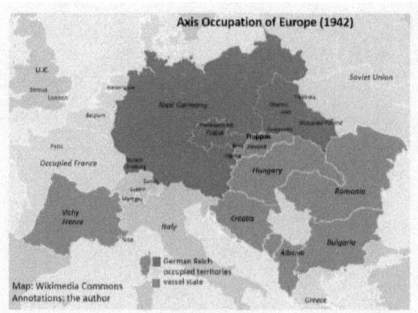

Europe 1942

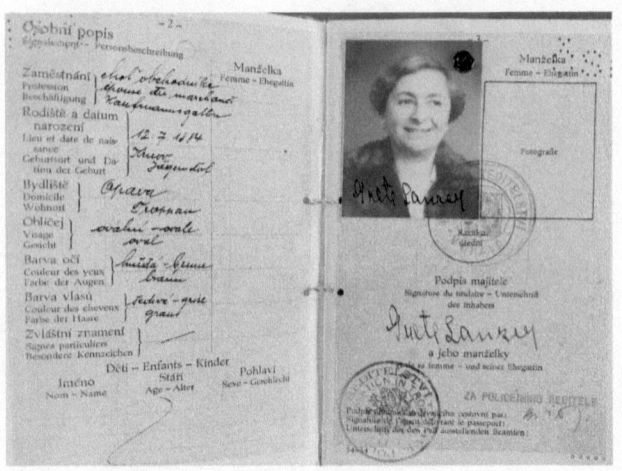

Grete Lanzer's passport, issued 1935.

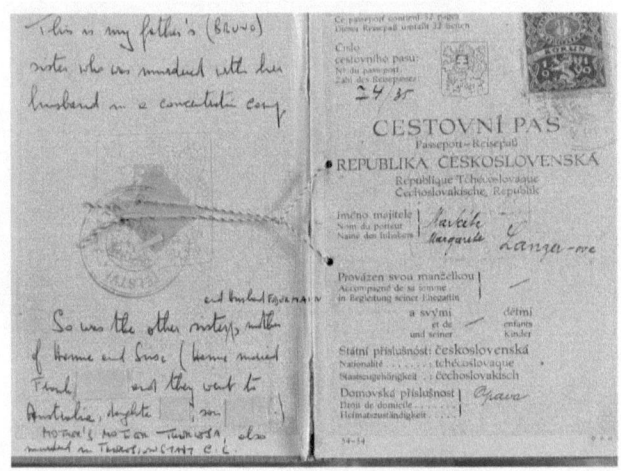

Grete's passport with my father's message.

The photo in my grandfather's study I stared at as a child. I thought it was Irma, but later discovered it was my grandfather's mother, Johanna. Probably taken in 1930, for Johanna's 70th birthday.

Irma, Alfred, my father, and me as a baby, 1958.

Marianne, cigarette in hand, with my father after he joined the Czech division of the RAF in 1943.

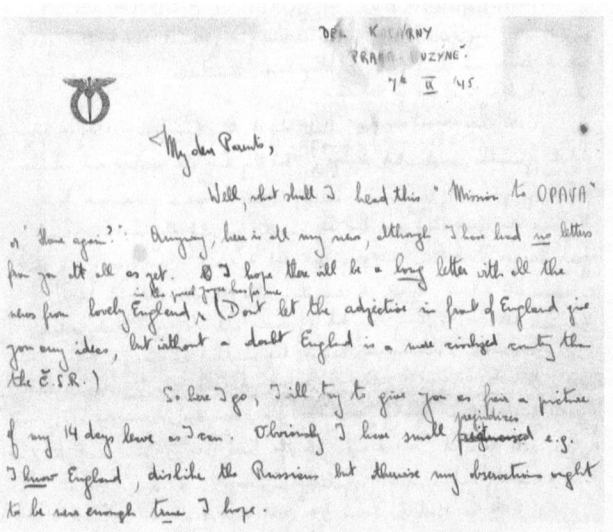

The start of my father's letter he wrote upon returning to Czechoslovakia after the war. September 1945.

Therese with her grandchildren, Hans-Peter and Eva, 1929.

Family photo: back row Alfred, Melitta, Marianne. Seated Bruno, Gert, Eva, Hilde with Claus on her knee, my father (standing). Behind my father, Eduard Hellmann. 1930.

Marianne Wilhelm, my grandmother, around the age of 25.

The family in Opava, possibly taken on my grandfather's birthday, July 1930. The lawn mower, lower left in the picture, must have been his birthday present.

The Vogel family two months after arrival in England.
May 1939.

The card documenting Grete's fate.

The card documenting Else's fate.

The card documenting Karl's fate.

The card documenting Therese's fate.

Great-grandmother Johanna's family. On Johanna's right is Ernestine, her mother.

Johanna, Grete, Else and Irma, 1910.

Hilde and Alfred, around 1927.

Hilde Wilhelm, Paris, 1939.

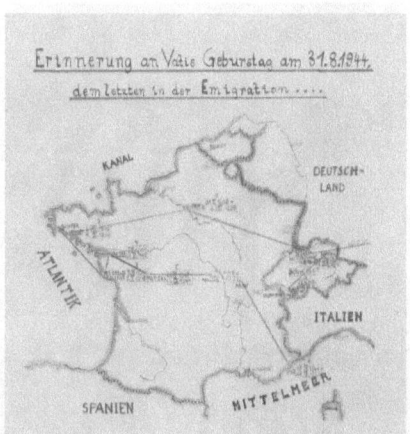

Claus Wilhelm drew as a 15-year-old how the Wilhelm family moved around in France during their exile. The sketch was a birthday present for his father entitled *'For Dad's birthday, 31. August 1944, the last one in emigration.'*

Claus Wilhelm's Hitler caricature.

A postwar family photo. Everyone was smoking apart from my father.

Queen Elizabeth, the Queen mother being introduced in 1971 to Bruno at the Gütermann factory reopening after the fire.

Oskar and Martha Weishappel after the war.

The Wilhelm and Vogel family met again after the war. Late 1940s.

The stylised MBV initials of my grandparents on the wall surrounding their house in Opava. Photo from 2016.

Julia and me having a weep on the steps at the family house's garden, 2016.

Eva sitting on the same steps with her dog, Bobby, around 1935.

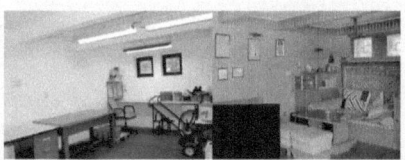

The same room in the house that had belonged to my father's family in the 1930s and 2016.

Julia and me at the house in Opava, 2016.

Eva's carving documenting the family's fate. She made it for her parents' 20th wedding anniversary. Note the red stylised MBV initials interwoven with a yellow 20. 1942.

The memorial to Therese and her husband Ludwig in the Jewish cemetery in Opava. Photo from 2016.

Me, Eva, and Julia, 2013

Else, Grete and Therese. Else was looking into the camera when the photo was taken and suddenly, when I found her photo, it was as if she was looking straight at me, down through the years.

9 EVA
1923–2013

... the shadow is a hovering presence that will not go away, binding those who were not there to those who were, both dead and alive.

Ellen Fine[1]

Aunt Eva, my father's sister, died aged ninety in August 2013. I went back to England for her funeral. The day before the funeral, Julia and I went to Eva's house in Surrey to prepare for the celebration of her life after the service. The house felt empty and quiet without its owner, and memories flooded back of family gatherings which had taken place there during my childhood. Two mad dachshunds, Archie and Percy, had raced around, and Eva had loudly and collectively called 'Boys!' to them. I heard Eva's laughing voice in my mind; she was an energetic person and had spoken with conviction in (not quite authentic-sounding) upper-class Oxford English, which she lavishly sprinkled with swear words.

---

1. Ellen Fine, *Third Generation Holocaust Representation Trauma, History, and Memory*, p. 47.

The day before the funeral was warm, and the garden was brimming with colour. I busied myself making little posies of flowers to decorate the tables for the celebration, arranging them in Eva's large collection of small vases. Julia and I pottered around, taking time now and again to chat and reminisce. We had so many shared memories of our grandparents and their children: my aunt and her uncle – her mum and my dad. The stories tumbled out of us. Julia gave me some objects she had found while clearing the house up. One of them, a little book, led to my finding Else, Bruno's other never-mentioned sister. I tell about that in the next chapter.

The funeral service itself was jam-packed with people who had known and loved Eva. Some had to stand in the aisles as all the seats were full: at least a hundred people attended. It was a moving event, with people struggling to fight back their tears but also switching with ease to loud and hearty laughter. This was because of Eva's well-developed habit of swearing, and people paying tribute to her mentioning that. Julia's husband, Trevor, Eva's son-in-law, said with perfect timing and intonation during his tribute: 'the only aspect of English culture she seemed *not* to have picked up, was the judicious use of euphemism'; the room roared. In my mind, I heard Eva's loud voice in her cultivated upper-class sing-song: 'The bloody bastards! The buggers! Bloody hell ... !'

Eva was fifteen when Bruno and Marianne fled with their children to England in 1938. She was old enough to remember her life in Opava before leaving and young enough, like my father, to begin a new life in England with relative ease. Eva was two years older than her brother and spoke more about the past than he did – not to me but to her daughter, my cousin Julia.

Eva made a carving for her parents to commemorate their twentieth wedding anniversary in 1942, and it gives insight into what she and the family had experienced. The object is small, 11cm in diameter, only 3mm thick, and Julia gifted it to me in 2018 for my sixtieth birthday. I had never seen it before. This present touched me deeply, and her mum's artisanship and the story it had to tell impressed me. Eva skilfully integrated the figure 20 (in yellow) at the perimeter. She carved a symbolised M, a V and an upside-down B (in red), which connect the object's parts: the initials of her parents, Marianne and Bruno Vogel. Eva took on this symbolism of her parents' initials from something sculpted on the wall at her childhood home, as the reader will discover in Chapter 16. The house in Troppau is at the centre, and directly below it are four figures who seem to be hurrying. The car they drove on their way to Prague, their first stop as they emigrated, is to the right, and Eva painted a tiny 'Praha' sign indicating their destination. At the top of the carving is the Gütermann factory in England, and the Welsh dragon symbolises Irma and Alfred's growing business in Wales with IVO Tapestries. To the left are various objects; I puzzled about the clock: did it simply represent time? The dogs (lower left) had to stay in Opava when the family left.

Possibly within months of arriving in England, earlier than the anniversary carving, Eva had made a carving showing her dream of returning to Opava and her happy childhood. The small object shows her in bed asleep. Behind the open curtains she depicts her dream. She is walking in nature, under the skies, between two women: her mother, Marianne, and her grandmother, Therese. Eva's eye for detail shows; she included a posy on the bedside table and a little blue carpet on the floor in front of her bed. She looks tiny and snug in her green wooden bed with lots of pillows, sleeping in a room with a reddish (possibly wooden) floor.

Eva, born 22 April 1923, went to boarding school for fifteen months after the family arrived in England in 1939. She then attended the Girls High in Stroud, Gloucestershire, a grammar school, from June 1940 to July 1941. She was a day girl and lived with her aunt, Irma, at the house called Ravingdon in Pitchcombe near Stroud. She passed her Cambridge School Certificate straight away, an exam qualifying her for university entrance. This shows how quickly she became proficient in English. A year later, she passed the Cambridge Higher School Certificate with distinction in German. Although she won a scholarship to Westfield College, Oxford University, she started to study languages at the University of London, but only from September 1942 to December 1943. She gained an intermediate BA in German and Latin, a grade then awarded after a year of study. Eva also regularly joined my father for working stays at a farm owned by one Tom Lewis.

After that, aged twenty, Eva volunteered for the Auxiliary Territorial Service (ATS), the woman's branch of the British army, during the Second World War. When the war was over, she did not follow up on her academic possibilities because, as Julia shared, she 'faced up to the fact that she hated the discipline of writing essays'.

Despite her dislike of academic writing, Eva nevertheless wrote the following compelling account about her trip to Prague in October 1945. It shows, among other things, her command of English and that, like my father, she had an urge to record her experiences in writing and to tell stories. She called it 'The Return of the Native':

'Will you be going back after the war?' They always asked that, whenever Czechoslovakia came into the conversation. Free again ... home! I never thought or dreamt about anything else. I lived for it, all those [war] years. Home.

Not a large town, Opava, but the dearest, most beautiful. A proud town – proud of her historical past, her taste, her theatre, her schools. A peaceful town. My hometown. We lived just outside [the town centre] *on the way to Kylesovice. 'The yellow villa'. 'Down the hill', they used to say when directing a stranger, Down the hill, then pass the yellow villa .... Home .... I could see it so clearly, so vividly. The long curve of wall – a high wall, yellow too – with clusters of purple-velvety clematis foaming over the top. And beyond the heavy iron gates, the house, with its steep roof. And the garden – how I had loved the garden.*

In all, I have now been back three times and if ever I should go there again, I know it will not hurt anymore. I went home the third time to get it all out of my system. I was stationed in Vienna and a friend took me in his jeep. We drove to Prague and then days later turned east to Moravia. We visited all the places of my childhood – the forests, mountains, and villages in the vicinity of my home. Now memory haunts me no longer and I am at peace. But it was the first visit that mattered. The wonderful chance, the moment I had lived for came five months after Czechoslovakia's 'liberation'. I was on leave from [the ATS] in Italy and by some great luck I was given a passage on one of the Czech repatriation liberators, and war office blessings with permission to stay a few days.

It is Monday, 15th October 1945. We are flying high up above the clouds. Germany is below but we cannot see any land. I am so thrilled, so excited, that I cannot keep still, and hardly feel the cold. The babies are awfully good, asleep most of them, on the laps for their mothers. British wives of Czech soldiers; they are going home too, but for them it is the unknown. They sit in the bomb bays calmly as they might sit in a London bus, yet they have left behind everything dear to them, dear and familiar. They are off to a strange land with strange customs and an alien language. How will they fare? I wonder for a brief moment.

Standing beside me by the tail window is a diplomatic courier from the London Embassy. To him this trip is routine and my impatient enthusiasm a diverting amusement. 'Just think', I keep repeating, hardly grasping it, 'I'm going home!' 'I'll take you to a night club in Prague', he smiles indifferently. 'Oh, how wonderful!' I had been a child when I left – no night clubs for children.

'There's good food if you know where to go – we'll have dinner first.' Dinner in Prague – a real Czech dinner! 'How lovely, thank you!' He looks at his watch: 'We should be there soon now' and once again I glance over to my luggage. One of the cases is heavy, with saved up tins and soap and presents for those left at home. The Czech crew are in cheerful attendance. 'Don't you run off with a dashing Russian!' I laugh – but I had forgotten for a while that the Russians were still there.

We dip into enveloping greyness – we are going down. I swallow hard because my ears seem to be bursting and – Prague, down there is Prague! I hop out into a dull, dismal afternoon. Czech voices of Czech officials. I could hug every one of them. 'Welcome to Prague'. I'm so happy, so happy. Cold wind and raindrops against my face. I breathe deeply and the Czech winds' sting is a caress. With a pang I remember the sunny afternoon when we took off – for six months [in 1939] as we then thought, the six months of Father's [work] commitments in England. 'Seven years' I think and yet it only seems yesterday ... the bright buildings, the glistening planes from all over the world, the smooth voice over the loudspeaker and announcements in many tongues, handkerchiefs waving, all the world's flags on ground poles. There are flags now, too, rattling in the wind. Ominously side by side, ours and theirs – the Russians'.

Husbands dashing forward – husbands and wives together again. 'Darling, welcome home, darling'. One girl alone – holding fast the sleeping baby. Perhaps he didn't get the telegram, perhaps he missed the train, perhaps ... wide eyed, bewildered but no fuss, no scene. She is so alone – but she is British. They're giving us thick slices of black bread, with pink sausage and a cup of nasty coffee. I love the bread, Czech bread.

It is getting dark when we are shown to the bus which will take us to the YMCA. Those not from Prague are off to the YMCA for the night. We go in a coach, my yellow labelled luggage in the rack above. Suburbs. Silent streets lined with trees – I had forgotten! The wind driving the leaves and clouds of dust. No dust in England. Bumpy, cobble pavement – home too, I think at every jolt, home – and I'm thinking it in English. Not many people about; too cold and windy. An untidy mound of rubble – familiar sight of blitz times. Why don't they clear it away? The dimly lit streets are empty, and I don't know any of the parts through which we are passing. Queer to not know Prague well – queer to be a stranger in my own capital.

We are there. A tall modern building. The driver rings the doorbell and men come to help with the luggage. Sullen men but strong. German? Did I hear them speak in German? Then I see the 'N' stitched on their front. N for Němec (German). They are German and the tide has turned. That is how they made the Jews wear 'J's' and now the tide has turned. I hated the Germans. An eye for an eye, I used to say in England, they had enslaved my country, they had enslaved Europe, shot my grandmother. The first German I see, I'll spit in his face, I used to say in England. Now I'd seen them I felt pity and disgust. Humans being singled out.

I am lucky – I have a room to myself. An iron bed, a chair, and a washbasin. I try the taps, taps with Czech inscription, but only the cold works – and it's icy. 'Good old army training' I think gratefully as the water is running. When I go down, he [the man from the plane who invited Eva out] *is waiting for me, proudly waving a handful of meal coupons. We set out, first to have some dinner. Now the streets are crowded, and we turn into Wenceslas Square. Shop windows are brightly lit, and people are strolling up and down leisurely – it hasn't changed. There are many Russian soldiers and I just want to look and listen. Czech advertisements and Czech words.*

Suddenly I see a group of soldiers in British battledress with Czech Brigade Flash.[2] *I don't know them, but we shout hello, and they are asking eager questions about England. Queer – the first strangers I talk to in Prague are not strangers because they've been in England too, and we're speaking English to each other. The novelty of it all leaves no time though – I just accept the facts. I am intoxicated.*

We go into a large restaurant – an orchestra is playing at the far end but the buzz of Czech voices is almost drowning the music. Suddenly there is a hush, and everyone is looking – looking at me. Then the headwaiter beckons at us, and we are ushered to a corner table. Waiters rush to assist with the chair. And as I see the menu my momentary embarrassment is forgotten. All these Czech dishes.

We go to three different night clubs. I've never been to one at home before – I was too young then. People are staring again but I am taking it in my stride more. We drink and dance and I'm enjoying every minute of it. Many tables are occupied by Russian officers – but only very few have women with them.

After a while the band leader comes over to us, makes a deep bow and asks what the gracious lady would like them to play. The lady is amazed and chooses various Czech and Slovak folk tunes. The band obliges and the 'lady' feels like crying. One last request – the band leader bows again. 'Do you know 'Tipperary'?'[3] *I ask in a shaky voice and the violin gives the*

---

2. The 1st Czechoslovak Independent Armoured Brigade Group was an armoured unit of expatriate Czechoslovaks organised and equipped by the UK during the Second World War in 1943. A 'flash' is an identifying coloured patch worn on uniforms.
3. 'It's a Long Way to Tipperary': a First World War marching song with an

lead. Then everyone – everyone except the puzzled Russians – join in. They all know the words and as they sing, they raise their glasses to our table. I sing too with a quivering chin and tears rolling down slowly. Back in my bare little room I suddenly realise how tired I am and as I curl up between the clammy sheets, I don't feel the cold ...

Two thick slices of dark, dry bread spread with black plum jam and acorn coffee are the breakfast. I will have to waste today reporting to various military officers. Prague in daylight – I walk the streets slowly, drinking it all in. I notice the general shabbiness, not one elegant woman to be seen and the fashions seem three years behind.

I am taking it quite for granted now that people turn to look at me – it's the British uniform and I suppose that I must be the first ATS girl seen in the streets of Prague. I come to a [?] and as I approached, a policeman salutes. Was that meant for me, a mere one pipper[4] – the girl who until '39 had felt the customary suspicious respect every continental has for the police? There is no-one behind me, so I return the courtesy. Making my way to St Wenceslas Square, where I shall catch the 22 tram, I will have ample time for reflection. 'I am back' I keep telling myself, back after all these years. That's what I have been waiting for – but I feel lonely – isolated. I am not one of my own people – I am a stranger and merely speak their tongue. Their Tongue? My own tongue – Czech. It's just that I don't know Prague very well, it must be that. Wait until I get to my hometown, to Opava. All policemen salute, and Czech soldiers too – my right arm is kept busy. The trams are overcrowded, there are no queues. I'd forgotten that – horrible,

---

irreverent and non-military theme with characteristically British qualities of cheerfulness in the face of hardship.
4. 'One pipper': military slang for a person wearing a single star on the shoulder of their uniform, implying a lower rank.

the way one has to push and scramble. Squeezed inside, people are asking me who I am.

Either Eva never got round to describing her return to Opava, or the rest of her report has been lost. Her account reveals her state of mind before and during her return. She is observant of the people around her; her voice comes over clearly, as does her eye for detail. Her memories at the start of her report seem to echo carefree childhood days, and it was quiet, outdoor visual impressions that came to her mind. Eva commits to paper the painful loss of her home and that she had visited the house three times to resolve her loss. Reflecting, she emphasises that another visit would not hurt anymore. However, it sounds a little as if she was trying to force acceptance upon herself of the loss of her childhood home.

Her account then focuses on Prague and describes her return. The Second World War had ended five months previously. Eva writes about Czechoslovakia's liberation in inverted commas: a clear jab at the Russians. Her mind wanders, as she observes her fellow passengers, to how it had been when she left the familiar for the unknown in 1938/1939 when the family fled.

Doing a bit of name-dropping, Eva records her exchange with a diplomatic courier from the London Embassy, and how he invited her out. As a twenty-two-year-old woman, she recalls that she was a child when she left, and maybe she was sensing her adulthood and how time had passed as she self-confidently accepted his invitation. As they descended towards Prague, she was again reminded of the Russian presence in her home country, and, while she doesn't openly write it, uneasiness about that lies between the lines.

As the plane descended Eva experienced discomfort, but her excitement about returning continued to infuse her. Briefly, Eva contrasts the winter weather with the sunshine when the family departed for England, and she experiences 'a pang' as she remembers. That may have been longing for days gone by before the war, for her childhood. Eva writes that she and her brother had been told that Bruno's work at the Gütermann factory meant six months in England. It seems credible that the children were not told that the trip was an emigration because of the Nazi threat to the Jewish family.

The account contrasts her previous years in England with Prague, and Eva was surprised because she realised that although she was thinking about being home, she was thinking in English. This reveals how comfortable she felt with the English language. But for the first time, there's an inkling of disquiet, and it has to do with identity. She calls herself a stranger in her own capital, and this experience contrasts with her joyous, almost childish expectations evoked during her journey there in the plane. She was bothered that more rubble had not been cleared away from the roads in the aftermath of the war. In England that must have been the case. There may have been a demonstrative aspect to not clearing the roads in Prague, which was not badly damaged during the war – a sort of 'we suffered too' message.

Eva commits to paper her first encounter with a German and lists the reasons for her vengeful impulses. She acknowledges the murder of her grandmother, Therese, but her 1945 narrative is incorrect. Therese's fate had not yet been clarified, or if it had been, Eva didn't (yet) know. She counts herself lucky because she had a room to herself at the YMCA, and, simple though the room was, without warm water, she roots herself in British 'tough army training'. For Eva, even the tap at her sink, like the wind upon her arrival and the bread, had a Czech identity.

She was surprised that the first people she encountered on the streets of Prague were soldiers in British battledress with a Czech Brigade flash. They spoke English with one another, and another implicit identity issue seems to have arisen. Eva again notes that Russians were in the nightclubs, and she also noticed that they were not accompanied by many women. This observation seems to point to

Eva sensing their presence as unnatural; for her they were not a normal part of society, because their female partners were absent. The Russians did not belong.

Eva then vividly records what seems to have been a tribute to the British for defeating the Nazis in the war, triggered by Czechs seeing her uniform. She briefly alters her writing stance and moves to the distance of the third person, writing about herself in inverted commas as a 'gracious lady'. This she may have taken, like a cue, from the bandleader, who had probably addressed her as *milostivá paní* ('madam'), a third-person form with an extra layer of deference that people in service used at that time. Additionally, this experience, being addressed in this way, touched Eva's change in social status; as a fifteen year old (when she left), she would not have been spoken to like that. She was encountering the reality of having grown up coupled with the gallant status of having served abroad. Multiple layers of challenging experiences seemed to have jarringly come together in this moment, and she captures that: it was important to her to record it. Some of the tension from the war seems to have been released as she cried while 'Tipperary' was sung. It was an intense moment that she saves in words. Several things happened within her: the song in English catalysed an emotional release, and possibly she sensed comradeship and her British identity which had developed during the war and had saved her and her family. Perhaps her loss came to her mind; she had survived the war, but her grandmother (and two aunts and their husbands) had not. She probably also experienced relief that the war was over.

Although she received respect from policemen and others when they saluted her the next day, Eva seems to have felt lonely and confused. She observes that Prague was generally 'shabby' and noticed there were no elegant women walking the streets, that fashion seemed to be three years behind. Eva was comparing how the women on the streets of Prague looked to the last time she was there, before the war left its devastating traces. The atmosphere on the streets in post-war Prague comes over. Eva was comforting herself in her disorientation, by envisaging her return to Opava, hoping that her longed-for homecoming would be as joyous as she anticipated. This part of her account suggests that she was experiencing a sobering disenchantment, contrasting with the almost childish joy and hope while on the plane to Prague. The surviving page of the piece ends with criticism of people for not queueing, a custom in British society but not on the continent. She had forgotten that.

Eva visited my father in 1946 in Czechoslovakia, and the meeting did not go well. His letter to her after the two-day visit belongs to Chapter 11 and gives insight into their distant and, at times, destructive sibling relationship.

Eva in England after the war

Julia told me that Eva had a good and interesting career and worked for various theatrical and advertising agencies before meeting Michael Waring in 1951 and marrying in 1953. She lived in Cyprus while Michael, who was in the army, was stationed there, and she worked for the local police as the station secretary and then moved around with Michael. She also lent her artistic skills to book cover illustrations. She stopped working after her marriage and became a mother in 1959. After marrying, Eva's life was tragically peppered with four miscarriages.

In 1965 after twelve years of marriage and when Julia was six years old, Michael died of cancer. Julia told me something of her mother's life once she was widowed: 'Her active interest in politics came about when a local conservative MP wooed her after Michael's death. He took her to the House of Commons, and she became involved in local politics. She was a natural Tory fuelled by her attitude towards Russia.' Eva did not remarry and threw herself into her support of the Tories and work in the Citizen's Advice Bureau.

As a child and teenager, I saw Aunt Eva regularly when birthdays and Christmases were celebrated. I liked her eccentricity and liveliness but was aware of tension between her and my parents, although I didn't understand it. Michael's death occurred the same year as Alfred's death in the fire and Irma's suicide six months later. These multiple tragic events were buried from the younger generation and became part of the unspoken family history. Or, expressed otherwise, the younger generation was intentionally shielded from the tragedies – but we nevertheless picked them up atmospherically.

I gained deep insight into Eva and her way of dealing with the past when I spoke to Julia and transcribed our recorded conversation which makes up this book's penultimate chapter.

The next chapter focuses on Eva's and my father's aunt, Else, Bruno's younger sister.

10 ELSE
1887–1941 (?)

Today, 45 people died in the ghetto. No births were registered.

Łódź ghetto resident [1]

It was a little book that led me to Else, Bruno's younger sister. I was at Aunt Eva's house in 2013 after she'd died, helping Julia prepare for a celebration after Eva's funeral. Julia was sorting her mother's possessions at her home in Surrey and showed me some old books written in German which had probably belonged to Irma; they must have brought the books with them when they emigrated to England in 1939. Eva inherited them after Irma's death in 1965 – and she kept them. One of the books, *Brachvogel*, by Friedemann Bach, had belonged to Eva's aunt, Else. Until now, I'd only known this sister of Bruno by surname, Federmann, which my father had noted in Grete's passport. The book was small, old, leather-bound, and as I opened it, I saw the bookplate on the first right-hand page – a

---

1. Lucjan Dobroszycki (ed.), *The Chronicle of the Łódź Ghetto, 1941–1944*, p. 14. Hereafter *The Chronicle*.

silhouette image of Bruno. That spoke to me, and I thought that Else must have been close to her brother. The bookplate declared the book to be part of the library of Else Vogel, and for the first time, I realised that my great-aunts and I had shared the same maiden name: I had grown up in England as Nicola Vogel. Julia smiled quietly as we looked, and she gave me the book. I paused as I held it and imagined Else holding it while reading decades ago.

Else was the most remote of the three relatives that I searched for. I knew of her existence because my father had noted her in Grete's passport, but I only had her married surname. Now I had her first name. Initially, I had no information about Else apart from the names of her daughters and her husband, which my father had noted in Grete's passport. I found nothing about Else in the suitcase at my mother's house. Back in 2004, when Grete's passport came into my life, I'd easily found documents online relating to Grete but could not trace the other people my father had listed. Admittedly, I'd not tried very hard. In those days I was not yet ready to go in more deeply; that came much later, in summer 2021.

However, back in Freiburg, after my journey to England for Eva's funeral in 2013, I started researching Else more earnestly; she was not to be found. I hadn't thought of searching for Else using the Czech version of her name, which I did not know, so I couldn't have done it anyway. In the end, I found out more about Else's fate only by searching for her husband, Karl Federmann. When I finally found documents relating to Eliska Federmannova – it must have been in 2014 – bewildering sadness overcame me again. Else's card, dated 21 October 1941, was the first document I found, and it showed that she and Karl were transported from Prague to the Łódź ghetto in October 1941.

As I started to understand more, the following picture emerged: Else had lived in Ostrava with her husband Karl, their daughter Suzanne, called Susi, and her stepdaughter Hanne, from Karl's first marriage. I had already met Susi and Hanne through Irma's account of Susi's arrival in England. Ostrava (Ostrau) lies about 35 kilometres southeast of Troppau. Karl's first wife, whose name was also Else (which confused me for a while), died in 1919 aged thirty-two, leaving him alone with Hanne. As Hanne's birth date is given as 1917, Karl must have cared for Hanne as a toddler for around two years; perhaps his family helped him in this tragic situation. Geni.com[2] documents these dates, and that Hanne was Great-Aunt Else's stepdaughter is further backed up by various family documents. Likewise, genealogy websites record Susi as a half-sister to Hanne. Hanne emigrated to England before Susi arrived in March 1939. As my chapter on Irma relates, Susi tragically killed herself in 1940. There is no way of knowing if Else and Karl knew this before their own tragic and untimely deaths.

I had never heard of the Łódź ghetto, and I only had sketchy knowledge about the largest Nazi ghetto of Warsaw. So again, I had a lot to read and learn. Since I knew so little about these family members, I strongly felt I owed it to Karl and Else to begin to understand the conditions of the ghetto, their existence there and their deaths.

The Łódź ghetto

The ghetto was self-administered, like Theresienstadt, with various administrative departments. It was cut off from the outside world in May 1940. By the end of 1942, almost half of the people incarcerated there had been murdered in the death camp Chełmno/Kulmhof. M.C. Rumkowski was the head of the Jewish Council of Elders, a disputed leadership figure who aimed to make the ghetto of economic benefit to the Nazis by being productive, thereby saving the inhabitants. His plan was unsuccessful: the ghetto was liquidated in the summer of 1944, and the remaining people

---

2. www.geni.com/people/Elsa-Federmann/6000000020571564129.

were sent to Auschwitz to be murdered, Rumkowski included. The extermination of the Jews of Łódź and the surrounding area in Chełmno continued on and off until January 1945.[3]

Maria König (1921-2019)

Maria König was someone who survived the Łódź ghetto as well as Auschwitz and the concentration camp in Bavaria, Flossenbürg.[4] Her book about her experience of the Łódź ghetto promised to give me insight into what Else and Karl had experienced there. As she was approaching her hundredth birthday in 2018, Antje Leetz, a friend, interviewed Maria in her care home and recorded what Maria related about her survival. Maria died a year later. My following summary in English of Maria and Antje's book (published in German) gives an impression of the Łódź ghetto.[5]

In the 1930s, Łódź was a large industrial city with around 600,000 inhabitants located south-west of Warsaw. It was known as the 'Polish Manchester' and had textile companies with dyeing factories. Łódź was ethnically divided into Polish, German and Jewish thirds. Much of the poor Polish, German and Jewish population was concentrated in a slum area. In those days, Christians and Jews had little in common. Maria's mother didn't allow her to play on the street because she feared non-Jewish children would pick on her and start a fight. Maria grew up aware that the Polish civilian population did not like Jews. Long before the war, there were posters stuck on fences that shocked her: *Jews out! Go to Madagascar!* That thing with Madagascar remained a life-long puzzle to Maria. It referred to a plan to forcibly relocate the Jewish population of Europe to the island of Madagascar, to the east of southern Africa. This was seriously

---

3. www.yadvashem.org/de/holocaust/about/ghettos/lodz.html#narrative_info.
4. www.gedenkstaette-flossenbuerg.de/en/history/flossenbuerg.
5. Maria König and Antje Leetz, *Marisha – mehr als ein Wunder: Eine Überlebensgeschichte* (*Marisha – More Than a Miracle: A Survival Story*).

proposed in the summer of 1940 by the Nazi German government but shelved in 1942 as the *Endlösung* came into action.

The Nazis invaded Poland when Maria was still a child, and she remembered the start of the Second World War, a warm summer day in early September 1939. She became a witness to Nazi brutality, and the threat of arrests grew. The family knew that they could not flee as they didn't have the financial means, and there was nowhere to go anyway. They soon received the notification that Jews had to leave their flats by a specific date and move into the ghetto.

Many Jewish people lived in the area of Łódź which became the ghetto, along with the poor non-Jewish population. The ghetto was part of the oldest quarter of town, called Bałuty. The non-Jewish poor who lived there were moved out to other areas of town. Maria recalled that people arriving from Germany couldn't speak Polish, and for them, it was even more difficult than it was for her family. A lot of Yiddish was spoken because not only Polish Jews lived there but also German and Ukrainian Jews.

The roads there were small, the flats old with inadequate or no sanitation. Maria's family was transferred to the ghetto at the end of November 1939. They had to leave their furniture behind and only took small private possessions and a blanket for each person. There was no preparation: they couldn't take food or winter clothes; everything happened quickly, and the winter of 1939/40 was very cold. The outer limits of the ghetto were set up with barbed wire, and the inhabitants were literally trapped inside. Everyone was registered, and each family was given a room regardless of the family's size. Maria's family – six people including her grandmother – lived in one room, sharing a three-room flat with three other families.

The family's first flat in the ghetto was on the edge of it, and when Maria went outside, she saw German soldiers marching backwards and forwards, ensuring that nobody fled. Sometimes the soldiers spontaneously shot people who came out of their houses, so it was dangerous to go out on the street. Some people took their own lives because the situation was intolerable.

The adaptation to ghetto life was difficult to put into words, and Maria wondered as she spoke to Antje how it was possible that tens of thousands of people lived in an area where only a tenth of that number had previously lived. Nobody could imagine how crowded it was and that so many people lived together in a single room. Typhoid became endemic.

In time, Maria recalled, people got used to their very bitter situation – ghetto life was a plunge into a totally different world. The inhabitants settled in remarkably quickly, and Łódź became self-organised by its inmates. It was forbidden to own a radio; some who did were publicly hanged. Maria told Antje that the ghetto was a world with hardly any books. Maria was eighteen when she was sent there, and her hunger for knowledge and reading comes over when she relates that there was, nevertheless, occasionally, the possibility of reading a book. But one never received the whole book: it had been divided into three parts and you got the next part when you finished your section, and so three people could read one book simultaneously.

There was a ghetto currency in marks to buy wood in winter for heating; wood was also used for cooking. Food was rationed; there was bread, no butter and no other fats either, but there was a type of oil that was dark with onions, which was spread on bread. There was a portion of flour once a week; sometimes there were a few miserable potatoes. Many people, including Maria's younger brother, died. He starved in front of her eyes, and decades later the memories of that still filled Maria with anguish as she spoke to Antje about her experiences.

There was hardly any furniture in the flats, and people were grateful even to have a place to sleep. Blankets and clothes had to be acquired, and there was active trade and markets where things were bought and sold. But things like shoes or a pan to cook food in were difficult to come by. Some people sold their possessions to buy food. Jews had to wear a yellow star with the word *Jew* on it, and there were many rules that Jews had to follow or face the threat of death. For example, nobody was allowed onto the street after 8pm. Maria cited Jurek Becker's novel,[6] which describes every aspect of the ghetto situation well, including the loss of orientation regarding time. Maria quoted from Becker's book as she spoke to Antje: 'Well ... it's evening. Don't ask me the exact time. Only the Germans know that.'

More and more people continued to arrive. Illnesses broke out, and many people died because there was no help for them. Transports left for the East; initially one didn't know what happened to these people, and then ghetto inhabitants heard that people were being murdered with gas or were sent to the death camp Majdanek.

People tried to create a trace of normality within the ghetto. Children went to school, and many good teachers were employed there; that helped people to keep going. The idea that carried people through ghetto life was 'it's difficult now, but at one point, the war will end, and my children will survive'.

By the time the war was in its third year, some people knew they were ruined; they could no longer even walk and were just waiting for their death. Sometimes people just died while walking on the streets, and their bodies would be collected up. Sometimes the desperately crowded conditions lessened when transports to Auschwitz or other ghettos took place. There was a continual coming and going: some transports brought people, others took people away.

The Chronicle of the Łódź Ghetto, 1941–1944 is a remarkable document of major historical interest. Its authors regularly documented everyday happenings in the ghetto, sharing a wealth of devastating information. A group of ten to fifteen people were the

---

6. Jurek Becker, *Jacob the Liar, a Novel*.

lead authors, and they wrote with caution, wary of what the Nazi authorities would do if discovered, but it seems that the Nazis were not aware of the existence of *The Chronicle*. The introduction to the English version of *The Chronicle* explains that the book was edited and represents about only 25 per cent of the original, avoiding repetitions (for example, about the weather) to promote flow while reading. Nevertheless, it is a huge tome of 565 pages.

The story of how *The Chronicle* survived the war is remarkable. Nachman Zonabend had been a postman in the ghetto; while the ghetto was being liquidated 1944, he had the task of supporting the Nazis in covering the tracks of their crimes. He did the opposite: upon locating bundles of writing and suitcases full of archival content, Zonabend moved everything into an unused well and covered the valuable documents with bedding. He buried the largest suitcase under blankets in the courtyard of the building where he had found everything, trusting that no one would search. In January 1945, after the Red Army freed Łódź, Zonabend recovered the documents.[7]

The contents of *The Chronicle* included whatever appealed to the chroniclers as worth recording: the events of a certain day, the weather, the arrival of food, disease in the ghetto, deaths and suicides, births, shootings, arrivals of newly interned Jews, and the transportation of inhabitants ('resettlements'). The mood within the ghetto was also recorded, but the impersonal description of developments appears suspended in a void. The Nazis were seldom mentioned and were not subject to critical inquiry by the authors, who avoided writing about the context of the existence of the ghetto; there was no sense-making of what was happening. No conclusions were recorded, only facts and descriptions of events. This makes for an uneasy, uncanny reading experience which I found confusing: it

---

7. http://geb.uni-giessen.de/geb/volltexte/2008/6084/pdf/SdF-2008-01-26-35.pdf.

filled me with disbelief while I concurrently knew what I read to be true.

Around mid-1942, reflections in *The Chronicle* on the gravity and hopeless situation of the inhabitants increased. There were now about 160,000 people in less than four square kilometres. In the following, I share three particularly disturbing extracts from *The Chronicle*. The entries are about potato peelings, suicides and shootings.[8]

> *May 9–11, 1942 [p. 168]. A much sought-after item*
>
> *Potato peels have become a much sought-after item. The soup kitchen directors are approached in a wide variety of ways and all strings are being pulled, just to somehow or other obtain a little of this food, which is the only nourishment apart from bread for some people.*
>
> *12 May 1942 [p. 171]. Sign of the times*
>
> *People are gathering in front of the entrances to the soup kitchens in search of potato peels, they accost the help[ers] for them; they will not leave the managers in peace. Thus, the latter were pleased by the ruling of the Department of Soup Kitchens on the 11th of this month, forbidding the distribution of potato peels to anyone whatsoever. Potato peels may be obtained solely on the basis of medical certificates stating that they are necessary to the restoration of a given individual's health and when approved by the director of the Department of Soup Kitchens, Mr Kaufmann, who, at the same time, sends them to one of the soup kitchens. So many formalities for potato peels!*
>
> *Saturday, May 16.1942 [p. 173]. Potato peels*

---

8. Permission to quote requested by email on 4 September 2024.

The demand for potato peels, obtainable with medical certification, has recently been so great that the director of the Department of Health was forced to forbid doctors to issue any more such certificates. However, it is not always possible to refuse to give people cards. By Friday, the Department of Soup Kitchens had given out 350 authorizations for potato peels and various public kitchens. Control of the potato peels in workshop kitchens, which are exclusively for the workers employed in those enterprises has been left to the directors.

THE MONTH OF MARCH, 1942 [p. 133]. Suicides

The universal mood of depression and panic that reigned in March as a result of the resettlement action provided fertile soil for acts of desperation. The following chronicle of suicides committed in March illustrates the state of affairs.

On March 1, a married couple, Wiktor and Daisy Heller, settled here from Prague, committed suicide together by taking an overdose of Luminal. Wiktor Heller was born in Bohemia in 1882 and his wife in London in 1886. In the ghetto they lived in the collective at 10 Jakuba Street, which is where they committed suicide. The husband died before the doctor arrived, and the wife, a few hours later in Hospital No. 1. They left a letter from which it appears that Heller was driven to his desperate act by illness and anguish, while his wife wished to share her husband's fate.

Gabriel Frydman, the insurance agent who jumped from the fourth-story window in February in an attempt on his own life died in the hospital on March 1.

On March 4, Sara Tenebaum (of Gnieznienska Street), born 1886 in Brody took her own life by leaping from the bridge over Zgierska Street near the church.

The names and circumstances of fifteen other people who had died by suicide were additionally reported in this entry.

THE MONTH OF FEBRUARY 1942 [p. 129]. *Shootings*

On February 24, at 6 PM., Ludwig Rabl, born in 1881 in Bohemia, was mortally wounded in the head by a sentry's bullet in the vicinity of the barbed wire at the intersection of Franciszkanska Street and Smugowa streets. The wounded man lived in a collective at 13 Franciszkanska Street, that is, in a building in the immediate vicinity of the incident. Physicians from First Aid found the body as it was already growing cold. By order of the German sentry, the body was taken to the mortuary at Precinct 1 [Hospital No. 1].

Two other shootings were recorded in this entry: of Edyta Czerkowska and Fiszel Wolf Kuperman.

Of some 210,000 people forced to live in the Łódź ghetto, perhaps some 1,000 to 1,500 survived.[9]

Documenting death

So, this was the ghetto where Else and Karl were sent. Another involuntary society; another place of intense human suffering. It is difficult to imagine how it was, suddenly living in dire conditions behind barbed wire with soldiers standing on the corner ready to shoot.

I unsuccessfully searched lists of the Łódź ghetto's inhabitants for Else and Karl's names, using their German and Czech spellings. I turned to Axel Braisz from the Arolsen Archives[10] for help; I had got to know him while researching Therese's fate. He sent an

---

9. https://encyclopedia.ushmm.org/content/en/article/lodz.
10. www.arolsen-archives.org in English and German.

alphabetical list of people registered in the ghetto under the Polish versions of their names, including Ehlisa (Elulsa) Federman and Karol Federman. That is why I had been unable to find them. Their address in the ghetto was Sattler 3. Finding Else's last known address was meaningful to me, and a sense of quiet earnestness overcame me when I read her name on the list. For a while, I did nothing as I digested the information; for long moments I was just very still.

When did Else die? The transportation date from Prague to the Łódź ghetto is 21 October 1941, and this is the date given as the end of her life on the walls of the Pinkas Synagogue. This date is also given on a family tree, with the note 'transported'. A more probably date is 15 November 1941, which is the date next to her address on the list of the ghetto inhabitants in the column headed 'Notes'. I believe this was when Else's life ended. I don't know how she died, whether it was illness or starvation, possibly both. Whenever it was, it was a desolate, desperate death, one among millions of other deaths that the Nazis were passively responsible for. It's as if Else just faded into history – all traces of her sad end vanished: there is no grave, nothing. Her nameless corpse was, perhaps, thrown onto one of the piles that survivor Helen Colin so graphically and tragically describes in her testimony.[11]

Karl's fate

Karl, who carried a title and had a PhD, possibly survived longer in the Łódź ghetto than Else. On various ancestry websites, for example, Geni.com,[12] his date of death is given as 12 September 1942, and the person who added this data wrote that Karl was murdered in the Chełmno (Kulmhof in German) extermination camp. MyHeritage.com gives his date of death as 13 September 1942. I

---

11. www.youtube.com/watch?v=gqLjAP5cUOY.
12. www.geni.com/people/Dr-Karl-Federmann/6000000020571544154?through=6000000020571487187.

have not discovered who posted these dates, but I sense that the timing is an accurate, likely possibility, just one day apart. Yet another source, the list of ghetto inhabitants, corroborates 12 September 1942 in the 'Notes' column. This date range carries significance because around 12 September 1942, almost 16,000 people were deported to Chełmno and killed within a five-day period.[13] Karl was possibly one of them. Perhaps someone who survived the Łódź ghetto shared this with members of the Federmann family, and eventually it found its way online.

Józef Zelkowicz's diary recorded impressions of these deeply shocking and traumatic days.[14] Zelkowicz noted in his account that the deportations started on 7 September and lasted for approximately seven days: each day, 3,000 people would be deported. The Nazis' target was 20,000 people within a week. Mainly children under ten and people over sixty-five were herded together and selected for extermination, but others were additionally included so that the target would be reached. In September 1942, Karl was sixty years old. Inhabitants realised that, as Zelkowicz recorded, only people who could work would survive and be allowed to stay in the ghetto: 'Diejenigen, die nicht arbeiten können, gehen zum "shmelts"' ('Those who cannot work go to the "shmelts"').[15] *Shmelts* is Yiddish for 'the oven' or 'the rubbish pile'. At the start of September 1942, the ghetto's hospitals were evacuated. Zelkowicz asked himself 'Warum, in Gottes Namen, wirft man die Kranken wie Stücke unkoscheren Fleischs auf die Lastwagen?' ('Why, in God's name', he asked himself, were patients 'thrown on lorries like pieces of unkoscher meat?').[16]

---

13. www.holocaustliteratur.de/deutsch/Chronologie-zur-Geschichte-des-Gettos.
14. Jozef Zelkowicz, *In diesen albtraumhaften Tagen: Tagebuch auf Zeichnungen aus dem Getto Łódź/Littmannstadt, September 1942* (*In These Nightmarish Days: Diary Entries from the Łódź/Litzmannstadt Ghetto, September 1942*). Hereafter Zelkowicz.
15. Zelkowicz, p. 14. For copyright reasons, Lena Hartmann from the Wallstein publishing house requested that I used the German original followed by my translation into English (personal correspondence by email, 22 December 2022).
16. Zelkowicz, p. 13.

The Germans themselves searched the ghetto for people to murder, and this operation surpassed everything known until then. With unbelievable brutality, children and old people were rounded up and thrown out of hospitals onto the street. Zelkowicz graphically wrote about the inhabitants' fear, anxiety, and panic. His words for Friday, 4 September 1942 are: 'Kein Wort, keine Kraft, kein Ausdruck vermag es im Geringsten, die Stimmung wiederzugeben, die Klagen und die Panik, die das Getto seit Tagesanbruch beherrschen' ('No words, no faculty, no expression can in the least convey the mood, the lamentation and panic that have dominated the ghetto since daybreak'[17]). After this wave of deportations, 89,500 people remained in the ghetto, which had finally taken on the character of a pure labour camp; only those who could work had a right to exist.

The extermination camp Chełmno/Kulmhof

Man will das erbärmliche Leben weiterführen mit der Hoffnung: 'Vielleicht wird es besser werden'. Vielleicht wird man doch noch überleben und weiterhin Mensch bleiben.

(You want to go on living your miserable life with the hope: 'Maybe it will get better'. Maybe one will survive after all and continue to be human.)[18]

As I researched the Łódź ghetto and the subsequent transportations to Chełmno, I again felt the compulsion to understand more about what had happened to family members. Karl was Bruno's brother-in-law. I'm not sure if he was murdered at Chełmno or died from another cause while in the ghetto, but it seems tragically likely that he was transported and murdered with thousands of others. It took me days of reading to comprehend the abysmal horror and systematic annihilation of human beings in this death camp. It took equally long

---

17. Zelkowicz, p. 22.
18. Zelkowicz, p. 19.

to digest what I had read, and several disturbing and intense weeping sessions so that I could summarise and write about Chełmno.

Where to start? The facts seem the simplest way to get to grips with what kind of unspeakable place it was. Chełmno was situated 65 kilometres north-west of Łódź in Poland and was set up to start murdering people in December 1941. It was here that the Nazis experimented early on with their extermination plan, and it was the first, initially secret, camp in Nazi German-occupied Poland. Carbon monoxide was used in these early days of the Shoah to kill the victims when they arrived. Figures regarding the number of murders committed vary between 150,000 and 340,000. Transports from the ghetto to Chełmno were not officially documented.

Upon arrival in Chełmno, at 'the palace' – a large manor house – deportees were stripped of their possessions. About fifteen Jews were forced to work there sorting and unpacking the victims' belongings. The people to be murdered were transferred to vans. The vans were large, up to 5m long, 2.2m wide and 2m high. The inside walls were lined with metal, a wooden grille set into the van's floor which had an opening to be connected to the exhaust fumes through a metal pipe. When some fifty people filled a van, the van doors were closed, the engine started, and the exhaust fumes were transferred to the interior through the pipe. To protect themselves, the van drivers wore gas masks. Asphyxiation took up to ten minutes; the screams of the dying could be easily heard. Then the vans with the corpses were driven four kilometres to the forest camp. Sometimes the van was in motion, and the people were killed by the same method while being driven to their burial pits in the forest. A Sonderkommando recruited from incoming transports excavated mass graves, and the bodies were thrown in. On average, about six to nine vanloads of dead people were transported daily.

In this way, the Nazis murdered hundreds of Poles and Soviet prisoners of war from January 1942 onwards. Sinti (a subgroup of the Romani) from the Łódź ghetto were gassed here as well, and thousands of Jews from Germany, Austria, Bohemia, Moravia and Luxembourg. The trenches were quickly filled, and due to the number of corpses, the smell of decomposing bodies soon began to permeate the surrounding countryside and nearby villages. The SS therefore ordered the exhumation and burning of the bodies in the forest. The Jewish Sonderkommando had to do this atrocious work. The bodies were cremated on open-air grids constructed of concrete slabs and rail tracks. Jews from more recent transports replaced the members of such Kommandos, who were regularly executed so that they could not bear witness to the Nazi's barbarous crimes.

There is evidence that in the mid-1970s, Bruno and Marianne officially documented the fate of their relatives. I found Else's and Karl's cards online, and on the back, Bruno, in his familiar handwriting, had written his name, the date and his address: 13 Castlebar Hill, the address I was so familiar with as a child, a place of fun, safety and happiness. Seeing it on the back of these cards is disturbing and triggers deep sadness about my relatives' fates. I don't know how it came about that Bruno signed the card; a staff member of the Arolsen Archives suggested that Marianne and Bruno had visited Prague and signed the cards there. Two dates are noted in Bruno's hand: 25 March 1974 was on Karl's card (but he wrote Marianne's name) and 8 August 1974 on Else's card, where he wrote his and Marianne's name. It is noteworthy that Marianne undertook no such confirmation of her mother Therese fate's, or at least I found no such card with a signature. Why? It might have simply been too much for her.

In the next chapter, I turn to my father. He was the person I knew the best and the family member who, in his letters, eventually revealed the most about all the hushed Holocaust stories embedded within my family.

11 HPV: MY FATHER
1925–2005

When did I feel the first tremors of what was going on around me – when did I feel the stable and peaceful world of my earliest years begin to shift?

Saul Friedländer[1]

There were several fires during my childhood; I've already written about Alfred's death in a fire when I was seven, in Irma's chapter. When I was about twelve years old and already in bed one evening, there was a short phone call, then I heard my father open the front door, slam it loudly and roar off in the car. As he was a placid driver, the sound of him accelerating like that was frightening. I jumped out of bed, looked out of the window, but he was already gone. I called down to ask what had happened. My mother answered in a shocked voice, 'The mill is on fire'. My father, the businessman, navigated this catastrophe successfully, and there is a photo of him and Bruno

---

1. Saul Friedländer, *When Memory Comes*, p. 12.

celebrating the reopening of Perivale Gütermann with the Queen Mother in the early seventies, only a year after the factory fire.

My father occasionally shared some of his childhood memories with his children, but they were disjointed; he did not tell a story that made sense. For example, we knew he didn't like being tucked in at night at his boarding school and that one of the first English phrases he learned was 'Shut-up-and-mind-your-own-business'. But as a child I asked myself, why did he have to learn English anyway? Occasionally, when he was in an exuberant mood, he spoke a few Czech words: he told us they were Czech, but I didn't understand what 'Czech' was. I remember him once talking about the stickiness of resin from the pine trees in the country he came from, something that the deciduous woods of England did not have. And then there was the mammoth at the house he'd 'left behind'. How strange, but I didn't ask so I could better understand. Many years later, I understood that the skeleton of a mammoth had been found when the foundations of the family's house in Opava had been dug.

When I was ten years old, my father gave me a German course on 45rpm records that I liked listening to: 'Guten Tag, das ist ein Buch ...'. But he never spoke German with me at home, and I can't remember him speaking German with his parents. He spoke English well, and there were only a few words where, if you listened carefully, you'd notice that English wasn't his first language.

My father had an astute mind with two basic modes. Mode One was enthusiastic and convinced: occasionally he went on a mission and then tended to preach to those around him, but he got things done. He was always ready to help and advise if asked, and he could evaluate situations rapidly and fairly from all sides. Mode Two was quieter: he then appeared preoccupied or withdrawn and could fall asleep at any time during the day. He just switched off. The older I got and the more he worked, the more distant we became. In the end, I'd say my father was an absent one.

My father was a widely travelled, English- and German-speaking British gentleman of Czech-Jewish ancestry who had been brought up as a Catholic. He was called Peter in England, but he signed himself with the initials of his full name, Hans-Peter (or Hanuš-Petr) Vogel, thus 'HPV'. He reclaimed his Czech nationality towards the end of his life and polished up his Czech language skills. He joined creative writing classes when he retired and developed his passion for writing, but in English. Brexit would have shocked him: he was a European.

But who was the person I didn't know, the person he was before he became a father, the thirteen-year-old refugee who was thrown into English culture? The letters I found in the attic in 2011 gave some answers to this question and revealed what he had experienced as a boy and young adult. The letters also helped me to unwind relationships and discover the family members I had never heard of. I grew to understand who the various people he wrote to (and about) were; some of my discoveries were surprising. In the following, I illustrate these facets of his wartime experience by creating a narrative out of his letters and quoting from them. Further topics emerge on the sidelines, such as how he transitioned to a young man, his identity and language issues.

1939: First year at boarding school

Marianne was making decisions about the private education of her children while the family was still in Zurich after they had left Opava in late 1938. She received four pages of suggestions for various boarding schools from a company called Gabbitas, Thring & Co Ltd in England in a letter dated 14 January 1939. The company still exists. Prices per term were included 'FOR THE GIRL' and 'FOR THE BOY', eight suggestions for each child. My father was involved in weighing the pros and cons of the sixteen different schools, as documents that my brother Sam owns show; mother and son filled out columns in a table listing the schools and noting a variety of parameters to help them choose. Eva and my father were, therefore, prepared to go to boarding school when they got England.

I wonder what Marianne and Bruno's motivation was for sending the children away. It seems quite drastic and unsettling for them to be separated from their parents after the upheaval of leaving Opava, living away from home for several months in Prague and Zurich, then the journey to England and their arrival in the new country. However, I gather from my father's first letters written in German to his parents at the end of March 1939 that he took the transition in his stride. He went to Cliftonville School in Margate, Kent. He was not homesick; he seemed quite happy trying to learn English on his own with a dictionary, picking up new words and looking for someone to spell for him when he wanted to write a new word down. He missed going for walks and didn't like porridge because it was too sweet. He wrote to his mother, Marianne, that the milk was water to which powder was added. He described how all of his lessons were with different teachers and that one teacher could speak a bit of German. That teacher had lent him the dictionary and taught him 'I am', 'I was', 'I want' and 'I have', and he writes: 'ich kann alles ganz perfekt' – 'I can do it all perfectly'. He told his mother that he could ask for everything at mealtimes and already used the most common expressions such as 'go away', 'stop it', etc. He said he felt left out when a teacher read out something funny: the whole class laughed, but he didn't join in because he didn't understand what was funny. He reported to his mother that he had gone to the headmaster's study, knocked, entered, stood in front of him and said, 'Plies sör ai wont reiting päper', which delighted the headmaster. In these first letters to his mother, he wrote that he hoped to be able to make himself understood to his teachers after the Easter holidays, only a few weeks away. He requested a clothes brush and sewing thread and mentions that shoes were never cleaned. He concluded that he had a lot to learn, and, sounding a little doubtful but prepared to try, he wrote, 'Ich hätte gar nicht gedacht dass es so schwer ist Engländer zu sein' ('I'd never have thought that being English would be so difficult').

He mentioned unfamiliar bedding in a letter from April 1939 and wrote that making his bed with five thin layers was tricky, as the bedclothes would scratch him at night if he didn't make them up right. He was used to a duvet (*Federbett*) and had not yet grasped tucked-in sheets and blankets. Poignantly, he wrote one time about waking up feeling cold in the depth of the night because his bedding had fallen onto the floor. He also wrote about planning a letter to his grandmother, Therese, at Easter. As I read that, I thought, 'she is still there ...'. By the time I had begun to seriously read and write up this chapter on my father's letters, I knew of Therese's fate and had become accustomed to Therese as absent, deported, killed.

Hans knew that Marianne read his letters aloud, and, with a vertical line, he marked where she should no longer read aloud because he was about to write about his bowel movements: 'jetzt kommt Clo' – 'now the loo'. He wrote in a coded way that the topic was 'mediocre', which I interpreted to mean that he was constipated, although he wrote that he drank so much that he was not hungry at breakfast time. He assumed that dehydration was the reason for constipation and didn't know other causes of sluggish peristalsis. He wrote that the toilets were filthy, which was more likely to have been the cause than anything else. My father reported that he was asked about his bowel habits on the first school day and, once he had answered positively, no one inquired again. He thought suppositories might be a good idea and requested that if Marianne sent them, they be wrapped in neutral packaging. The letter is then marked with another vertical line to indicate that reading aloud again is now okay.

I was familiar with Marianne's concern about children's bowel movements from my experience with her as a grandmother when, decades later, I stayed the night with my grandparents in Ealing. Luckily, although my father readily shared his situation with her in his letters, he did not take up this monitoring habit with his children and it was not passed on to further generations. The inclusion of this topic in his letters does, however, suggest a trusting mother–son relationship in that he – a thirteen-year-old – openly reported and shared his concerns on such an intimate subject. But he didn't want anyone else to know about his worries and warned his mother not to read these parts aloud. He seems to have expected interest in this topic from schoolmasters, and it is almost a complaint that he was only asked once about it at school. Hans reassured Marianne that he'd quickly got used to everything, and so it seems. Reporting on his first bath, he hesitated to describe how the baths looked and thus indirectly conveyed how dirty they were. Furthermore, he wrote that he had no underwear but strangely said that he didn't need any. Nor did he have a tie or belt. 'Apart from that', he wrote, no one was particularly looking after him; but the teachers were 'double nice', and the food continued to be good. He signed himself off from these first letters as 'Hans'.

In later letters from this period, my father wrote about walks on the beach, which he enjoyed; it might well have been his first experience of a coast. With wonderment, he reported that people went swimming in the sea. In another letter to his parents he stiltedly wondered what he would be doing during the upcoming holidays. He was 'talking' to his parents through writing – but he avoided directly asking about being with them. It seems strange that it was not the natural course of events that he'd spend time with them during the holidays. At some other point, his parents were planning to visit him, and he was keen to show them around. He mentioned answering a letter to his cousin Susi, responding to her immediately because he was almost dying of boredom. His boredom suggests being cut off through language, and there are other indications that, while he was learning English fast, he was certainly not yet part of the crowd. He wrote of a positive encounter with a boy who gave him a ping-pong ball and some chocolate but stated that they could not understand one another. He wrote that everyone listened to the news, but he could not understand anything. A few months later, still in his first year at school in England, Hans started weaving English words into his German sentences, and the quality of his German spelling, even of simple words, declined markedly. I noticed how his handwriting changed, and Marianne, avidly but in good humour, started correcting his spelling; more on that topic later. In these letters, he reported participating in French and Latin lessons. He asked for some photos of his sister Eva, saying he wanted to send them to Tante Grete and 'Grossmama' (Therese), who were still in Troppau. I wondered about this bit in my father's letter as Marianne could, of course, have sent photos of Eva directly to Grete and Therese. My mother shed some light on this mystery. I gave her a draft of this chapter in 2022 and after reading it, she recalled my father telling her that photos of attractive older sisters were sold to older boys to pin on their walls to pretend they had a girlfriend. The businessman seems to have emerged early in my father's life.

He reported openly to his mother what he was spending money on and how much things cost; he was being accountable and honest. While at school, my father wrote to other family members as well. He wrote to Tante Litta (Melitta), Marianne's sister, his cousin Susi and Heinz Gütermann's family in Switzerland. He stated that he'd heard from his aunt Irma and his sister Eva.

Later in my father's first year in England he reported that he was cold all the time, and in a letter to Irma and Alfred, written on 1 October 1939, he noted that his school would be 'really nice' if it weren't cold and dirty. The school he attended was now called South Down College, as the letterhead reveals. He was no longer on the vulnerable English Channel coast at Cliftonville School but on the southern coast in Eastbourne. In this letter, he also wrote that football was on Tuesday, Thursday and Saturday afternoons. However, he said, regretfully, that he had so much learning and catching up to do that he couldn't join in. Another sporting activity was boxing; he sounded confident about his abilities during a boxing match. Hans became a Boy Scout and was proud of his uniform. The letters continue to be newsy, with few complaints and with no hint of homesickness, although he was excited about seeing his parents when a visit was planned. The lack of complaint seems authentic; he was not glossing things over – it's as if he was taking everything as a great adventure. He reported about other refugee children in his class from Poland, Switzerland, Germany and Chile, and two from Czechoslovakia. Why a refugee from Chile was in England is unclear. Interestingly, he used the word 'other' in this context and it implies that he understood his status. In the class below him, there were four more boys from Czechoslovakia and one from Austria. He added that these younger lads were nasty.

Some struggles shine through. In October 1939, he wrote that many boys were more stupid than he was but teachers repeatedly explained things until the pupil understood. And he noted that if one had still not understood, one had to ask again and then things were explained again. He referred to a letter from Bruno about fractions that had 'helped enormously' and wrote directly to his father, thanking him for sending half a crown and saying he'd go to the cinema with the money. Someone gave him a very fine, warm scarf in school colours, but he didn't otherwise know how he could warm himself up. My father wrote this letter after the outbreak of the war, and his parents had sent him a gas mask case which he found 'marvellous'; he commented that it had probably cost a lot of money. Presumably, the school had provided the gas mask itself. Sport turned up again in his letters, and he would be playing in the first eleven team of his house against other schools. He wrote that practising for an air raid at night just meant getting up and going downstairs, past a window against which sandbags had been stacked up, and gathering with others in a safe area. He drew a tiny picture of stacked sandbags in front of a door. The war seemed to be coming closer.

First names, handwriting and spelling

Besides revealing my father's wartime experiences, the letters brought to the fore facets connected with the activity of writing itself. Things such as his developing identity showed in how he signed off and in how his inner state was reflected in the quality of his handwriting. His script transformed markedly during the first fifteen months in England, changing from a childish to an adult hand. That appears to be a big step in a short time, from a nearly fourteen-year-old to a fifteen-year-old. Furthermore, his handwriting altered drastically sometimes – for example, to a tiny script when he reported on his closest encounter with a bombing attack. Then his hand became strikingly meticulous when he wrote to his father to beg to be given a bike.

The different languages also influenced and 'interfered with' one another in the process of writing. Basic spelling mistakes of simple words in his first language, German, increasingly appeared during his first period in England, when he had to write in German because he was not yet proficient in English. Learning English affected how he wrote in German. Later, his spelling in English was understandably shaky, and Marianne often tried to support him here, correcting him, but with limited success. Some humorous exchanges occurred in this realm.

Identity issues echo in the absence of a consistent first name to sign himself off with in his letters. In his first letters, he sometimes signed off with 'Hans', sometimes with the initial 'H' in a stylised form or 'HV'. As a seventeen-year-old, he practised an elaborate 'HVogel' signature, joining the H and the V together, and also used 'H.P.V.' for Hans-Peter or Hanuš-Petr Vogel (pronounced 'Hanusch'). By 1944 he usually signed off with 'HPVogel' but he had a phase in mid-1944 of calling himself 'Honza', the Czech nickname for someone called Hans. At one point, after the war in 1947, he signed himself off as 'Hanus, Hans-Peter, Michael – as you wish'. Michael was my father's second name. He seemed aware that he had not decided what he wanted to be called (or he didn't yet know who he was) and light-heartedly offered a selection for his parents to choose from. Finally, at the age of twenty-five, in 1950, letters were signed off with 'Peter', which became his English name and identity.

Understandably, shifts in the content of my father's letters to his parents took place through the years. The most obvious is the change in voice from that of a child to that of a self-confident young man, and his letters then started with 'Dear Parents' or 'Dear Family' – instead of 'Dear Mutti'.

1940: Correspondence in English

A letter dated 13 March 1940 is one of the first in English. He had a health issue, but he didn't know what it was:

Dear Mutti!

Thank you very much for your letter and the Sardellenpaste [Sardine paste]. You are always so quick in Erfüllung meine Wünsche [fulfilling my wishes]! Now before I answer your dear letter, I must tell you some-think which (is that right?) is not very pleasant. Monday morning at 10h we had Mr. H. till quarter to 11. During the lesson I had a lot to scratch myself, which bought my on the idea that I have possible German measles. Specially behind my ear I had a place full of (Wimmerlen) [pustules]. So I went on the end of the periot to Mr. H. and asked him how German M. start. He took me emiditately to Nurse. She looked at me for a long time. Then she sendet me out and had a long talk with Mr. H. Then she took my temperature and said; 'it's no use to put you to bed, you can go out but must'n com together with the other boys at all'. On my spots Nurse put me some Iodin.

It was a beautiful day and so I worked busy in ouer garden. This is lovely. But yesterday and today it is raining and I can not go out therefore. That is awful because I have got nothing to do.

Till yesterday I thought I am suspect of German M. but Nurse told me that she is not sure, but she things it is 'Ringworm'.

What this is I do not know, but you can see is because it lockes like a ring. And this form had this spots behind my ear. But she told me more than 100 times it is nothing bad at all!! And I want to tell you this too! I feel perfectly allright, but am so long incalated [incubated]*, till this spots finish. I am sleeping all by me self in a little room. If I have very long time I box the wall, till I swet. Better made can this spots only be made throu Iodin, which I receive every morning and evening. But I want to tell you one more, that I feel perfectly allright. By the way, I even do not know if I will be able to send this letter. Because I would spread my desies.*

Ringworm is not a worm but a fungal infection that can appear anywhere on the body. My father must have experienced anxiety at the diagnosis, which he didn't understand. However, it comes across yet again that he's coping. He proactively clarified the issue and reassured his mother twice that he felt fine. He was suffering only from boredom. It is heart-wrenching that he wrote about punching the wall until he broke out in a sweat. His writing shows that his English has grown within only a year so that he could express himself, although many sentences have German structure, and his spelling was often way off. Again, there is detail, and he took the time to share the chronological steps leading up to how he felt while writing the letter. He was telling a story. He felt free to write to his mother in English; he was not ashamed of making mistakes, and it seems Marianne was already proficient in English. The second page of the letter is missing.

In one letter during this period, he shared that he had some dreams, 'not wishes': a bicycle and an air gun to use at the shooting club at his school. He emphasised that these were dreams and that to dream about these objects was 'very nice'. He was dropping loud hints but gently and respectfully, trying not to pressure his parents while nevertheless expressing his hopes.

In a letter from 6 July 1940, he mentioned going to church, not because he had to but because he wanted to. He would be going to Sherborne, the nearby town, with 'all the other roman Catholic boys'. By explicitly writing down his religious identity, it is as if he was reassuring himself (and perhaps others) that he was Roman Catholic and not Jewish. He stated, 'The school I like here every minute more'. Again, he reported how the family was staying in contact: he had received letters from Irma, Alfred and Eva. He wrote about air raids, one just after tea a few days previously where there was a quick 'all-clear'. A crash had woken everyone that morning. A boy visiting Sherborne had spoken of two bombs that had fallen into a field; he'd seen the craters. Then Hans wrote, 'Now may I ask you something. Could you include in every of your letters, what is getting on in the world? It is not a very nice feeling this island feeling.' His school was not informing pupils about the war, possibly wanting to protect them, but Hans was interested and wanted to know, and his use of language is creative.

It seems that his school had moved again, this time from Eastbourne to Somerset, and in a short letter on 12 July 1940, he wrote:

> *Thank you very much for your postcard. I actually have nothing much to say, but you want me to write, so I will. If I only think to be able to make you breakfast pleasure I must write of course! I am very glad you like* [the sketch of] *'my' room very much. So does Vatti* [Daddy] *I hope. Therefore you are excused for not writing. You write to much already anyway. But better write only short and tell me some news. I just had a haircut. The weather is very wett and I do not know jet quiet, which is worse, Eastbourne or here. Else there is nothing much to tell. Many kisses and love. HV*
>
> *P.S. Am just going to write now a essay on: The autobiography of a cigarette.*

A couple of weeks later, on 21 July 1940, Hans wrote about noticing a poster near his school. A local farm was looking for farmworkers; boys could also apply. He had a friend, Helman, who 'too liked this idea very much, so I wonder if you could write to Mr Cottingham [the headmaster] if it would be possible to arrange something for Helman and me. That is of course, if you don't mind. I would love to. Helman will ask too.' In the same letter, he reported on a nice new teacher, who said his essay was very good, and his teacher was 'very content'. 'Real school' would soon finish, and many boys would be leaving, having completed their exams. Again, it seemed that he would not return to his parent's home during the holidays: 'But we too will do some work during the holidays.'

Hans reported on his first close scrape with the war in a letter dated 1 August 1940, mentioning ten air raid warnings, of which six were during the day. He concluded that if anyone said that where he lived was a 'save aria', then they must be stupid or liars. The next town, Yeovil, had factories and laboratories that 'glisten' and an aerodrome – meaning that he heard planes humming all the time. He saw two squadrons of Spitfires going up and twelve planes, probably German, on the horizon. Fire was 'intense'. He then reported on an occurrence four days previously, very early on Sunday morning. Mr Cottingham had said it would be best if the boys stayed in bed that morning. However, Hans had been woken by the telephone that rang to warn of an air raid. He lay in bed, and through the closed window shutters he saw light gleaming and thought it was daylight. But it was searchlights. He then heard planes, remarking that that was nothing unusual. Then there was a sudden tremendous noise, and he jumped out of bed and closed the shutters, which had flown open. He saw another flash, and the air compression was so strong that it almost threw him off his feet. He woke everyone in his room; the alarm was already ringing, and the boys went to an outbuilding they used for shelter during air raids. He had to run through the open and saw about twenty searchlights, and it was 'not a nice feeling to run over'. But everything was okay, and thirty minutes later there was an all-clear. Between the lines, his fear is perceptible as he wrote of this closest encounter yet with bombing and the war. He added in this letter that he was not sure he'd be able to come to see his parents in the holidays.

That Bruno rarely corresponded with his son seems to be confirmed in a letter from 8 September 1940, which started, 'My dear Daddy, I was awfully honored to recieve once for a change a few lines from you'. My father's English had become more fluent, and he reported on a stay at the farm owned by Tom Lewis, who had previously advertised for workers. His parents expressed worry that he was doing too much, but he was assertive and, now aged fifteen, wrote, 'I am now old enough to know how much I can do' – challenging his parents, who must also have expressed concern about him becoming a bike owner. He wrote, 'even about the bike you are afraid! I got some sence (I hope)'. In a short letter from 3 November, he wrote that Eva 'because she is a prefect now, I think, she thinks, there is no need to write to her brother'. He seems hurt.

Towards the end of 1940, he caught chickenpox and could not make it to a family gathering over Christmas in Stroud, where Irma and Alfred lived. He was not feeling ill and wrote that he was 'perfectly normal looking, except about 7 spots in my face, and my hair is not very nice, because I can not make it [do it], because I got quite a lot of spots in my hair'.

1941: The war becomes real

In a letter dated 13 February 1941, Hans told Marianne they had to write an essay called 'Is the invasion of this island imminent?' There would be a debate about 'invasion' at his school club; he wrote the word in inverted commas. In the same letter, he asked for some soap. The meadows were covered in snowdrops: he'd love to send his mother a bunch, but Hans supposed she had plenty already. Three days later, on 16 February 1941, he shared more about the club and the latest meeting.

> *We had to promise by raising a left hand to what our principles were. It was very ceremonious. We then had a speech by Mr. Evans about going into the RAF and what it was like. Then we had a few short speeches by the other masters, sorry, I meant to say vice-Presidents, about their experiences from the last war.*

The promise Hans wrote of was to 'Service, Chivalry and Truth'. He added that he felt 'quite grown up' as it was the pupils' club and it had nothing to do with school, meaning that he experienced his teachers as individuals and not in their roles as teachers. The headmaster was collecting money for the club, and Hans asked his father if he would contribute. If so, he told him, he should mention that he is a Rotary member, adding politely – cautiously – 'mind you, it is only a suggestion'. Hans wanted to send his mother a notebook in which he was keeping up with his German, so she could correct it. This letter closed with 'I too listened with enthusiasm to Mr. Churchills Speech. Smashing, was it not?' 'Smashing' is less widely used now but was common slang during the period.

Paper seemed to have become rare. Marianne wrote in a letter from 20 March 1941 that Hans should reply on the other side, which my father did, in pencil. These surviving letters from mother to son give insight into their close and trusting relationship. In a four-page letter from March 1941, Marianne wrote tightly; two lines of her handwriting are pressed into one of the lined paper she used. My father answered on the empty back pages of hers, and that is how Marianne's writing was saved in the cache of my father's letters to his parents. Marianne praised him for interesting content and told him about recent encounters with people they knew in London. She wrote in German, weaving some English words in, and my father wrote in English, weaving some German words in. Marianne wrote that her sister, Litta, was content living with the family in Wimbledon who had taken her in; she was working in the household. Marianne told her son that she had received two cards from someone who had heard from 'Grossmama', meaning Therese, in Troppau. This person reported that Therese was fine and that Gert, Melitta's son (Therese's other grandson), visited her every Sunday. Furthermore, Gert had spent two days over Christmas with his father ('Onkel Edi', the German and Gentile) in Troppau, and had even gone away for three days to see Tante Martha. Marianne expressed surprise that Gert had gone 'so far away' to visit Martha during wartime. This news about relatives in Troppau suggests that Marianne and Therese had no direct exchange. More news came indirectly and was passed on. Marianne wrote that she'd heard that Therese had heard from Alfred (Wilhelm), her brother; his family were all fine. She went on to explain English spelling rules and corrected 'really', which Hans consistently spelt 'realey'. Marianne complained that she'd corrected this mistake numerous times. She then praised Hans's writing, only to point out in the following sentence that he often wrote 'my' when he should write 'me', concluding, 'so sieht man, daß es nur eine matter of aufpassen ist'. This sentence combining the two languages means 'so one sees that it's only a matter of being careful'. A few sentences from Marianne-the-pharmacist followed, suggesting how he should treat his chilblains. She then returned to correcting his English, illustrating with examples from the Czech language; Marianne was fluent in Czech. A visit was being planned, Marianne stating that decision-making was difficult at present due to the war but adding that a meeting in Stroud where Irma and Alfred lived would be possible. The upcoming School Certificate exam was a topic, and this may have been the reason for Marianne's concern about her son's spelling. She asked if he felt ready to take the exam in December and whether other boys in his class would be sitting exams then too. Towards the end of this letter, Marianne reported that she'd be visiting the Czech Institute. (A Czechoslovak Institute had begun operating in London in January 1941 to promote the country's culture and inform the British about the country.) She wrote about the food she would send him and that the nights were quiet, meaning no bombing. Marianne signed off her letters with 'DeineM' ('yourM'), the 'M' standing for either Mama, Mutti or Marianne. Both parties carefully dated nearly all of these letters.

The school was preparing the teenagers to join the armed forces. My father wrote about participating in an event:

> *... just imagine it, we had (the whole school) an hour's talk by a Fighter-pilot who is brother of one of our boys. I think it was the most interesting talk I ever heard. He was in France and had shot down 2 and damaged a German Fighter. He told us all the experiences, realey it was super.*

Hans reported that his former school, South Down College in Eastbourne, had burned down. There were plans for him to go to Stroud for the holidays and meet everyone again. After receiving much critique of his spelling, Hans corrected his mother's spelling of 'attack' in good humour, as she had spelled it in two different ways: attaque and attac. He signed off happily that it was only seventeen days until they would see one another. To the end of his life, when dealing with uncertain spelling, which remained an issue, my father had a strategy: he wrote clear letters at the start and end of a word and squiggled in the middle. The reader was left to decipher what he meant, making reading his handwriting challenging. This habit started manifesting in the letters to his mother written in 1941. Eva's handwriting was even more difficult to read, but she didn't have spelling issues like my father.

In a letter from 18 May 1941, my father wrote that a sports day was planned for July. Where Marianne and Bruno could stay during their visit to the sports day was being considered, and in a grammatically quite sophisticated sentence Hans wrote, 'you shall have to come down. But I do not know how that will be able to be arranged'. Appearing unperturbed at poor exam results, my father reported them, explaining that the position was always out of twelve boys in his class: arithmetic 8 per cent, position 12; algebra 3 per cent, position 12; geometry 40 per cent, position 5; English literature 34 per cent, position not known; English language 41 per cent, position unknown; English history 57 per cent, position unknown; science 17 per cent, position 6. His geography result was also not known. He reassuringly wrote, 'we are starting from the beginning now in Maths again so I will work hard to keep up'. There was no sense of disappointment; he seemed very factual about his performance and seemed not to expect reproach from his mother for what might be considered bad results. From my own experience at school, I cannot ever remember him talking to me sternly about working harder for better marks when I'd had a bad school report (which was often). One of my brothers even commented upon his uncritical attitude in his tribute to him at our father's funeral in 2005. My father's stance about exams was do-your-best-and-don't-worry. This attitude seems to have developed early on in life and to have stemmed from Marianne's tolerance and warm-heartedness; she was seldom harsh, hurtful or critical of her children (or her grandchildren).

On 15 June 1941, my father expressed gratitude and appreciation for a birthday parcel, which included the following: tennis balls; an identity disc (a pendant) which was 'simply lovely' and cooled his neck; a comb, 'nice and so elegant', just the thing he wanted; a sponge bag; 'smashing writing paper'; and a rucksack. He asked, 'How did you come on that rucksack idea? I did need one, and you guessed it.' The gift of food, which he listed in his acknowledgement, included a tin of pineapples, Coke, a bag of sweets, biscuits, chocolate, Lion Bars, wafers and butterscotch. All of this would have been extremely difficult to come by; how did Marianne procure such goods? One wonders if there were connections to the black market. He wrote: 'Well, my vocabulary is not wide enough to thank you for everything'. Eva had also written and sent him a gift of two razor blades, which must have been difficult to come by, for his developing beard. Tante Litta had sent chocolate and three shillings. He'd also heard from Irma and Alfred and his step-cousin Hanne.

He was considering his summer holidays and hoping to attend a scout camp. Debates were still going on at his school, and he wrote in a letter from 6 July 1941 that the subject was 'Should we bomb the axis's civil population?' (The Axis powers were Germany, Italy and Japan.) Hans suggested travel dates on the same line, and the normality of violent topics in wartime alongside everyday life comes over. Letters continued to be only to his mother.

My father reported to Marianne about working on Tom Lewis's farm during the summer holidays in a six-page letter dated 23 August 1941. The wheat was being harvested, he'd helped put up sheaves, and it was 'a mighty hard job'. He'd fed seventy pigs, brought in a cow that was calving, collected loose corn, cut nettles in the back garden, driven the tractor, fetched a horse to be shod, cleaned up the cow stables, which he noted was 'neither easy nor pleasant', and labelled milk. He wrote about the work in the stables: 'I whish all the 27 cows which get milked in there could have a Pfropfen at a certain place. That's just between you and me!' – *Pfropfen* is German for a plug or a bung. He often wrote of the farm owner, his boss Tom Lewis. The relationship was to become life long: years later, as a father, he would often mention Tom Lewis to his children, and Tom became godfather to Sam, my youngest brother, in 1966.

Refugees were limited in how they were allowed to move around the country. My father had written for official permission from a local authority to ride a (presumably borrowed) bike to Dorchester and was happy to have very quickly received a positive answer. Now he wrote that he had to wait for an official response from Yeovil, a smaller town nearby.

Over that summer, the tone of the letters changed from polite and considerate to cocky. Feeling very pleased with the amount of work he'd been doing on the farm, he signed this letter off with an exuberant, large 'Hans' and then added the following:

> *Please send this to all the leading newspapers, so that everybody knows what I am doing. If anybody wants my autograph being a national hero tell them that they may have it for 2s6d. By the way, [Eva] the poor dear can hardly walk. But that is too bad! Now you must be careful! Please see that she never sits in the draft! You should watch her moving like a weasel if I should be near. Oh yes, I want to ask you. Do you think I could have every day news-bulletins of the whereabouts of that labil heart. Does it move regularly? I should register its movements by latitude and longitude. I know where I shall be when I see her next. The reason being the bit of paper I am including. If you would send me a translation, I'd be thankful. Of course you shall tell me about the poster and I will be really pleased. (Do I get the V.C.* [Victoria Cross] *for spelling that correctly?)*

Eva had also been staying on the farm but in my father's eyes had not been pulling her weight. She was, nevertheless, so tired that she could hardly walk. His sarcasm took flight, and he warned his parents she must not sit in a draft, to avoid catching a cold. His comment that Eva moved like a weasel if he was near seems to mean that she was avoiding him. The mention of a 'labil heart' seems to be mixing languages; 'labil' means unstable in German and asking for the location of this heart (longitude and latitude) might have been showing off using these words. Increasing the intensity of his sarcasm, he said he knew where Eva would be when they met next, the reason being 'the bit of paper I am including'. This seems to refer to a letter he'd received from Eva after she had left the farm, which he passed on to his parents. He asked for 'a translation', suggesting that her writing was not legible, which is another unfriendly jab at Eva, but he also breached trust by sharing her letter with their parents. Was he competing with Eva for his parents' approval and attention by putting Eva down and elevating himself? He praised himself for his correct spelling of 'really'.

Marianne wrote to her son in German using a typewriter on 17 September 1941. This may have been to signal important content. The original letter and a carbon copy of it have survived the years. In it, Marianne complained that she'd not had confirmation that he'd received her telegram. She confirmed that he could remain longer on Mr Lewis's farm, sent him ten shillings for the week and noted that she had informed the headmaster that he would be back at school on 24 September. She hoped Hans was being diligent about his schoolwork. She then came to the serious part of her letter and the real reason for writing. Mr Cottingham had written to Marianne and Bruno that if Hans was to be prepared for the School Certificate by December, he would need private coaching at the cost of five guineas a lesson. (Marianne added an exclamation mark here, which is understandable: that was a lot of money for the time. A guinea was one pound and one shilling.) He would have to spend most of his free time studying. An alternative would be to postpone and take the School Certificate in summer 1942. Marianne wrote openly about her surprise and confusion because Mr Cottingham had previously said how very promisingly he'd viewed Hans; he'd expressed interest in keeping him at the school to prepare him for a university scholarship. Marianne urged her son to immediately answer before she contacted the headmaster: did Hans feel he should have the extra lessons? She pointed out that it would be a demanding term, with little time for sports. Did he think he could manage without coaching? Would it be better to do the exam the following summer? Marianne wrote that she would be answering the headmaster to express how amazed both parents were at this news, contrary to previous statements about how well Hans was doing at school. She urged Hans to share how prepared he felt, compared with other boys in his class.

Mr Cottingham had pointed out that sixteen was young for doing the School Certificate, even in one's first language, and seems to have suggested that taking the exam next summer would be the best solution. My father's answer, which he wrote on the original and sent back to his parents, was brief: 'Don't worry, the first 2 letters must have been circulars, which were sent to all parents.'

Marianne was away in Cardiff at the start of October 1941, retaking her pharmacy exams in English. (In a letter from 24 January 1942, there was confirmation that she was now a fully qualified English pharmacist.) Bruno was alone at home, and his son wrote, 'I expect you are a bit lonely and as I have a few minutes to spare, I thought I might as well tell you about a marvellous football game'. His team lost 4-7 to the army, but 'it was surprising what a clean and decent game the Army played. Extremely gentle and there was not one foul during the whole game.' In a short sentence at the end, Hans mentioned being surprised at having received a letter from Paul Ritter, 'he who lived in T. Grete's house. He reminded me of all sorts of things ...'

In a birthday letter to his uncle, Alfred (Irma's Alfred), on 26 October 1941, the new elements of sarcasm and attempts at being linguistically smart reappeared:

> *Before I say anything else (If I say anythink else) will you please tell me why you and Auntie Litta must have a birthday on the same day? It is hardly fair especially as there are 365 days to choose from! Well, Uncle Alfred, how are you? I have not heard from you for ages and have not seen you for at least ages 2x. I do hope this is no fault of mine, but if I recall rightly, it was I who wrote to you last. How are your chickens getting on or is this Auntie Irma's subject. Anyway this reminds me of something and as Lord Beaverbrook wants all the 'wasted paper' (eg. my letter) I better fill it fast.*

On the third page he wrote:

> *In my birthday letter I can not very well ask if my sister is behaving, as I do not want to spoil it, which is very considerate of me, don't you think. Perhaps it would interest you that we won our first house match on Saturday 4:2. And that the time of wonders is not past, as we are having half an orange each for breakfast this morning. What else can I tell you? That I have a nail sticking out of my football boot and that I have not combed my hair yet?*

The dig at Eva indicates rising tension between the siblings. He closed after a not very good poem about his sister with, 'Well, I shall close now, wishing you once more all the best in the world, lots of presents and no more nephews like this one, I remain yours, Hans'.

The question of when to take the School Certificate seems to have been resolved, and in a letter from 13 November 1941, he stated to his parents that it was only three weeks to the exams and he was

> *... rather surprised that my hand is so steady under the circumstances. But what it is like to take an exam when you have as much chance of passing like you have these days of buying a banana, you know, I expect. But I have not given up hopes by long as I believe the times of wonders has not passed. (Proof of that is that we had oranges for breakfast a few days ago and that my darling sister sent me a bar of schoko.) I do hope Father has not forgotten that bike! And was it a Spitfire he promised me if I should get the Matric[ulation]?!! (Or was it a good hiding if I should fail?)*

Addressing his father directly in this letter, he thanked Bruno for the tip about maths which he had 'taken to heart and all I can say is that I am doing my best'. He noted that he had realised for the first time what perfect handwriting his father had.

In a letter to Marianne dated 24 November 1941, Hans's teacher Ernest Tonkinson, who was giving him extra lessons in preparation for the exams, wrote that he was worried about him. Mr Tonkinson thought Hans would pass unless he was 'extremely careless and frightened'. Hans had spells of 'absolute silliness' when he just gave up and said that he was going to fail. 'His great difficulty is English.' This was hardly surprising, as he had only been in the country for less than three years, and to let him sit the exam in December 1941 instead of in summer 1942 appears pedagogically reckless.

My father reported to his parents that the worst was now over on 8 December 1941. He felt that he had not done too badly overall but wrote that the English exam was terrible, and he did 'not do at all well'. He reaffirmed that the whole School Certificate would be failed if a pupil did not pass in English. He prepared them for the worst. His use of language was very poor, and his stress and tension comes over. As I later discovered, Eva passed her School Certificate on her first attempt in 1940, and perhaps for this reason the alarm bells had not rung in Marianne and Bruno's minds.

1942: Aged sixteen and seventeen

In a letter from 25 January 1942, my father wrote only to his father; they had an exchange about the Rotary Club, of which Bruno was a member. The letter's tone is somewhat deferential at the start, and the reason becomes evident in the third paragraph: he wanted a bike, and he made a case for this. It seems surprising by today's standards that a teenager had to beg his father for a bike. He wrote:

> *Now about the bike. How much I want it, is needless to say. But as I can only have it if I passed School Cert., it seems out of the question. What do you expect me to say? Obviously I want one, and looking at it from a practical point of view, a bike on the end of the summer is not quite as useful as at the beginning of it. And in any case by then they might be much*

more dearer and harder to get, but I expect you know all that. And if I was an ordinary onlooker, I should say that if I pass next time, I could not deserve it any more, because one can not do more than one's best, and that I did last time. Well, how much I want a bike you know, but of it of course depends on you.

It is an old-fashioned practice to promise a child something special if they pass exams, and my father challenged Bruno's approach. Giving one's best and finding that it is nevertheless not good enough is a difficult position to be in, and the way Hans asserted himself seems courageous. This suggests he had some self-assurance, while accepting his dependency on his father's good will.

At the beginning of February 1942, he was getting over having failed the School Certificate and wrote, 'Meanwhile, letters of condolence pour in', and after a 'marvellous' outing to Yeovil that all the boys who sat the exam undertook as a treat, he said, 'I am beginning to think it was really worth while taking the exam'.

On 11 February, writing to both parents, he strangely moved to the distanced third person, as if he was not (yet) who he was: 'Meanwhile, here is the beginning of the news, and this is H.P.V. writing it.' Towards the end of this short letter, he added, 'I do not know why, but I do not seem to be able to write a decent letter anymore'. He sounded a little despondent, perhaps because of the exam results and possibly due to the war news. The concluding sentence in this letter showed that he was up to date on war happenings; he wrote: 'Well, hoping that when you read this the *Scharnhorst, Gneisenau* and *Prinz Eugen* are sunk'. An internet search told me that these ships were part of the Channel Dash. This was a German naval operation whereby Hitler recklessly ordered three warships to return to a German port from the west French coast via the English Channel instead of taking the long journey circumventing the British Isles. The British had failed to detect what was happening for twelve hours, and the ships got through the Channel, although not unscathed. The Channel Dash was an embarrassment to the pride of Britain, with its long-standing British naval superiority, and the news of what was happening must have broken while my father was writing to his parents.

Mid-March, my father received some good news: his plea for a bike, possibly with support from Marianne, had been successful. He excitedly wrote that he was 'looking out of the window, whenever a car comes up the drive now, with more than a beating heart!' A bike was on its way. He wrote to Bruno on the evening of Wednesday, 18 March 1942, saying that it was:

> ... *super, marvellous, stupendous, excellent, glorious, magnificent, splendid, delightful, charming or in other words it is like a dream come true. The only difference between my dream and the bike is, that I never would have dared dream about a bike anywhere near the beauty of the one I now have. It still seems very hard to believe it is my own and I actually woke up this morning wondering whether it is really true. Oh! It is marvelous!! And this reminds me, that I have still not said 'Thank you'. Words can hardly express my thanks, but still, I can try, Well, thanks a million.*

In an undated letter that arrived on 21 April 1942 (noted by Marianne and which arrived seemingly on the same day it had been sent), from Tom Lewis's farm, the conflicts with Eva turned up again, as did my father's sarcasm. Eva had apparently entered his room without knocking, and he wrote, 'You can also tell her, that I would be very grateful if she could possible rake up enough energy to knock on a door in future'. The expression 'to rake up energy' seems quite an advanced use of English, as if he's flexing his writing muscles. He continues on the topic of his sister:

> *Personally I think it is high time Eva starts having 'Dates' Now when I was young ... (Ho Ho!) And talking about Eva and thinking about the weather, I realized that charming young thing has her 19th birthday anniversary tomorrow* [Eva's birthday was 22 April]. *'Pray convey my deep and hearty congratulations to her, I am tooo busy, anyway I shall be seeing her on Monday.*

The sentence which aligns talking about Eva with thinking about something as superficial as the weather suggests disdain. He seemed to elevate himself by referring to her as 'that charming young thing'. Again, his use of English surprises: 'Pray convey ...' is hardly everyday English, and he sarcastically uses this official style. He ended the letter by asking if he could spend the night with his parents. But instead of just saying that, he wrote:

> *The other thing of importance is, that I would be very pleased if I could have your kind invitation and blessing to stay Thursday to Friday night under your roof at 62 Hanger Lane.*

Marianne wrote to Irma and Alfred on 25 September 1942, and Irma noted having received the letter on 29 September. The handwritten original found its way into the collection of my father's letters to his parents. She explained that having failed again in summer, the plan for her son's third attempt at the School Certificate was now clear. Bruno had approached Loughborough College in early September 1942, with a plan that did not come to fruition. Tom Lewis suggested that Hans do a practical year on his farm and study with a teacher from Sherborne during this time. He had left school and would take a correspondence course and have individual coaching. Marianne wrote doubtfully, 'wie das nur gehen wird!!' – an expression which means 'however will that work?' – and added a mixed-language sentence: 'Bruno took it very favourably und so worry ich auch nicht zu sehr.'

A letter to his parents from 9 October 1942 explained how things would work when Hans was studying for the third sitting of his School Certificate with Cambridge University. He sounded optimistic because everything was clearly set out. Summarising, he wrote: 'If one only does what they tell you to do and also as they tell you, I can not see how one can not get on well'.

By now, Marianne was despairing at her son's spelling and corrected the numerous mistakes in this letter in red. Before Christmas 1942, in an undated letter, he reported that he'd had feedback from the English literature teacher on an excellent answer, but in maths he was only just at the pass level. He asked about the 'Xmas programme (if any)' and wondered how long he would stop at Hanger Lane. He asked if he would even be staying there or somewhere else, and this suggests that the Hanger Lane flat was too small to put up the whole family.

Letters as Hans grew older often began with apologies for not writing more often. The content altered too. By 1942, there were no references to staying in contact with his grandmother in Opava. After four months of imprisonment in Terezín, Therese had been murdered in Treblinka at the end of 1942. While the destinies of relatives who had not escaped to England might have been spoken of when the family met, there is little trace of their fates within the letters I have. It is possible that letters I haven't read in detail, in the hands of my brothers, contain information that would pinpoint when my relatives stopped communicating or even report on their deaths. I can only assume what my relatives in England surmised based on how reports on the Holocaust were unfolding in the media. News of the systematic killing of Jews that trickled into England was greeted with disbelief. No one could comprehend that even the Nazis could initiate state-organised mass murder violating fundamental laws of humanity. The Allies took (too much) time to realise that the genocide was occurring. The *Manchester Guardian* published an article on 30 June 1942[2] stating that over a million Jews had already been murdered in Nazi-occupied Europe. This is the latest date by which the state-led genocide must have become public knowledge in England, but the information may have been too monstrous to accept. On 15 June 1944, the BBC reported on Auschwitz after Rudolf Vrba and Alfred Wetzler escaped from there in the spring of 1944.[3] If they had not before, Bruno and Marianne knew now with certainty what was happening.

1943: To the Czech army

In a letter dated 28 March 1943, my father reported from the farm that 'There is going to be a huge raid on Germany tonight, our planes, all heavy ones, have been going over for the last one and a half hours in one continuous roar. One can see them from time to time passing the moon.'

He wrote that he would tell all about farming when the family came together over Easter and shared that he was now also a ratcatcher and got '3d per rat!' Furthermore, he was now (at last) the bearer of the Cambridge School Certificate. Everyone must have been relieved, above all my father. The idea was being floated of his applying to the University of Reading to do a two-year diploma in agriculture. He didn't think he would be accepted, and he preferred to volunteer for the Czech Air Force if he could get in. He asked his family to 'write soon about the Czech RAF', meaning that he wanted their opinion. His future was uncertain; the next step was unclear.

In a letter from 25 May 1943, he wrote, 'First things first, and when one is on a farm then farming comes first'. He was respectful to his parents but mindful of his own space. He continued by describing how he envisaged the future. That involved having a medical and a

---

2. *VEJ*, vol. 6, p. 398, document 136.
3. www.pbs.org/wnet/secrets/the-vrba-wetzler-report/45.

dentist appointment, a visit to Irma and Alfred, and a visit to his parents in London, and having 'a generally good time and then into a new atmosphere – the Czech army. The more I think of it, the more I am looking forward to it!! I wish to be in a Czech squadron.' Still in the farming world, though, he asked his parents for a 'very good second-hand book on pigs, pig keeping, management etc'.

In a letter addressed to 'Dear Mother and Father' dated 23 June 1943, he named himself in his letterhead as 'Hanuš P. Vogel', identifying as Czech by using the name Hanuš. New language challenges were on the horizon because he was now in Peterborough at the Czech Army Department. He thanked his parents for the first letter he had received at his new location, in his new life away from the farm. He wrote that,

> *I was rather dreading its arrival, as one has to march to the důstojník [officer], salute etc. when receiving a letter, but all went well. I really have a lot of spare time now, but right now it should not be spent writing letters as I have a devil of a lot of Czech to learn by heart. Ranks, command, are all slowly settling in my head. I did say slowly! Drill, rifle cleaning, sewing on buttons, polishing shoes 'cvičení' [exercise] 'posluha' [service] and more drill are among the working items, while eating, swimming, ping-pong, and even tennis [are] possibilities from the lighter side. We are of course not to talk about any military things, so there is not much to tell, not in a letter, anyway. But I don't think I shall harm, when I say this is a super place, more like a holiday camp than anything. We get up at 7, Sundays at 8!! Drill from 9–12, rest 12–2. Work 2–4, Czech till teatime, 5 o'clock. After that one is free! The food could not have been better cooked by [someone called] Gusti. So what more does one want! I am, of course, as a 'nováček' [newbie/novice] confined to camp for the first two weeks, where one spends one's free time peeling potatoes, sweeping rooms etc., but everyone is really nice and takes a*

personal interest. The officers are very kind even if one is very daft. My sergeant and many others are old 100% Czech soldiers, many having served five years in the Foreign Legion. Newcomers are arriving daily. Many of them have been in our country less than a year ... The stories are ghastly, but highly effective. The Czechs here are mostly young, and have a terribly good name in the town, with right. We learn here to be proud of our nation and ourselves, and we are. I must say we are really smart and well destined. Discipline is, by the way, very, very strict, we wear British battledress here. 10 of us attend Czech lessons, never up to now has anyone shown any anger, when I did not understand them. English is spoken quite a bit, German, although almost known by all is spoken very little. But we were, for example sworn in in German! And if the officer does not know English, he often talks German.

It is unclear what he was alluding to when he wrote about ghastly stories, but he probably didn't mean that the newcomers brought stories of systematic state-led murder of Jews in concentration camps by the Nazis: the genocide was kept secret. There were a range of other highly disturbing stories, such as the destruction of Lidice in reprisal for the killing of Reinhard Heydrich as well as battles. 'Highly effective' must mean that the stories convinced the troops of the righteousness of fighting the Nazis. His enthusiasm came over again; he was ready to serve and was adapting flexibly to a new environment, new tasks and a new role. It is interesting that he already referred to newcomers having been in 'our country' – meaning England – for less than a year. He was motivated to improve his Czech, the language he had had little contact with since leaving Opava in autumn 1938, four and a half years previously.

A letter from my father congratulated Bruno on his birthday on 16 July 1943. It was Bruno's fifty-seventh, and my father pinned a newspaper clipping to the letter about a table tennis match between his companions and a local team. I took the pin out of the letter, realising that it had been holding the pages together, doing its job, for nearly eighty years. It was, unsurprisingly, a little rusty, and it felt strange, a little intrusive, taking it out of the letter where my father had put it all those years ago – as if I'd disturbed the pin's resting place.

His present to his father was forty American cigarettes, which Czechs in the USA sent on Zborov Day.[4] He had some news about meeting someone from Troppau:

> *His name is Senzer. He is one of our sergeant majors here, he is a really nice man and it is great fun to talk old times over with him,* he was the owner of the inn, 'Krone' or 'Korona' [Koruna is correct] *in Troppau and he says he knew Irma and Alfred especially well. He's not big, he is strong, and he also had a villa on Gilschwitzer Berg. He's very nice to me and very popular with everyone.*

After mentioning the Krone, my father switched to German, and I have translated. He then added: 'Funny, I wrote German without realising it'. He continued, mentioning that the civilians in town were 'sweet' to the Czechs and that 'it is a real pleasure to be a Czech soldier'. He was not yet decided about joining the Air Force; he couldn't join straight away because his Czech was not yet good enough. He was working on a local farm to complement the 3s a day the army paid him, and he felt valued.

In a letter from 16 November 1943, my father reported to his parents on a meeting with his commanding officer to protest about not being part of an aircrew because his Czech was not yet good enough:

---

4. Commemorating 2 July 1917, during the First World War, when a successful skirmish with Russian soldiers took place in Zborov (as an internet search told me).

But he was also ~~good~~ rude enough to hint that I am not yet to train, because I could do more good in the translation office. My work there, by the way, is very interesting and everyone is extremely nice. I think I will enjoy my work and its surroundings for the time being. But all this means goodbye to dreams, anyway for now. I have already had a hint that lots of important work is expected around Christmas, which might mean cheerio to leave for a bit longer. Well, family, cheerio for now; to everybody's reassurance, I am, now that I have real work, feeling mentally much better.

There are several interesting points here. My father's second language had become English, and his previous second language, Czech, had become his third language. He was experiencing frustration because this shift in his abilities was hindering his joining the Air Force. He had been feeling down, perhaps a bit depressed, seemingly because his sense of purpose was affected. He had been given translation tasks, and having an assignment seems to have positively influenced his mental wellbeing. Notably, he assured his parents that he was now feeling better, which implies that they knew that this was not previously the case. Furthermore, he mentioned in this letter that 'home' was Czechoslovakia.

The tussle with English spelling continued, and on 11 February 1944 my father wrote to his parents: 'Oh before I forget I must at once tell that one spells heavy like this and not havy. Now you are the one that spells how one pronounces!' He had been sent an iron and his sarcasm resurfaced: 'Many thanks for your technical explanation about the iron. I really would not have known what goes where, if you hadn't told me, I think I would have connected it to the gas jet.'

He again shared his feelings with his parents: 'You know, I feel fine today. Perhaps it is because, being on duty I missed a test, perhaps it is because it is such a lovely day today. Perhaps only because it is

Saturday tomorrow.' He also reported that he had received a charming letter from his step-cousin Hanne.

I found a tiny telegram among my father's letters, dated 18 March 1944. It had been lying snug in its envelope for decades, a trace of a long-lost form of communication, written in pencil. It was flawlessly preserved, a bit brittle, and the paper had yellowed. I imagined people's excitement, and possible dread, when a telegram arrived. He was asking where the family would meet during his leave: where Irma lived (in Pitchcombe near Stroud), at Tom Lewis's farm (Sidwells) or in London at his parents' place.

By August 1944, in a letter from the 19th, he had achieved his dream of joining the RAF but was struggling with something else: air sickness. He wrote, 'The weather isn't so good now, rather a lot of air holes. You can imagine how I react!! The exercises get harder, too, of course. I hope I'll make it, it doesn't look too good just now because to be sick and catch a Morse message at the same time needs quite a lot of ability.'

Uncertainty about his future turned up again, and he shared that he was undergoing a 'battle of words' about staying on for the mechanic's course. His superiors wanted him to sign up to stay in the wireless department after the war, and it was explained to him that he must stay in the forces anyway 'at home' (in the Reserves) and that it would be a great plus to be well trained.

In a letter from 1 September 1944, he wrote that flying was a 'thing of the past for a bit' as he had failed part of the Morse test before even finishing it. Putting his failure in context, he added that the other two sitting with him had already failed twice. He would be having a different test soon and was unsure whether he would pass it the first time: 'Good job that they don't mind when one passes as long as one does sooner or later.' He was not sure that he would be trained further, but as he was nevertheless to be sent to the Bahamas, he didn't mind. However, my father did become engaged in active service before his trip to the Bahamas. His squadron surveyed German submarine activity from the air around the British Isles (something my mother told me that my father had told her).

He commented in this September letter on the family news that Hanne was pregnant, and he closed hoping that the nights for his parents were 'still quiet', meaning without bomb attacks. Amazingly, I was to meet and talk to Hanne's child almost eight decades later via a Zoom meeting in 2022.

1945: The end of the war

In a letter dated 11 March 1945 written from Nassau in the Bahamas, memories came to my father from his time at school. His parents had told him that they had seen the brother of someone who had been at school with him. Recalling those days, he wrote with astonishment, 'Gosh, don't those days seem as if they are from a different century or era'. How much had happened and how he had changed, became clear when thinking back to his school days. The 'Czech Club', as he called his squadron, forty in number, were having a day off together, and there was a lot of fun with singing, running, playing cards, jumping and, of course, swimming. The girls usually joined in; there was a 'lot of healthy fun', he wrote. There had been some exchange in their letters about politics, and my father commented: 'I am glad Beneš[5] left a good impression in his last message. There is no doubt about it, he is a truly great man.'

His parents – or more probably just Marianne – had been worrying about his seasickness. He calmed them: 'Please don't let my seasickness in any way bother you. If you want to feel as I do now you must feel 100% fit, sunburned, full of energy and full of good temper.'

---

5. Edvard Beneš (1884–1948). Czech politician and statesman, president of Czechoslovakia 1935 to 1938 and 1945 to 1948. He led the Czechoslovak government in exile from 1939 to 1945 during the Second World War.

My father wrote to his parents from the Bahamas on the day the war ended in Europe, 8 May 1945, also known as VE Day, for 'Victory in Europe'. He headed his letter 'End of World War II':

> *Dear parents, the time 8.15, the day – V.E. Day and the place the services club. Below me singing in progress, outside singing, everywhere happiness. Pity it is, in so many cases, a drunken happiness. I am thinking of you all in England. I bet London is full of flag! Is there a Czech one fluttering from our windows? Pity not all of us can be together this day, still we will be soon. Meanwhile I could very well imagine you by the wireless while the King spoke. When you rose this morning, I was sitting in the rear turret[6] of [our ship], one of our kites taking drifts. We were on a night navigational trip. A rear turret is a glorious place to do a bit of thinking – nothing but stars above with vague water below. We landed at 5.15 which by my calculating is 9.15 your time. I awoke. The first thing I heard was the distant looming of Mr Churchill's speech. I missed most of it though. Once being up I went over to Paradize [beach], an hour's journey from [?] Field. There I bumped into Maxine who took me to dinner with friends of hers. Very charming people, there dinner was concluded with champagne. For the first time I had any. There was lots of talking of course. Then the King's speech at three and another dip into the sea. Feeling no urge to get drunk (that's most probably because I don't know what it's like) I left them all and headed here for a read and a meal. In a while I'll go to the pictures to finish V.E. day. Funny, all of us, I mean the crew, feel terribly out of it all. We just can't celebrate like all these English by just getting drunk. Through the window I see they*

---

6. Turrets were weapon mounts made to protect the crew and mechanism of the artillery piece, able to be aimed and fired in various directions – a rotating weapon platform.

are letting some rockets [fireworks] go. Reminds me of Opava and the skating rink. That was quite an occasion for us then. I wonder what the future has in store for us?? I do hope you had a really grand victory celebration. You Mother and Father have done as much as anybody in winning this war, we young ones haven't really felt it all much. See you in five weeks, Love HV.

There seems to be a wistful undertone to this letter, and although the intense strain of the war was over, my father does not seem overwhelmed with relief. It was over, but now the war's consequences had to be dealt with. He could not celebrate with the English by getting drunk: that was not his thing, and none of his crew felt like doing that. His thoughts were with his family in London. His mind even went to Opava, and childhood memories surfaced. He'd sipped on some champagne, trying it for the first time, although his dislike of alcohol's effect would be life long. He was far from his family, far from home, and where 'home' was – he had often brooded on this – was unclear. He was musing about the future, which was unsettled. He credited his parents with contributing to winning the war as much as his generation, saying that he had not felt it that much. That seems to allude to his parents' losses weighing more than his, possibly also meaning that he could adapt more easily than they could.

His next letter was written on the way home from the Bahamas; he had already celebrated his twentieth birthday, on 12 June. He seemed to be playing with words when he wrote, 'Still "all at sea" although I am one week into my 21st year. Tomorrow, I expect to have terre ferme once more beneath me.' The letter was received on 22 June 1945, and he had met someone during the journey home. He told his parents that Judy Joyner, a twenty-four-year-old American Red Cross girl, might contact them, and he commented: 'very charming. Hard to decide whether more charming than intelligent or vice versa. She crossed the ocean with me. My first platonic love! I'd like to show her London.' By platonic he probably meant that they didn't kiss. It occurred to me that my father had never mentioned a girlfriend before in his letters. He'd been at an all-boys school and then in the army; there had been no opportunity to have a relationship. He closed the letter in an exuberant but reflective mood: 'Oh! It'll be grand to be with you all again. I think I have grown a little out of my childishness these last few months. Hope you'll think the same.' It is again touching how much he openly shared with his parents.

1945–1947: Czechoslovakia after the war

Two months later my father was in Prague, and he remained in Czechoslovakia for more than two years. He was still in the army and wrote that his free time was limited. This first letter (in my possession) from Prague was dated 18 August 1945. He had found someone to help 'solve the problems', which must mean reclaiming the family house. His reception was positive , 'everyone is especially nice', and it was easy to find somewhere to sleep: 'As for rooms to live in, if I am in this uniform there isn't a single person in Praha's streets who wouldn't let me willingly sleep in their flat or house for a very reasonable sum. We are the "very braves sons", didn't you know?' Plans for his future were on the table again, but he would have to improve his Czech to study at university. The letters from this period change markedly in voice: they become long, written with detail, and my father seems to have flourished back in the country of his childhood. Part of this development may have been due to his family status. He was now in charge of things and making decisions to do with his family's house, but also with Irma and Alfred's house and the Lanzer and Federmann properties.

The exiled Czechoslovakia government in London under Edvard Beneš returned to Prague on 16 May 1945; democracy was back. Albright summarises the insecure situation: 'Czechoslovak democracy died with Munich and was resurrected when Beneš and his government returned to Prague. In less than three years, it would be buried again.'[7]

An undated letter to Eva in English reveals a breakdown in the relationship between the siblings. My father must have written it in mid-1946 after he had started studying agriculture at the University of Brno in October 1945, when Eva visited. As always, I have not corrected his spelling. Interestingly, Eva kept the letter; Julia sent it to me in 2022. Without even reading between the lines, it is clear that my father was highly indignant about his sister's behaviour during her visit to him. The letter shows that he was hurt and offended, but also judgemental, offensive and aggressive towards his sister. One sentence shocked me:

H.P. Vogel.

St. Brno, Videnshka 29

Dear Eva!

Thank you for the money. If that was the only reason why you came to Praha then I am sorry that I did not make it clear enough that I was not in need of money. What else shall I write to you. How dreadfully you disappointed me. How terribly rude you are, how conceited, how stupidly trying to be English with the result of being just terribly Jewish and nothing else. You are the type of person I hate and I think that if I had to live with you just as you are now I should learn to dislike you heartily.

That you brought a 'friend' with you, well, that was the first ridiculous thing to do. (he's married, [you] stupid thing, high time you found something decent and young, not that the major isn't really damn nice chap). That you didn't express

---

7. Albright, pos. 5136 (chapter 26, paragraph 1).

interest, [in] how I live, how my studies look like and my school is almost unforgivable. That you smoke like a chimney is stupid.

That you so rudely snubbed Vlasta was heartless. Poor girl cried about two hours, and you didn't even find time to ask who she is. I'd heartily smack your face, really. All the things we did. Collected eggs, flowers as well, a hundred of small things but it would be stupid to tell you that. After such an excellent breakfast to say that 'you know, I do like toast these days'. You silly girl. 'English papers please', you poor darling, why come at all to Č.S.R?? If you cannot read Czech anymore then stop wearing Czech medals [unclear] oh dear!!! Your letter to me, I fully imagine, if you find time to write, which I doubt, I can very well imagine [it will be] full of sorrow of how I look. You idiot. And if you have such opinions, then please keep them to yourself. If you must talk, then not behind my back.

Listen, if today there is, real bean coffee for parasites like you, butter of which each citizen only gets a small square, eggs we get for a month etc. then it is only here because not one Sunday has been kept, most people work even [on Sundays] for the nation. No one gave us wealth. Every bit of order, organisation etc. was a result of hard work, something which you do not know! And you, stupid painted doll of no importance will air your views on communism. They did a damn good job even if I don't agree with them. If Vlasta had any guts she should have torn your Č.S.R [flash] from your shoulders. If I look different now as I used to then that is only a small something which work demands. You think that the 10 months I've lived here were all as plentiful as the two days you kindly spent here. Well, there were months when everyone was hungry.

But enough. Unless you change and stop floating in mid-air and come down to earth, (you are nothing else and will smell just like Communists when they put you in your grave) I wish to have neither correspondence nor conversation with you. What you need is hard fysical work, damn hard work. And, I beg your pardon, it wouldn't hurt if one or two Russians would rape you. You are not a daughter of my parents. Father would be unhappy if he saw you! The sooner you get out of the army, or away from all those officers anyway, the better. If you don't, you better get married soon, or no one will want you, doll, and read a bit about Č.S.R and stop representing it. Hanuš

A previous chapter addressed Eva's way of navigating her life, which greatly contrasted with my father's, and this letter dramatically illustrates some of their differences. Eva had already taken on a (very) British persona while my father was maintaining and cultivating his Czech identity, and this was seemingly a source of conflict. There were many other reasons for my father's indignation towards Eva: in his eyes, she was putting on airs. Eva was twenty-three at the time and was already denying her Jewish heritage. She had a relationship with an older married man, which shocked her brother. Eva showed no interest in Hans's studies during her visit; he'd expected some attention and perhaps moral support. Furthermore, she didn't relate positively to Vlasta, his girlfriend, and Eva seemed to have no idea how meagre rations had been saved up to provide the visitors with good meals. Supplies after the war were poor, and he mentioned everyone having been hungry. She seems to have mentioned him looking thin to their parents and this additionally infuriated him. Her demonstrative Britishness, the comments about toast and British papers, grates, and part of his anger is understandable. He criticised how Eva looked, calling her a painted doll; she must have worn lipstick. Perhaps his most perceptive sentence is the second part of the line, 'Unless you change and stop floating in mid-air and come down to earth'. Although he threatened Eva here (not wanting anything to do with her), he also indirectly credited himself in this sentence with being down to earth, and there is probably accuracy in his judgement here. Considering the gender roles of that time, his spiteful comment that 'no one will want you' if she doesn't get married soon are nevertheless somewhat understandable – she would have no means if she didn't find a husband.

The sentence that shocked me and is inexcusable was his suggestion that rape (by one or two Russians) 'would not hurt' her. He slightly diluted his statement with a pseudo-apologetic 'I beg your pardon' phrase at the start of the sentence. This part of his letter strongly suggests that my father was aware that Russians were raping women in post-war Czechoslovakia. Nevertheless, this reference to intentional violence against women being potentially helpful to make Eva wake up, in some way to bring her (or other women) to their senses, is deeply disturbing.

Eva responded to her brother's letter, point by point, as faint numbers written in pencil in her striking hand besides his paragraphs indicate. This letter, too, has survived the years; it is twenty-eight pages long and beyond the scope of this book. The tension between the siblings remained unresolved during their lifetimes, but the rift was not openly aggressive. As a child, I just knew that they didn't like one another; there was no fun or closeness between them. Criticism and grievances expressed behind Eva's back were also no rarity, and the intense tone often surprised me as a child. Then, I had no access to their common history as I do now.

Post-war Czechoslovak politics were enormously complicated, with the country caught in the East–West divide. Madelaine Albright's book *Prague Winter* gives a lucid portrayal of this period. In the following, I briefly sketch the political developments and juxtapose my father's activities in the country of his birth.

Russian troops didn't stay in Czechoslovakia after the war but left with US troops at the end of 1945. The communists were nevertheless strong: the absence of Soviet occupying soldiers did not mean that Stalin had no influence. With a high turnout (nearly 94 per cent) and 38 per cent of the vote, the Communist Party won the May 1946 elections, possibly, Albright suggests, because they had more control than their democratic rivals over the media. (That sounds eerily like the second decade of the twenty-first century – social media, Brexit, Trump and Putin's war in Ukraine, which was sold to the Russian population as a 'special military operation' by state-led media.) May 1946 marked the last democratic election in the country until 1990. Klement Gottwald was then the Communist leader. He formed a coalition government with cabinet members, nine of whom were Communists, three were Social Democrats and a dozen ministers from more moderate democratic parties. Two ministers did not have a party affiliation. Albright notes: 'The delicacy of this political equation would have a major impact in future months'.[8]

My father witnessed the expulsion of Germans from Czechoslovakia based on the so-called Beneš Decrees. He wrote, in a letter dated 2 October 1946, probably quoting a newspaper's figures, 'that the last transport of the Germans has left, all in all 2,143,167 have gone. Leaves us with about half a million I think.' My father seems very matter-of-fact about the expulsion of Germans from the previously multi-ethnic country; possibly, he condoned it. He was not alone here: most people did, including democratic parties. Countless innocent people lost their homes, starved to death, were subject to violence and were killed during this revenge. Was he aware that Bruno would have been counted as a German? I think not. Marianne and Bruno were not German, but they were German speakers. The policy of aggressively driving out Germans, often innocent people, must have played into my grandparents' decision not to return to their home country. Albright, herself of Czech-Jewish heritage, points out that only in the 1990s, after Václav Havel (1939–2011)

---

8. Albright, pos. 5304.

became president of Czechoslovakia in 1989, was this politically controversial period of post-war collective reprisal addressed. It is difficult to comprehend the immense impact of how Czechoslovakia was subject to three great catastrophes within only fifteen years: the war and the Holocaust, the ethnic cleansing and post-war expulsion of Germans, followed by Stalinist suppression and communism.

In a letter to his parents dated 3 March 1947, my father noted that politically, things were 'rather boiling' and there was 'quarrelling' as Slovakia wanted autonomy. Sensitive to this development and no friend to communism, he was also musing about applying for nationalisation in the UK. Again, a sense of uncertainty about the future hung in the air. These events must have been hugely alarming to Marianne and Bruno in London, not only because their son was in the middle of it all but because the chance of returning to their home in a liberal democracy was dwindling daily. In May of the same year, my father congratulated his parents on their twenty-fifth wedding anniversary. He mentioned planning to spend Christmas 'at home', but he meant with his parents in England and not Czechoslovakia. Reassuringly, he wrote on 15 June 1947: 'hope Mother wasn't worried about those reports re. occupation of the CSR. Here [Brno] was 100% quiet and normal life.'

When exactly he left the country is unclear; it seems that after a trip to Sweden, he did not return. In letters my brother Sam owns, we found evidence for him applying for a Swedish visa in July 1947. Furthermore, he did not enrol for his university course in October 1947. So, my father must have left his homeland forever between late July and October 1947. My mother remembers that my father had told her he had left via Sweden and it was six months before he arrived in England. On 25 February 1948, non-Communist cabinet members resigned from the government in protest at the tightening Communist grip on the country, and the Communists then came into control of Czechoslovakia. By 1948, it was therefore clear that democracy had no future in Czechoslovakia, and my father must have seen this coming and he left in time. The progressive, multi-ethnic Czechoslovakia my father and Eva grew up in morphed into homogeneity. Leaving after communism had taken over would have been almost impossible.

1948–2005: Back in England

As there was no need to write because the family saw each other regularly, letters from this time are scarce. Hans wrote to his parents only when he was out of the country. In a letter from 11 December 1950, at the age of twenty-five, he identified as British. His address was Gutach; he had become an apprentice at the Gütermann Company, and the name he wrote at the top of the letter was 'H. Peter Vogel'. That was how he remained: during the rest of his life, he kept a quiet 'H' in his name; whether in his mind it stood for Hans or Hanuš, I will never know. In 1953 my father met my mother, who is English, and two years later they married. He was already sales manager at Perivale Gütermann when they met.

The wedding photo captures a tense-looking Bruno. When I studied the photo, and with the knowledge I've gained from writing this book, I wondered whether Bruno was still grappling with the dispossession of his house, home and factory ten years after the war. With this marriage, it was clear that his family would stay in England. When I was born in 1958, it was a time still marked by loss and painful memories, many of them suppressed. My life started in a specific post-war emotional landscape, but I didn't know that. The war had been over for thirteen years, but its traces could not be simply shaken off.

My father worked himself up through the company in England. Eventually, he became managing director, and although his work was a far cry from agriculture, I believe he had a satisfying and varied working life. After the fall of the Iron Curtain in 1992 he visited Opava and the house and home of his childhood. He sought out

Therese's memorial, and a photo was taken. I wonder how he felt as he travelled back in time. I have no way of knowing – we didn't talk about that.

I was in Greece on holiday with my two youngest children in May 2005 when I spoke to my father for the last time, five days before he died on the 24th. He was going into hospital, as caring for him at home was now too much for my mother. I wept during the exchange and his last words to me were telling me to take it easy.

This chapter about my father and the chapter about his sister, Eva, belong together with their themes of refugee/émigré experiences in England as teenagers, how they dealt with their Jewishness, and their return to post-war Czechoslovakia as young adults. My father was a citizen of Czechoslovakia only for thirteen short years, Eva for fifteen years; nevertheless, after the war, Opava was home for them both. Their writing shows that the siblings had in common a strong identification with the country of their birth. They both commented on the Russians, and manner in which they did so seems to predict Czechoslovakia's eventual status behind the Iron Curtain. Eva adopted her British identity more rapidly than my father; he might have stayed in Czechoslovakia had the country not become communist.

My father wished to remain in Czechoslovakia and rebuild the country, which is interesting because he was the younger sibling. Jewishness troubled his identity less than it did Eva, which meant he had fewer issues with his past. There was continuity with his origins, in contrast to Eva, who wanted to make a clean cut and start anew. They went through different processes as they took on their British personas and did not seem to have been mutually supportive of one another during this period.

In 2018, my mother visited Prague. She had been invited there by the son of my father's RAF pilot while he was in the war. She was shown the Winged Lion Memorial, which commemorates the Czechoslovak

RAF airmen who served during the Second World War. Perhaps I shouldn't have been surprised when she sent me a photo of the names listed. Still, I was, and I smiled to myself because my father is recorded for posterity in the public realm with a variation of his name that he never used in his letters: Hanuš Petr Vogel.

12 THERESE
1866–1942

Die Erde speit Knochensplitter aus, Zähne, Dinge, Papiere, sie will das Geheimnis nicht Bewahren.

(The earth spews out bone splinters, teeth, things, papers, it does not want to keep the secret.)

Wassili Grossman[1]

In June 2021, ten years after I had found my father's wartime letters and was launched by them into learning about my family's history, I intensified my research on the paternal side of my family. My urge to research and write had been sharpened during three previous years of doctoral study. I started consistently taking time to investigate what had happened to Grete, Else and Therese, something I had not previously committed to.

That summer, a friend whom I'd told a little about my family's

---

1. Wassili Grossman, *Die Hölle von Treblinka* (*The Hell of Treblinka*).

history recommended a book in German.² The author is the granddaughter of Claus von Stauffenberg, the man who tried to blow up Hitler on 20 July 1944. The Nazis shot him and his co-conspirators on the night of the failed attempt. I bought the book, but the writing style did not grip me and having read six of the twelve stories, I laid it aside. I picked it up a week later, perhaps a little dutifully – if my friend had recommended it, I wanted to check it out properly – and continued reading. In the seventh story, something happened: there was mention of the Arolsen Archives in central Germany, which had been set up originally as the International Tracing Service,³ which was new to me. (I have already mentioned these Archives in Else's chapter although, chronologically, I first used them when researching Therese.) So, I thought I'd again try to find Therese, my father's maternal grandmother. Until now, I had not been able to trace her final fate as I had with Bruno's sisters, Grete and Else. My father had written in Grete's passport that Therese had been murdered in Theresienstadt, but I had found nothing to verify that, and she had remained a ghost.

It was 5am on an August morning in 2021 when I entered 'Therese Wilhelm' into the Arolsen Archives database. Twelve women came up with the same name. I started checking each of them, but they were all too young to be my great-grandmother, and I could also see from their places of birth that they were not Therese. The last entry on the list gave me goose pimples. I paused; I knew it was her. The name listed was not Therese Wilhelm but Terezie Wilhelmova. I hesitated before clicking on the link, wondering again at how the names of German-speaking Czechoslovak citizens had been changed. Seeing a relative's name turn up on your computer screen nearly eighty years after their death as a victim of the Nazis is deeply disturbing, and I sensed that although I wanted to know, I also didn't.

---

2. Sophie von Berchtoldsheim, *Mein Großvater war kein Attentäter* (*My Grandfather Was No Assassin*).
3. www.icrc.org/en/document/international-tracing-service-and-icrc.

As I dithered, I looked out of my bedroom window towards the rising sun. Weak morning light fell into my room through the trees in the woods near my flat. It would be another warm, sunny day. My mind wandered to the issue of first names, which are especially important to a person's identity; they represent who someone is, the essence of the human experience of being. I was remembering Grete's document that I had found online, where the Czech version of her name had been crossed out and altered to her German name.

I took some breaths before deciding to press the enter button on the link, which would lead me to more information, and then ... there it was. The scanned document told me that Therese had been transported from Terezín to Treblinka on 22 October 1942. Everything went very quiet within me. I did the maths: she had been seventy-six years of age when she was murdered. She'd been in Theresienstadt since 20 June of the same year. I had found her at last, after searching for her dozens of times. Slowly, a kind of peace infused me, but then tears came to my eyes. Even writing this fills me with anguish, pain and sadness, echoing what Jews were put through during the Second World War and Nazi persecution.

In my mind, I saw Therese arriving in Treblinka. I saw her getting out of one of the wagons she'd been herded into with a mass of others. She was scared, cold, starving and very thin. She was weak and ill. She knew she was going to her death. I saw her being sent to the queue for the gas chambers, violent SS men forcing her to strip off her clothes, her hair being shorn. And then she walked and stumbled with fellow victims to her extermination. Some people were screaming, some were weeping and some were quiet. I imagined her thinking of her children – Melitta, Alfred and Marianne – and her grandchildren. In my mind, she was dignified as she went to the gas chamber. But perhaps she wasn't quiet; perhaps she screamed.

Once again, I was driven to learn more about a relative's fate – this time, Therese's fate. I wanted to know, to look away no longer. Abraham Krzepicki (1915–1943), a survivor of the Treblinka death camp, managed to escape with three other prisoners on 13 September 1942. He had been sent to work in the nearby forest, and the flight for his life succeeded by hiding in a freight car full of the murdered Jew's clothing.[4] In his writing about Treblinka, he tried to put the unspeakable into words and described his experience on his way there from the Warsaw ghetto.[5] Over one hundred people were packed into his airless, sealed freight car. People pushed one another to get to the smallest chink in the floorboards to the outside and some air. Almost everyone was lying on the floor, and people were defecating, making the stench unbearable: he called his car 'one big toilet'. People lay gasping, trembling and shuddering as they fought for breath and their lives. Some, he noticed, were already inert and possibly dead. He estimated that his journey took about twenty hours; Therese's journey would have been far longer, as Theresienstadt is about 800 kilometres from Treblinka; Warsaw is 'only' 100 kilometres away. Having read Krzepicki's report, I wondered if Therese had even survived the transport. There is no way of knowing.

If she endured, the following excerpts from Chil Rajchman's book, *The Last Jew of Treblinka: A Survivor's Memory 1942/43*, give an impression of the final moments of Therese's life. Rajchman (1914–2004) was Jewish and forced to work as a 'hairdresser' at Treblinka. Upon arrival, a small number of young men were selected to constitute the *Arbeitskommandos* or *Judenkommandos* to manage the incoming people and their possessions. So-called hairdressers were members of these *Kommandos*, made to cut hair before people were sent to the gas chambers. Rajchman escaped during an uprising in

---

4. www.holocausthistoricalsociety.org.uk/contents/treblinkadeathcamp/survivorsandescapees.html.
5. Abraham Krzepicki, quoted in 'Gas Chambers at the Aktion Reinhard Camps', in *Belzec, Sobibor, Treblinka: Holocaust Denial and Operation Reinhard*, edited by Jonathan Harrison, Roberto Muehlenkamp, Jason Myers, Sergey Romanov and Nicholas Terry (Holocaust Controversies, 2011), https://holocaustcontroversies.blogspot.com, p. 299.

the Treblinka death camp on 2 August 1943, with about one hundred other prisoners, and hid until the war's end. He took his writing with him when he emigrated to Uruguay, where he married, had a family and built a new existence. His records for posterity are deeply harrowing, powerful and authentic first-person lived experiences of his ten months in Treblinka:

> *The same boxcars appear, the doors open, the occupants are driven out, as always, with rifle butts and whips. After a few minutes, the chief murderer of the camp comes and shouts, 'Hairdressers, fall in!' ... Naked women appear. In the corridor, an assassin instructs them to run to us. He mercilessly whips them, screaming, 'Faster, faster!' I look at the victims and can't believe my eyes. Each one sits down in front of a barber's place. A young woman approaches me. My hands are paralyzed, I can't move my fingers. They sit across from us and wait for us to cut their beautiful hair. Her crying is heartbreaking, the next woman is already sitting in front of me, she takes my hand and wants to kiss it: 'Tell me, what are they going to do with us? Is this the end already?' She cries and asks if it is a painful death, if it will take a long time, if one is gassed or given electric shocks. I don't answer her. She pushes, she really wants to hear it from me, because she knows she is lost. I can't bring myself to tell her the truth, and I reassure her. The exchange of words lasted only a few seconds, no longer than cutting her hair. I turn my head away, for I am ashamed to look her in the eye. A murderer next to me yells, 'Come on, cut the hair faster!' So, hundreds of women pass by me, screaming and sobbing. I have been transformed into a diabolical automaton who takes away their hair. Fearing the blows, some begin to sing. I am horrified: Next door people are being gassed, and we are supposed to sing ...*
>
> *The entrance to the gas chambers begins at the barracks opposite the platform. It is called the 'Schlauch' – the tube. It*

is lined with shrubs and looks like the avenue in a public park. Everyone has to walk naked along this path, which is filled with white sand. No one comes back from there. Everyone is brutally bludgeoned and bayoneted. After that, the avenue of white sand is full of blood. At the door, SS men herd people inside. They constantly move their arms and shout in a devilish voice: 'Faster, faster, go!' We are frozen to the spot. After a few minutes we hear desperate cries ...

The dead are welded together. The standing corpses are pressed together, arms and legs intertwined. During the suffocation and agony, the body bloats, and finally the corpses form only one mass. We try to separate another dead man from the pile. We succeed. We have grasped the technique. We hurriedly drag the corpses onto the bloodstained gurney and run in the same direction as the others. The lashes of the murderers, standing on either side of the path, accompany us. They are thrown into a mass grave together with 10,000 others. In this building the gassing took twenty minutes, while in the newer building it took about three quarters of an hour.

The number of people murdered in Treblinka is estimated to be 870,000.[6]

A new cache of letters came to light in April 2023. They were mostly post-war, from Alfred in Switzerland to Marianne in England. Shockingly, these letters revealed that Therese had a visa to leave Prague and Czechoslovakia. Why she didn't get on a train and escape, presumably to Alfred in Switzerland or Marianne in England, will remain forever hidden in history. Perhaps it had to do

---

6. www.holocaust.cz/de/geschichte/nazistische-konzentrationslager-und-ghettos/vernichtungslager/treblinka-2.

with her age and being alone; deciding to leave might have been too momentous for her. The rapid deterioration of the situation in summer 1939 must also have played a role. With the outbreak of war in September of that year, borders were initially closed. International travel was not possible, and her visa would have lost validity in the eyes of the Nazis. By spring 1940, Europe was in turmoil and by 1941, as a Jew, there was virtually no way for Therese to leave Prague without permission, let alone the occupied country. Therese became trapped.

In 2023, Julia found a piece of writing that my father had written in 1997. He'd done it in his creative writing classes, and it was full of musings on everyday life in times gone by. For two pages he recorded superficial chit-chat. When the company got on to talking about how marvellous grandchildren were, he wrote that his mind had wandered, and he recalled his grandmothers:

> *Father's mother, granny Johanna celebrated her 70th birthday in hospital.[7] All the grandchildren recited poems. My mother had been good at writing them. Funny that I don't remember her funeral; did they 'protect me from grief'? Mother's mother was called Theresa. I remember being fascinated by Grossmutti's velvet bands in many colours, which she always wore around her neck. I somehow imagined that it helped to hold up her head. The conversation on the table seemed to have fallen into a black hole. Into the silence I heard myself say, 'My grandmother was murdered. Much worse she knew for weeks, perhaps months that it would happen. She died in a concentration camp.'*

---

7. It must have been her seventy-first, as she wrote about her seventieth.

13 JOHANNA AND MARTHA
1860–1931 AND 1884–1972

Those who do not remember the past are condemned to relive it.

George Santayana[1]

I found a photo in the suitcase at my mother's house; it was probably taken before the First World War. Johanna is in the middle, surrounded by her daughters. Grete has her arm protectively around her mother and is leaning towards her. Else, on the right, is smiling relaxedly into the camera. Irma, at the back, looks a little tentative and not quite fully grown. Perhaps the photo was taken in 1910 on Johanna's fiftieth birthday. Irma would have been seventeen at the time. Bruno is not in the photo, and it may have been taken while he was studying in Mittweida.

My great-grandmother Johanna Vogel, née Schäffer, was the oldest of ten surviving children, and Martha was her youngest sister. Bruno often mentioned 'Tante Marta', also reverently called 'Great-Aunt

---

1. George Santayana (1863–1952): Spanish philosopher.

Martha', during my childhood, but I never met her. I did not understand who she was. Nor was it as if Bruno ever pointed to Johanna's photo in his study and explained anything. It was left to my imagination, and imagined I was looking at Irma. He had a family, though – that is (seen retrospectively) the point: nine uncles and aunts, and he must have had numerous cousins. In contrast, Marianne never mentioned her brother, Great-Uncle Alfred, to me, although he was alive and well and living in Switzerland.

I know the name of Johanna's mother: she was Ernestine, Bruno's maternal grandmother. Julia gave me a letter written by one of Ernestine's many grandchildren, Anneliese. Anneliese was Eva's (and my father's) cousin, once removed. I had never heard of Anneliese but, via letters, she stayed in contact with Eva and Julia, and many details of the family in this chapter are from a letter Annelies wrote to Eva and Julia in 2008. (The address on her letter was Nova Friburgo in the state of Rio de Janeiro in south-eastern Brazil. The town was named after Freiburg in Switzerland, not Freiburg in Germany, reflecting the connection to European immigrants.)

Isador and Ernestine Schäffer had fourteen children; four died very young. Isodor was presumably no longer alive at the time the family photo was taken, around 1912. Ernestine is on Johanna's right; she looks a little severe. Who Ernestine's children were, and who were spouses, is unclear. I think Martha is on the far right; she looks the youngest.

Johanna's seemingly well-to-do family lived in Branitz, a town formally part of the Austro-Hungarian Empire in the historical central European area called Silesia; the area today spans Poland, the Czech Republic and Germany. These days, Branitz lies entirely in present-day eastern Germany, to the east of Cottbus. I don't know when Johanna moved to Troppau.

Anneliese wrote in her letter that one of Johanna's brothers, her father, was called Max. He had married late, and Anneliese was born when Max was forty-nine. Anneliese had two older brothers, Robert and Franz. Max had a brother, Kurt, who also lived in Branitz. There were only two other Jewish families in the village. Anneliese said that although her parents were not religious, Max and Kurt's children were baptised to avoid discrimination at school. This suggests that antisemitism was rife, otherwise the step would not have been necessary. As Branitz only had a primary school, Anneliese went to a secondary school in a nearby town, a convent school. Everyone knew that her parents were Jewish, and Anneliese wrote, 'When it became intolerable because of the Nazis, I left school [in] 1938, then [in] 1939 we came to Brazil'. Anneliese's uncle, Alfred, one of Johanna's many brothers, was a chemist; he had been sent to Brazil in 1911 by the company Merck (presumably his employer). The First World War broke out in 1914, and Alfred stayed in Brazil in safety with his family. Anneliese's brother Franz, an engineer, could not get a job, 'being the son of Jews', and left for Brazil in 1934. The rest of Anneliese's family, her brother Robert and her parents, followed in 1939.

Johanna's 70th birthday in 1930

Another source of information about Great-Grandmother Johanna comes from recollections she typed on two pages; a copy of the document has survived the years, and I found it in the suitcase at my mother's house. A sense of untroubled times comes over from this retrospective piece that Johanna wrote, dated 26 January 1930, in which she recorded the preparations for the celebrations surrounding her seventieth birthday. I have translated it from the German and summarised Johanna's account of her experiences of the festivities in the following.

In the weeks running up to her birthday, her grandchildren Hanne and Susi came each Saturday from Ostrau under the pretence of joining ice-skating training. Troppau had an ice rink that both Eva and my father mentioned in their writings. However, Hanne and Susi were preparing a birthday surprise for their grandmother. Once, in the presence of their aunt Grete, Johanna gently challenged Hanne and Susi about where she could meet them after the ice rink closed, and the children (then thirteen and nine years old) were at a loss for an answer. Johanna well knew what they were up to. The children, unprepared for such a question and not sure how to answer, looked for help to their aunt, who was with them during the visit. Grete managed the situation competently, Johanna recorded, and did not let on about anything. This minute snippet of everyday life that Johanna touchingly captured in writing moved me, because up to now I'd exclusively encountered Grete in documents as a victim of the Nazis. Here she was helping her nieces out of a tricky situation; the normality of that was heartwarming. Johanna knew things were going on, but the secret of how her birthday celebration was to be was kept, and she wrote proudly about her other grandchildren, Eva and Hans (then seven and five years old), who also didn't let on, to Johanna's grandmotherly delight. Eight days before the party, Johanna had to avoid other rooms in her house apart from her bedroom, and a sense of happy tension must have existed in her household in Troppau, where she lived with two of her sisters.

On the first day of the celebration, flowers were everywhere in her home, which surprised Johanna; she wrote that it was 'magnificent!' She had been anticipating something, but this surprise surpassed her expectations. (And I wondered where the flowers came from in winter; this was in the days before imported flowers from Africa, but maybe greenhouses in Holland were already supplying and meeting a demand.) She recorded being delighted, surprised and momentarily speechless, reacting with both laughter and tears. Her birthday present from her sons-in-law (Eduard, Karl and Alfred) and her daughter-in-law (Marianne) was a radio, 'the newest system – a grand apparatus'. She recorded her pleasure at listening to the radio. This comment took me fleetingly back in time to days without today's communication possibilities, and I imagined the wonder of owning a radio for the first time at the age of seventy. It was yet another instance during this family research project when words from a different era spoke to me; the past wove itself into my mind in the present.

Johanna wrote about her pride at being given a special photo album, bound in leather, with 'JVO' embossed in silver on it. This was Irma and Alfred's idea, and Johanna wrote that it tastefully and lovingly documented the present state of her company in Troppau and Ostrau. The Latin phrase 'Per aspera ad astra' on the first page of the album means 'To the stars through difficulties'. (Did this allude not only to Ivo's success but also to her divorce, which was rare and courageous in those days?) Furthermore, she noted that page 17, 'Jvo around the world', was 'very interesting'. Bruno, with support from Grete, Else and Karl, had designed these pages, which included customer letters from China, America, Switzerland and Palestine. The company's international reach before the word 'globalisation' had been construed is indeed remarkable. It suggests a lot of hard work and a successful market niche for the company's tapestry product.

Another of Johanna's presents was a garden bench with her name on it and a matching garden table. She saw the furniture as having a deeper meaning, because Irma and Alfred would be buying a piece of land for a garden the following spring. Johanna commented that before anybody had even started working on the garden, Irma and Alfred were ensuring that she had a place in the garden. Johanna listed other presents: one of her brothers, Jacques, who lived in America, had sent a silver fruit basket; Martha had given her a silver breadbasket and tablecloths. Johanna wrote that she had been given so many gifts that she couldn't recount them all. In the afternoon, the Federmann family came, and the main celebration began. Around thirty people were there for the meal. Her grandchildren performed a delightful show. The text for the show had been written, Johanna noted, by her 'dearest and only daughter-in-law', her 'great pride', Marianne. 'It went so well, and it was so delightful that my youngest son-in-law [Alfred Karplus] broke into tears while my youngest sister [Martha] had the task of keeping me in line with her well-known humour so that I could show my joy without crying.' Johanna wrote that Grete had spent weeks practising with the children and creating the costumes. Grete also led the shadow image performance with great verve. Eva and Hans performed an enchanting part of the show: a group of moveable mushrooms, which Bruno had thought up. Eva and Hans danced to music while avidly blowing soap bubbles. Everything went so well and there was champagne. The adults danced towards the end, and Johanna summed up that it was a wonderful seventieth birthday party.

Irma and Alfred had organised something else; a celebration involving her employees. Johanna noted that 2 February 1930 was the date of the next phase of festivities. While at work, Johanna had felt that something was in the air. She had noticed little groups of people gathered about, but when she appeared, they quickly dispersed. At 9:30am on this day, when Johanna walked into her offices, the flock of her employees was waiting for her. It was an uplifting feeling: the whole room had been transformed into a flower garden, a tribute to '70 JVO' hung in the room, and everybody called out a thundering 'Hoch!' ('Hurray!') These were days before the singing of 'Happy Birthday'. Each department, instead of giving even more flowers, had collected money to set up a company fund. It had been Johanna's son-in-law Alfred's idea, to support anybody who needed rest and recovery. Viewed from a twenty-first-century perspective, this step seems modern and innovative. (This Alfred was Irmas's husband, not to be confused with Marianne's brother, who was also called Alfred, or the Alfred who was Johanna's brother.)

It was such a marvellous, animated atmosphere, wrote Johanna, noting that she could see in her employees' faces love and loyalty. Four employees had written poems, which were beautifully presented and spoken for her. She was moved to tears. There was a speech (who spoke is not clear from her account – possibly Johanna herself), thanking everybody for their contribution. In the speech, it was emphasised that everyone had enabled the company to expand to present heights. Spirits were high, wine flowed and there were further toasts. Again, it was Irma, Johanna noted, who had taken on the organisation with support from Alfred; all went well.

Johanna had thought the celebrations were over, but on Monday, 3 February (her actual birthday, as she noted), when she entered her company, she experienced further surprises: on her desk, the figure '70' had been laid out, made of flowers. Her chair was decorated, and again, a group of employees joined her and another thundering 'Hoch!' greeted her. She was delighted, and reasoned that not only her children but also her colleagues felt affection for her. Johanna concluded her piece:

> *What I did was my duty, I had the ambition to raise my children in similar surroundings that I had in my home, that is quite instinctive. But that you, my children and children-in-law, all recognise this and honour my age in such a way, that is touchingly kind of you. I have never had the feeling that I am too much. That makes me proud and happy, there are not many mortals who are granted such an age.*

There is much to be drawn out of Johanna's recollections. She had, for her age, vitality, she was healthy and above all, she felt valued by her family and employees. She had a keen ability to observe her surroundings. Although she was seventy she was still working, and her entrepreneurial spirit, which Bruno and Irma inherited, comes over. The inferred size of her company JVO, (not yet 'IVO'), about twenty-five years after it was founded, seems remarkable. The product, 'trammed' tapestries on a canvas sent out with wool for completion by the customer, belong to a long-gone era. Tramming tapestries means creating a guide for the user by 'sketching' with wool what colour should be sewn where. The actual needlework then involved sewing over the trammed areas to create a tapestry as well as filling in the background. Women frequently did needlework in the evenings back then, and I felt a fleeting longing for the quiet of those times. Johanna lived near Bruno, Grete and Irma in Troppau until she died in 1931 of diabetes.

Martha

Martha was born in 1884 and was only a year older than Bruno, although she was his aunt. She was baptised. Oskar Weisshappel, an engineer, Martha's husband, was Austrian and not Jewish. Anneliese wrote about her aunt that 'They survived the Nazi time in a small village near Branitz – Wanowitz. And just before the end of the war, they succeeded in getting away to Oskar's hometown Vienna.' The photo taken in September 1947 of Martha and Oskar says it all. Martha looks exhausted. They had lived through the war in constant fear of being found, persecuted and murdered by the Nazis. I have no idea how they managed to hide Martha's Jewish ancestry, whether they had help, went into hiding or lived under a false identity. The photo was made into a postcard, the one that I own sent to Bruno and Marianne by Martha. She wrote on the back 'unter dem Nussbaum', which means 'under the nut tree'. It was a walnut tree; a ripening walnut is visible at the upper right. Oskar's hunting hat is on the table, with a bowl of ripe fruit next to it. He is wearing a bow tie and traditional dress. The photo seems to have been set up and was probably professionally taken: the exposure is good, and it might well have been a 'we survived' message sent to Schäffer family members worldwide.

Twelve pages of Martha's will were also in the suitcase at my mother's house, and the list of people she named in it helped me to understand the large family. Anneliese had also sent Julia a family tree. The complete list of Johanna and Martha's siblings, with those who died, includes Max, Hermann, Jenny, Arthur, Kurt, Alfred, Jacques, Fritz, Heinrich, Dora, Salo and Ida.

The Weisshappels were undoubtedly wealthy: properties were mentioned in Martha's will, as were numerous pieces of jewellery. I know next to nothing about Martha or her life: no letters have survived. Martha was buried at the Grinzinger Cemetery in Vienna, near where she had lived at Cobenzlgasse 25 – far from the Jewish cemetery. Four years before Martha died, aged eighty-eight, in 1970, she gave me a chain of tiny, beautiful seed pearls. It had probably been made in the 1930s, as a jeweller once suggested to me. When my youngest daughter married in 2019, she wore the pearls as a bracelet – 'the something old' – as a tribute to the past.

14 THE WILHELM FAMILY

Another history, not his, not one he'd ever know, sifted its weight over him like ash.

Ehud Havazelet[1]

As a child, I had no idea that Marianne had a brother, Alfred, who had a son, Claus. Marianne never mentioned Alfred – she never spoke about her sister Melitta either – and I cannot remember my father ever talking about any of his cousins. He had four: on Bruno's side were Susi, Else's daughter, and Hanne, Else's stepdaughter; on Marianne's side were her sister, Melitta's son, Gerhard (Gert), and Alfred's son, Claus. In this chapter, I reconstruct part of the Wilhelm family's wartime story from two archives that came into my possession. One I inherited out of the blue in 2014. It was an old suitcase full of surprises, like the one at my mother's house. The

---

1. Victoria Aarons, 'A Kaddish for History: Holocaust Memory in Ehud Havazelet's *Bearing the Body*', p. 18.

second was a stunningly large official Swiss archive that I found by coincidence and gained access to in 2022.

Claus was the only cousin of my father of that generation who I ever met. It was the 1980s, and by then my father was gently encouraging contact, especially because Claus and his wife, Haidi, lived in Zurich, only a few hours away from Freiburg by car. I remember staying with Haidi and Claus in Zurich in November 1981 after emigrating to Germany. They had a large flat in the middle of town that was so sparkling clean and tidy that it astonished me. There was not a speck of dust to be seen. Haidi spoke a lot and Claus very little. I didn't feel at ease with them, and I don't think they felt at ease with me; we didn't know one another, and I didn't then really know who they were. Perhaps the unspoken or the unspeakable was between us. My father sent me a book (after I'd met them) that Claus had put together called *Die schnellen Jahre* (*The Fast Years*), as he had become a successful photojournalist. The book portrayed the world since the Second World War in four hundred images. As I also have a passion for photography, this would potentially have been mutual ground, and I now deeply regret that it wasn't possible to chat about his work and the past and create some closeness.

Claus died in 1994, but there was no travelling to funerals or anything like that. I contacted Haidi occasionally and planned to visit her in 2013 while in Zurich for a concert. She was now very old, but my sensitivity to the past and interest in researching family history had grown, and I felt drawn to getting to know her. However, she called me and cancelled our date at short notice, saying she did not feel well.

A year later, I heard that Haidi had died, aged ninety. A friend of hers, Alice Trier-Samuel, contacted me to let me know that I had inherited a family archive in Zurich, and I should collect it. Excited and not knowing what to expect, I went with my oldest daughter to pick it up. We drove the three hours to Zurich from Freiburg and located the storage warehouse. Upon our arrival, the person responsible for handing over the archive told us that the objects had been stored since the mid-1970s. A man gave us a large, old leather suitcase and an oil painting that didn't fit into the case. Several large photo albums with black-and-white images were part of the archive and were also handed over to me. That was how I became the owner of the Wilhelm suitcase of relics, another trove of the past.

We sat in the car where I had parked in the large, gloomy warehouse and started rummaging. The musty scent of old documents that had not seen daylight in over forty years wafted up to us. We found letters, memorabilia, small paintings, prints, drawings, etchings, school reports, old photographs of long-dead people, university certificates, newspaper cuttings, more recent photos of family members, ID cards and many *Heimatscheine* – official documents confirming the right of abode and a person's nationality. Everything was jumbled together. There was a receipt from a financial transfer in Troppau dated November 1930 that especially touched me. This tiny snippet of paper, perfectly preserved through the decades, witnessed normality and everyday life; but why had it been saved? There were jewellery fragments, and I wondered if the jewellery had belonged to Therese, Alfred's mother.

We spent the afternoon in Zurich with Alice, Haidi's friend, who shared some details about Haidi's past. She told us how difficult Haidi's relationship had been with her mother-in-law, Hilde. A raging jealous female feud seemed to have existed between the two, with Claus at the centre. 'I made him for me!' was what Hilde had more than once said to Haidi.

Back in Freiburg, in the following weeks, I spent hours sorting the suitcase's contents. That meant taking time, working to understand what I was looking at and puzzle together parts of the picture of the Wilhelm family's lives. I sensed that every item had meaning and was important to someone – it had been saved for a reason – but the meanings were often obscured because I knew next to nothing about the family. That slowly changed as I got to know the family through studying their archives. The oil painting (67 × 56cm) was of Alfred, and I knew enough about modern art to realise that it was a contemporary expressionist portrait that probably had some value. An Austrian artist, Ernst Schrom, (1902–1969) had painted it in 1966. Having his portrait painted suggests something about Alfred's understanding of himself: he had wanted to be seen by an artist and recorded for prosperity, and he had paid to get that done. I found the invoice in the suitcase: it had cost 4,000 Swiss francs, a considerable amount of money. However, Haidi and Claus had not wanted it in their flat, and I wondered why.

Spontaneously, while I was sorting everything and struggling to understand more about the Wilhelm family, I entered Alfred's name into an internet search engine and was surprised when a broad outline of Alfred, Hilde and Claus's fate during the war came up. The text was part of an archive in Zurich, the Archiv für Zeitgeschichte,[2] Eidgenössische Technische Hochschule – the Archives of Contemporary History. In the following, I call this archive 'the AfZ'. I have summarised the first full finding and share the brief (translated) biographies of the Wilhelm family here; most of this detail was new to me.

Alfred Wilhelm 31.8.1892 – 4.7.1975 Dr. jur.

Born in Troppau (today Czech Republic), israelite, son of Leopold and Therese née Sonnenblum; married Hilde Steinhart in 1928; one son; studied law; received a doctorate in law from the University of Vienna in 1920; ca. 1914–1938 worked as a lawyer from 1920–1938 in his own law office in Vienna; After the Annexation of Austria [by the Nazis] in March 1938 emigration with wife and son; 1938–1939 stays in Prague and Zurich; stays in France until September 1942. Flight of the family to Martigny, Switzerland. October 1942:

---

2. https://afz.ethz.ch.

separation of the family: Hilde and Claude Wilhelm accommodated in separate refugee camps to Alfred. 8.2.1943 private accommodation of son Claude in Küsnacht (Zurich) with Erika and Heinrich Gütermann. Summer 1943 family reunification in Küsnacht (ZH); 23.7.1945 to 1950 Alfred Wilhelm worked for the Association of Swiss Jewish Welfare / Refugee Aid (VSJF) in Zurich. Hilde Wilhelm-Steinhart: 20.9.1894 –1.3.1977. Born in Vienna, israelite, daughter of Salomon and Adele née Hacker; married Alfred Wilhelm in 1928; Claude (Klaus) Wilhelm: 17.11.1929 – 1994.

As I sifted through the contents of the suitcase and with the new information from the AfZ in my mind, I understood that Alfred and his family had not fled before the war and start anew in another country as Bruno and Marianne had done. Instead, before reaching Switzerland in September 1942, they moved around for over three years, arriving first (as had Bruno and Marianne) in Prague and then in Zurich, but then moving from place to place in France, continually endeavouring to escape the Nazis, before re-entering Switzerland, where they remained through and beyond the war. It was difficult to understand why their flight and refugee story had happened in the way it did. They moved from the occupied northern part of France to the unoccupied southerly zone, and the question that can never be answered is whether bribes and money were entailed or whether self-sacrificing resistance workers helped them, because what they did was dangerous. I again had a lot of research and reading to do to piece together what had happened.

I had the feeling that Therese had been an observant Jew, and documents in the suitcase show that Claus had not been christened after birth (as my father had) but only when he was five, in 1935. I thought that Alfred might have been closer to orthodoxy, too. Claus's parents seem to have given a lot of thought to his long name, which I found on his birth certificate in the suitcase: Claus Georg Leorene Sophokles, born on 17 November 1929. On 16 September 1935 he was christened Claus Georg Walter. In the suitcase there was a tiny 4.5 × 6.5cm framed photo of Alfred with his infant son on his knee. Alfred is beaming and looking proud. It was taken in springtime 1930. The photos I found of Alfred and Hilde in the suitcase suggested that they had a vibrant and sensual relationship. I have no pictures of my grandparents (or any other family members) in such happy physicality with one another as in the many images of this couple.

I got the impression that Hilde had a strong personality and knew what she wanted. It was a rare hobby in the 1930s for a woman to be a racing driver – but Hilde, as documents in the suitcase showed, was one. She trained as a model; there were numerous photos of her working: she modelled hats. She had her portrait done in Paris in 1939 after they had fled. In it, she looks pensive, perhaps a bit melancholic, but it is difficult not to also see a slight look of disdain in her expression, revealed by her thin, slightly raised right eyebrow.

Alfred's lawyers' office in Vienna was at Schwarzenbergplatz 18, as a saved newspaper cutting from August 1930 in the suitcase shows. As of 1933, antisemitism increased in Vienna, and tensions continued to rise during the 1930s. Alfred's nationality was an issue for him (and his family), and for me decades later as I tried to understand the dozens of documents I'd inherited. The many *Heimatscheine* in the suitcase seemed to clarify the question of citizenship, confirming his nationality as Austrian, not Czechoslovakian. For years, Alfred possessed only a residence permit for Vienna, and twice after the Second World War, in 1949 and 1968, he asked officials to confirm that he had a right of abode on a specific date: 13 March 1938. I looked up the date, knowing that the Nazis had entered Austria in March 1938. Indeed, this was the date that the Anschluss took place, when Hitler's troops marched into Vienna and Austria became part of the German Reich. These official confirmations of his right of abode related to compensation that Alfred applied for and received after the war because the Jewish family were forced to flee. After the

Anschluss, he returned to Czechoslovakia with his family, which seems a natural step to take. But then the Nazis 'came to Prague' (to use Irma's expression) in March 1939, and he fled via Switzerland to Paris with his family.

A very large archive

At the start of 2022, after I had found the AfZ archive about the Wilhelm family online, I reached out to the Institute für Zeitgeschichte in Zurich to request access to listed but unavailable documents. I hoped that further reading would help me to understand more about the family's experiences during the war. I received a prompt and friendly answer offering access, and the Institute said that it would contact me when they had digitised everything. A week later, they sent me two links. I clicked on them expectantly, and suddenly, out of nowhere, a mass of data was available to me about my great-uncle's family. I was inundated. I had access to over a thousand scanned pages to reconstruct the lives of Alfred, Hilde and Claus during the war (and some time before and afterwards).[3] The pages seemed like a silent monument that had been quietly, invisibly lying there, waiting for me. I was simultaneously moved and confused. As I gained an overview, by quickly viewing all the documents, it was clear that the AfZ archive bore witness to what the family had been through, the pain and trauma of flight and dispossession.

---

3. Doing justice to the extensive AfZ Wilhelm family archive is beyond the scope of the present book. It deserves research attention in its own right. I have excluded consideration of legal documents regarding dispossession, confiscation of assets, and later reclamation and compensation. Alfred's postwar work in Zurich is a further extensive part of the archive that I have not delved into. I inherited letters from Claus to Haidi written during the 1950s, which are revealing and a delight to read. Claus's work as a photojournalist, and his oeuvre, which I also inherited, are also outside this book's scope.

The archive came about, and its contents were summarised, as follows (I have translated):

> *The estate was given to the 'Archiv für Zeitgeschichte' by Claude Wilhelm's wife Haidi Wilhelm-Weber in 2000 and was supplemented in 2015 by a delivery from Alice Trier-Samuel. The correspondence during the period when the family members were housed in separate refugee camps in Switzerland documents the child's daily school life and personal consequences of the family's separation, and the regulations regarding compulsory education, upbringing in private foster families, and visiting rights for refugee families from 1943 onward.*

In a disturbing turn of fate, a kind of perverse synchronicity, on exactly the day I started writing about the Wilhelm family, Putin began his war on Ukraine. Within a week of 24 February 2022, over a million people had fled Ukraine. Their stories, fears, trauma, exhaustion and heartbreak were distressingly available to me via the news and television reports. Tears overwhelmed me again and again, for what the refugees were now experiencing and what Second World War refugees had experienced were churned into one endlessly sad place in my mind of what war means to humans. Again, as in Nazi Germany, a single person with too much power had brought death, terror, injury and desperation to Europe. Millions lost every sense of normality and security within a few hours as the Russian army attacked. Neighbouring countries, mainly Poland, warm-heartedly took the refugees in. Weeks or months of uncertainty and separation from loved ones stood before them. At least this generosity contrasted with how thousands of refugees had been dealt with during the Second World War in Switzerland (and elsewhere). As I started to explore the mass of documents the AfZ made available, I discovered with discomfort the Swiss official reaction to the Jews trying to escape Nazism. The Swiss state was repressive towards foreigners in the run-up to the war, during it and afterwards. I had not been remotely aware of this.

Alfred's persecution as a Jew started, of course, not in Switzerland but earlier. For example, the AfZ archive material included fifty-five scanned official pages listing the two thousand barristers, lawyers and solicitors in Vienna, lower Austria and the Burgenland region who were registered in 1938. I scrolled down through the pages and found Alfred's name included towards the end of the alphabetical list – he was a natural part of it. Scrolling further, at the end of this list there was a note simply informing Alfred that, according to various paragraphs of the Justice Department, he would be deleted from the list on 31 December 1938. By committing this list and the notification of his deletion from it, Alfred was making sure that his persecution was documented; it should not be forgotten.

I found a little notebook in the suitcase that came into my possession in 2014 which shows how well off the family had been. Their home address in Vienna was handwritten on the notebook's front, and the year, 1938. They had listed their possessions in detail: cutlery, plates, several coffee services, bowls of crystal glass, porcelain, glasses, vases, lamps, clothes, curtains, carpets, furniture, paintings, bed linen, mattresses and a diverse host of other objects. On the front, Hilde or Alfred (I think it was Hilde) wrote *'Pfutsch'*, which means gone/lost/destroyed/ruined in German. I believe that Hilde and Alfred reacted with understandable anger and bitterness to their persecution, especially Hilde.

As I slowly understood, their wartime story was roughly as follows: they lived three and a half years in exile in France, from January 1939 to September 1942 in Paris, Bénodet, Les Sables-d'Olonne, Nantes and Poitiers with the last twelve months spent in Nice. In July and August, their last two months in France, the Vichy regime in the southern part of France initiated the arrest and internment of over ten thousand Jews in compliance with the Nazi occupiers.[4] The Nazis occupied northern France; southern 'Vichy' France had been governed by Nazi collaborator Marshal Philippe Pétain since July 1940. The Vichy French government was extraditing foreign Jews to Germany (French Jews too, but to a lesser extent), where they faced almost certain death. The family's lives were in acute danger, and when two large waves of Jews took flight from Nice to Switzerland, the Wilhelm family were among those who fled. Claus portrayed this phase of the family's life in France and their various stations in a picture he made for his father in 1944, which I found in the AfZ archive. It gives an impression of how turbulent and insecure their lives must have been during those three and a half years. Further explanation about this drawing is given in a later section on Claus.

Switzerland's 'neutral' yet antisemitic stance

Despite its neutral status, Switzerland took an inhuman, restrictive stance towards Jews trying to escape the Nazis during the war; thousands were sent over the border to Germany and their fate in death camps. Regional canton governments and the national government treated the few refugees who were not sent back like unlawful people, despite their need for humanitarian aid. Their freedom of movement was limited, and they were held in refugee camps. Switzerland granted only temporary residence and defined itself as a transit country. A (potential) Jewish refugee had to have a residence permit from another country to enter Switzerland legally. This was, however, hardly feasible in Nazi-dominated Europe.

Six decades later, an independent commission of experts published a 361-page official document to reprocess and recontextualise this dark phase of Swiss history. It is entitled (translated from German) *Switzerland and Refugees at the Time of National Socialism*[5] and was published in 2001, which seems disturbingly late. It makes for

---

4. www.gedenkorte-europa.eu/content/article/544/-.
5. www.uek.ch/de/publikationen1997-2000/fberd.pdf.

uncomfortable reading. The report attempts to show how the idea that 'the boat is full' and the fear of *Überfremdung* arose. (*Überfremdung* is another German word that needs several in an English translation; it means having too many foreigners. *Über* means over, *fremd* means foreign.) The report dryly summarises that 'Thus the victims of Nazi persecution – even after the end of the war – were not at the centre of Switzerland's humanitarian engagement'.[6] Another argument for the restrictive position was that it protected the Swiss labour market.[7] Documents from this period also reveal that antisemitism was rife in Switzerland:

> *Many Israelites who have entered Switzerland immediately wish to engage in private business and trade. The correspondence of these persons clearly shows that they tell their friends and acquaintances to follow them to the Swiss paradise, and the reception of one in Switzerland enables ten others to follow him and settle with us. Their length of stay in Switzerland is quite problematic and indeed of very long duration ... These refugees are not very disciplined, and very often, it is necessary to take resolute action to make them keep the commitments they signed when they entered.*[8]

Israelite is an archaic and sometimes offensive synonym for Jew. On 13 August 1942, the Swiss government had more or less closed the border to Jews. The official document decreed:

---

6. www.uek.ch/de/publikationen1997-2000/fberd.pdf, p. 275.
7. *Flüchtlingsakten 1930–1950: Thematische Übersicht zu Beständen im Schweizerischen Bundesarchiv* (*Refugee Files 1930–1950: Thematic Overview of the Inventory in the Swiss Federal Archives*), edited by Guido Koller and Heinz Roschewski (Bern, 1999). www.bar.admin.ch/dam/bar/de/dokumente/publikationen/INVT11_Fl%C3%BCchtlingsakten-DE_BD1.pdf.download.pdf/INVT11_Fl%C3%BCchtlingsakten-DE_BD1.pdf.
8. www.swissinfo.ch/ger/fluechtlingspolitik-im-zweiten-weltkrieg_75-jahre-nach–das-boot-ist-voll-/43549998.

Political refugees, that is, foreigners who declare themselves as such when first questioned and can also provide proof, are not to be expelled. Those who seek refuge on racial grounds, for example, Jews, are not considered political refugees.[9]

Heinz Gütermann and the Wilhelm family

Heinz Gütermann, Bruno's friend, played a significant role in saving Alfred's family from being expelled from Switzerland to Germany. I found twenty-nine letters from Heinz to Hilde in the AfZ archive. Meticulously typed, the letters gave me a detailed insight into what Alfred, Hilde and Claus experienced during the war from 28 September 1942 (when they entered Switzerland) onwards. Most of the letters given to the AfZ archive were from Heinz to Hilde; perhaps Alfred did not keep the letters he received from Heinz. As I studied and analysed the letters, I was drawn into their fate and partook in their struggles. All the letters are in German; I have translated.

However, the oldest letter from Heinz Gütermann in the AfZ archive was not concerned with the Wilhelm family's flight to Switzerland. It is dated 22 July 1942, and Heinz wrote to Alfred about his mother, Therese, saying she 'has left, we have been unsuccessful'. He meant that the Nazis had deported her, and Heinz had tried to hinder her deportation. He informed Alfred that his letter of 11 July to Therese had been returned to him with the pencilled comment: 'Departed with transport 16./VI'. Heinz sent the returned letter to Alfred and expressed condolences about this grave news. He wrote, 'We have lost one great hope, but we are not hopeless'. It was heart-wrenching reading this letter; sensing how Heinz had tried to save Therese, tears came to my eyes. Heinz calculated the date of Therese's transport in this letter as between 7 and 16 June 1942. He was sadly close with

---

9. www.swissinfo.ch/eng/jewish-refugee-policy_-the-boat-is-full--75-years-later/43531288.

his estimate: Therese's card shows that 20 June 1942 was the date the Nazis interned her in Theresienstadt.

From further correspondence, I learned that Alfred and Hilde decided to take the risk of crossing the border from France into Switzerland illegally in September 1942. They did not go through the correct legal procedure, as urged by Heinz in his explanatory letter to officials. I wondered why Alfred decided to do this. He was a lawyer and committed to upholding the law, but going openly and forthrightly to the border would almost certainly have meant they would have been refused entry. Using his lawyerly reasoning, Alfred must have judged his chances of not being extradited as higher if he entered Switzerland illegally and presented himself with his family to the police. Alfred knew that Heinz would back him and do everything possible to keep them all safe when they were in the country, and that was exactly what happened, as I was to learn. How they could have entered is unclear: they may have paid someone to help get them into the country, with their luggage sent separately as freight.

The journey to Switzerland from the south of France took several days, as Martigny in Switzerland lies over 500km north of Nice. These days of travel must have been full of fear and uncertainty, not to mention the anxiety the family must have experienced when they presented themselves to the Swiss police, knowing they had entered the country illegally. With certainty, they knew that Swiss authorities extradited Jews to Nazi Germany. Claus's carefully composed sketch of the family's flight route states that they left Nice on 25 September 1942 and arrived in Switzerland on 1 October 1942. However, the date of a phone call, recorded in Heinz's correspondence to Alfred, was earlier, and this discrepancy may be a memory lapse of Claus's; he drew the sketch for his father's birthday nearly two years later, in August 1944.

Reading Heinz's letters, I pieced together how the family had been separated once they arrived in Martigny, Switzerland: Hilde and

Claus were interned at Institute Ascher in Bex, about 80km east of Geneva, a French-speaking part of Switzerland. Alfred, who had to work, remained in Martigny. It was over six months before the family was freed and reunited.

There is little doubt that the Wilhelms and Gütermanns had met (probably more than once), and perhaps they did so at Heinz's holiday home in Attersee in the 1930s. Still, Heinz kept mention of friendship out of his letters when dealing with the officials responsible for Jewish '*Emigranten*'. Instead, he took a pragmatic and business-like stance when writing to public servants within the state administration to try to help the family. Heinz emphasised that when he had worked in Vienna, Alfred had been his 'lawyer of choice'. Here was the competent businessman dealing with authorities in a confident, official tone. Writing to the state justice department and police department in the same letter in Bern on 28 September 1942, Heinz openly declared that this family, which he had long supported, had come from Nice and had illegally entered the country. He emphasised that he had recommended to Alfred that he should wait for the Swiss consulate in Nice to issue an entrance permit but that the pressure of circumstances seemed to have been greater than what Heinz called the honest will to wait for correct, official procedures – the *circumstances*, we can assume, being Vichy France's deportation of Jews to Germany. Heinz also reported in this letter that Alfred had contacted him on the telephone, openly stating that he and his family had entered the country illegally and they had already presented themselves to the police. Heinz said that he would support the family within his financial means to reduce costs to the state and wrote that he wished to see Alfred in the refugee camp as soon as possible. Heinz officially asked in this letter what should and could happen, and requested, in no uncertain terms, an answer regarding his proposed financial support.

On the same day that he wrote this letter to public authorities, 28 September 1942, Heinz also wrote to Alfred and congratulated him for escaping 'earthly hell'. He said he hoped to meet as soon as possible and that he had sent a telegram to Marianne and Bruno to assure them that the Wilhelm family had arrived safely in Switzerland. In a tone almost the opposite of his official letter written on the same day, Heinz suggested that his impression now was that there was no hurry; the family should catch up on some sleep and collect themselves. Then, the next steps would develop without anyone doing anything. He clarified that he had written to the police department in Bern, which was now responsible for them. He sent this letter off without having the refugee camp's address in Martigny, trusting that it would arrive, which it did.

Through reading letters Hilde wrote to Heinz, I sensed Hilde's indignation that these injustices were happening to her and how degrading they were. I felt her bewilderment that she'd been separated from her husband, the uncertainty and confusion of the time. Heinz gave psychological support when writing to her while she was in the refugee camps; his repeated message to Hilde was to hold on, be patient, and stay calm and confident. In a letter from 6 October 1942, Heinz assured Hilde that her stay in Switzerland would soon become more tolerable, and he informed her that he'd just rung Institute Ascher in Bex, where she and Claus were forced to live. Heinz wrote that he had confirmed with the camp's administration that he was prepared to support the family financially, as he had also stated when writing to the Bern police. He explained to Hilde that it was to be expected that the family would be separated and that Alfred would have to join the general labour force. Heinz reassured Hilde that her case would be processed, no one would be forgotten, and that it was only a coincidence that her family was searching for help in Switzerland: it could have been the other way around. Here, Heinz was playing with words and suggesting that, as his family was also Jewish, they could also have been the persecuted party. This seems a far-sighted point of view on his part. Heinz also suggested in his letter that Hilde should imagine Alfred was on a business trip to procure safe temporary accommodation. He was at pains not to appear sarcastic by making this comment, and he said so; he was trying to give her solace. He concluded by passing on a telegram message that he had received from Marianne in England regarding the notification he'd sent that the Wilhelm family had arrived in Switzerland. She'd written in English: 'Immensely relieved, congratulations, thanks and love'.

In a following letter, from 13 October 1942, Heinz was again empathetic towards Hilde, who had written that she was 'struggling with her nerves'. Heinz wrote understandingly that he could well imagine that the living conditions in Bex were primitive, more appropriate for men doing their military service. He agreed that things were difficult and could not be avoided, and he gently but directly suggested that 'some quiet heroism' on her part was necessary. He signed off, wishing her a happier heart and the ability to ignore petty daily aggravations.

Heinz was on a business trip close to Hilde's refugee camp only three days later. He dropped her a handwritten note saying that he had not been allowed to visit her. Again, he encouraged her to be patient: in Bern, where he had already written on the family's behalf, all cases were being individually dealt with. It is difficult to understand why visitors were not authorised to see refugees unless the view is taken that Jews who had illegally entered the country (to save their lives) were unlawfully there, in some way *guilty*, and therefore to be treated harshly. At the end of October 1942, Heinz and his wife Erica sent clothes, a thermos flask and a hot water bottle to Hilde and Claus in preparation for the coming winter. A letter that accompanied the package advised Hilde not to worry about the Gütermann family having used up their clothes ration cards because, apart from the trousers needed for the growing Claus, they had taken everything from their wardrobe, meaning that the clothes were second-hand.

Through Heinz and Hilde's letters, I slowly understood that the Wilhelm family had seventeen suitcases of luggage with them while in exile, presumably brought from Vienna and with them in France. Apparently, they arranged with a luggage transport company to send their luggage to Switzerland, but there were difficulties at the Swiss border control: official papers such as an ownership declaration were missing, and the luggage was held up and didn't come into the country with the family. I was surprised that Alfred's family had so much with them when they left Vienna. I knew from Julia and my mother that Bruno and Marianne arrived in England with next to nothing, although, as my mother recalled, they brought photo albums with them. There is also a story passed down about their au pair girl from Sion, Switzerland, 'Mademoiselle', who looked after Eva and Hans in Troppau. She travelled with the family and held on to Marianne's jewellery when they left for England. As Eva remembered and told Julia, they met with Mademoiselle in Switzerland after the war, and Marianne's jewellery was given back to her.

On 3 November 1942, Heinz wrote again to Hilde, saying that he had no real reason to write; he just wanted to make her happy with a letter. However, in this letter he did go on to detail seventeen keys to the suitcases he'd received from the luggage transport company. He described each key in detail, asking if she could remember which key belonged to which suitcase. When he received the suitcases, he would send the contents to her that she requested, if she could remember what was where and if she needed certain things in a specific piece of luggage. Reading this part of Heinz's letter, I suddenly understood that Heinz and Bruno shared a common attribute that must have contributed to their close friendship: fastidiousness. Heinz took the time to examine and then precisely type a description for Hilde of those seventeen large, medium-sized and small keys.

Heinz inquired about activities; what were they doing to shorten their waiting time, and could they work? He offered to send his 'small friend', Claus (whom he called Claude), some puzzles or quizzes, which he did in the same November 1942 letter, calling himself 'an uncle of Eva and Hans'. Still concerned about the family's luggage that had not yet reached him, he commented and explained that so much is 'flowing in from the West', meaning France.

In a letter from 9 November 1942, Heinz mentions that Alfred had been transferred to Schönengrund, Appenzell, which was 270km north-east of Hilde and Claus, who were still in Bex. Schönengrund is about 60km east of where Heinz lived in Küsnacht, near Zurich, a German-speaking part of Switzerland. Heinz judged this to be a positive development but stated that no contact with his close friend Bruno in England was possible, apart from sending a telegram. Heinz offered to subscribe Hilde to a weekly political magazine called *Weltwoche*. Heinz asked if Hilde was still not allowed to have visitors: he was on a business trip to Lausanne at the end of November 1942, only 50km to the north of Bex, but, as it turned out, he was again not allowed to visit. After he arrived home in Zurich, he sent her a package with food, and books for Claus to study.

Reading another letter from Heinz to Alfred confirmed my assumption that Alfred and Hilde were in regular contact with one another, but the only letter from Hilde to Alfred I found in the AfZ archive was dated 22 November 1942. Hilde wrote to her husband that she could not remember ever feeling so 'down':

> *That means something; you often complain that I'm so nervous, but now I feel it in every fibre and limb. I don't think [Claus] looks very good, maybe because he is so pale, but I can't do anything about that. It is difficult to understand why visitors were not authorised to see refugees unless ... I give him to eat what is available for us.*

These sentences reveal Hilde's tension and worry; being held in the refugee camp was draining her. Interestingly, Hilde used the English word 'down' to describe how she was feeling, in the middle of a

German sentence, suggesting that she spoke English. The letter is imbued with Hilde's struggles and her possibly depressive state of mind. She ended it with a question and a complaint that she was not getting enough letters from her husband. Her time seems to be dragging:

> *Do you know if Heinz has a date until one should be patient? I'm now waiting again for one of your rare and meagre messages, for the fact that evening and morning will come. Time passes so uselessly. In longing and love, your Hilde.*

In a letter dated 1 December 1942, Heinz responded to three points from Hilde's latest correspondence. She had expressed several wishes to which he answered: 'One can always have wishes, no more than what can ever happen happens. It's better to have an unfulfilled wish than no wishes.' His second point had to do with Claus; there seem to have been discussions about his family taking Claus in. Heinz stated that he was welcome any time. Heinz's third point was about their luggage. Two small suitcases had arrived at his house, and he would be sending Hilde and Alfred the towels they contained.

In December 1942, Heinz wrote to the Communauté israélite in Montreux (20km north of Bex) and again confirmed his willingness to support the Wilhelm family. He stated that this – and an offer of a deposit – had been communicated to state officials in Bern as early as the family's arrival in Switzerland. However, he disclosed in this letter that because official responses were stalling, he had approached this local authority hoping to get things moving. Unfortunately, the reaction on the local government level was that the Wilhelm family issue could be dealt with only if they had relatives in Switzerland, which was not the case. He had, however, received a half-hearted acceptance from a different local authority – they could be accommodated in a cheap hotel. With this letter, Heinz seemed to be officially documenting and laying open all of the steps he was undertaking. Clearly, he was doing all he could to get the family out of refugee camps. He further informed the Communauté israëlite that he had committed himself to take the thirteen-year-old Claude Wilhelm (Claus) in for the duration of his stay in Switzerland. On the same day, 19 December 1942, Heinz wrote to Hilde, and, for the first time, between the lines, there is a hint that he was feeling worn down and demoralised by the refugee issue. The family had been in Switzerland for two and a half months, and nothing had happened to improve their situation. Heinz shared in this same letter to Hilde that Alfred was still not in the Zurich area; that step he judged would be beneficial. However, Heinz was not sure if that would be possible and again reiterated that not having any relations in Switzerland was still the primary obstacle to their release from the camps. He sent a Christmas package to them, and then, in a letter dated 23 December 1942, he wrote to Hilde saying that, with Erika, his thoughts were especially with people whom world events had weighed down. Erika hoped for Hilde that her greatest wish would be fulfilled.

On the last day of 1942, Heinz wrote again to Hilde, saying that he had at last seen Alfred, who had successfully applied for a holiday. This marked a real change: earlier, Alfred had applied for a holiday and the censor pencilled in the margin of the application the word *'inutile'*, which translates simply to 'pointless'.

Heinz told Hilde that although he found Alfred to be in a positive state of mind, he could see the tension of recent months in him more than in Hilde and Claus. (This means that Heinz had, in the meantime, finally been allowed to visit Hilde.) In this letter, he mentioned having tried to reach Hilde on the phone in Bex and how delighted they had been when it had unexpectedly worked. On the same evening, they'd received a telegram from Marianne and Bruno: 'Loving wishes for Xmas and New Year to you all and good hope to Alfred's [family]'. Heinz had some positive official news which he judged to be good, although the issue of having no relatives in the country remained. Heinz believed they would be successful; his attitude was 'It just takes time'.

On 6 January 1943, Heinz reassured Hilde that Claus's missed schooling was minimal and should not worry her. His opinion was that knowledge would return to him, even if Claus forgot everything he'd ever learned. The most important thing was that Claus occupied himself with books; that activity was more important than success. However, some sort of teaching for children had been organised in the camp, and again, encouragingly, Heinz said he was happy to hear that Claus's interest was being kept awake.

In mid-January, Heinz wrote to Hilde about an idea as to how he could stay in contact with Bruno in England: he had a cousin in Argentina (a neutral country), and from there, his cousin could pass letters on to Bruno and vice versa. As Heinz mulled over the idea of corresponding via the Atlantic, I realised how lack of contact with friends and family weighed on civilians during the war. For us in a different world, with a selection of online messaging services instantly available at our fingertips, I suddenly understood how isolating and disconcerting being cut off must have felt. People lived in constant anxiety during those long, uncertain war years.

On 21 January 1943, Heinz wrote to Hilde that the 'Claude-Zurich issue' was being dealt with in Bern, and one '**had to**' wait until the authorities in Bern sent the application to the Children's Relief Organization in Zurich (Schweizer Hilfswerk für Emigrantenkinder, Zentralstelle). Then things would move very fast. The emphasis in bold type on 'had to' seemed to warn Hilde how important it was to wait and not do anything reckless. It was now, therefore, clear that Heinz and Erika would take Claus in. A week later, Heinz confirmed that Claus could come to live with them; that was the only sure thing, he wrote. Everything else remained unsure; the lack of relatives in the country was still a hindrance to improving their situation. However, if someone was not well enough to live in a refugee camp, they could be detained privately. Heinz asked Hilde if she knew whether she was fit enough to be in a camp. He apologised for being so direct but didn't know how to inquire otherwise. He encouragingly remarked that the wait for a solution no longer looked as endless as it once had.

At last, at the start of February 1943, Heinz had some good news for Hilde. He'd heard on the radio that the government would ease stipulations for refugees, and suddenly there was a ray of hope: Alfred could be declared unfit for a refugee camp and put up in a hotel with his son near Zurich in Küsnacht. Hilde would have the possibility of monthly visits and being able to spend some days with her family. Moreover, Alfred had located a certain Miss Regina Boritzer from the Verband Schweizer Israelitischer Armenpfleger (Association of Swiss-Israelite Caregivers for the Needy) in Zurich, who was prepared to work towards this solution that Heinz called 'a minimal programme'. Heinz reported that Alfred described her as 'proactive, [she] masters all difficulties and enjoys the confidence of the cantonal authorities'. Heinz wrote with a poetic flourish regarding these new prospects: 'Now we will get this new little horse to trot and hope it will take its obstacles. And should we get that far – maybe we will get even farther'.

By 9 February 1943, Claus had arrived at Heinz and Erika's home. Erika wrote by hand in a motherly letter to Hilde, describing Claus's arrival. Hilde had asked Claus to promise to write each day, and Erika confirmed that he had written the day before without being prompted. Heinz had written to Alfred on 6 February regarding schooling, which seemed to be the domain of the man of the house – but in another letter, Heinz told Hilde what was happening and reported details of Claus's new everyday life. Claus had to go into Zurich once or twice a day by train on his own, depending on whether he had afternoon lessons or not. (Lessons in the afternoon were not a regular part of the curriculum.) It was a pleasure to have Claus, Heinz reassured Hilde. The other issue in this letter had to do with rationing cards. Heinz asked Hilde to get the administration of the refugee camp to confirm directly to the official office in Zurich what the last date was that ration cards for

Claus had been issued. This was to avoid double issuing or no card being issued at all after Claus moved in with Heinz's family. This letter has an elated tone, probably because Heinz and his family had, at last, been able to help. Heinz sounded relieved and told Hilde that when Claus arrived from school, letters from both his parents would be waiting for him; he was anticipating Claus's joy at receiving the letters and hoping to reassure Hilde by telling her such a detail. Heinz also seemed careful not to encroach on Hilde and Alfred's parental roles in their son's life. He commented that Claus was quite orderly but 'inconsistent'. He mused that when regular, everyday schooling set in, sometimes with lessons in the afternoon and sometimes without, this would probably regulate itself. I imagined how simultaneously distraught but relieved Hilde must have been as she read this letter. She no longer had her son with her, but she knew he was in kind and caring hands and could attend school again.

Only three days later, in a long, two-page letter, Heinz acknowledged and thanked Hilde for immediately dealing with the ration card issue. Claus had compared Heinz to his father, and Heinz wrote that he was honoured. Heinz then put Claus's delight at everything (about which he'd written to his mother) into perspective, saying that it was understandable how happy he was now that 'the child had reclaimed his freedom'. Things, Heinz wrote, could, however, change from pink to grey when everyday school life set in. Heinz hoped that the teenager would be a good pupil and then explained reassuringly to Hilde how her son now went to and from school and added that a neighbour's child had the same journey, and they travelled together. Heinz wrote to Hilde about watching Claus on his way home through a window. As the young teenager walked towards Heinz's house, Claus stopped and took time to look closely at houses and their fences near his new home. In this comment, I fleetingly saw Claus the future photojournalist. I also saw Heinz watching and non-intrusively respecting Claus while he was observing; he didn't judge what Claus was doing as dawdling.

Hilde would be moving to a different camp and had expressed worry about that. Heinz calmly wrote (by now seemingly having some practice in dealing with Hilde), 'who knows if your fears will be confirmed when you get to Champrey!' Champéry is less than 20km north-east of Bex, and why she had to move is unclear. Heinz expressed faith again that the situation was gradually improving. He reasoned that if Alfred was outside a camp and Claus too, she would be able to join them soon. Heinz confirmed that the government in Bern was now navigating 'milder waters' regarding refugees. Quite bluntly but with refreshing directness, Heinz wrote to Hilde that worse outcomes had been avoided. Did he mean that they had not been sent to a concentration camp? I think so. He affirmed that Hilde's family had found a refuge and Claus had not missed essential schooling. He did not doubt that things could be improved, but that could now happen without the pressure of torturous deadlines. He added, the perfect gentleman: 'Please do not think that after these factual statements, we will be less concerned about your wishes, which are ours too!!'

Another handwritten letter from Erika is dated 24 February 1943, stamped, like all of the wartime letters, to show that it had passed the censor. Erika explained why Claus had not sent his daily letter: he'd been in bed with a cold and a high temperature. He was already back at school after two days off. Alfred had been able to visit, and father and son had enjoyed a walk together. How difficult it must have been for Hilde to be far away from her family, alone, reading those lines.

The following and last letter in the AfZ archive from Heinz to Hilde was dated two months later, 29 April 1943. Why there is an apparent two-month gap in the letters will remain a mystery. Heinz told Hilde that he understood that she was experiencing 'a certain depression', having arrived again at Champéry – meaning that she had been somewhere else in the meantime – and he was writing to say that he would be seeing Alfred that evening. Alfred had spoken to a commission regarding an extension of his holiday, which had been rejected. He had to work for another week, which Heinz did not see as bad because his discharge proceedings were now well underway.

Heinz wrote that he had travelled to Bern, over 100km from where he lived, to further her case to be released and join her husband. He had success and underlined what he wrote: 'The canton of Zurich has agreed to your residence in Küsnacht.' Furthermore, a phone call from the army had reached him with the news that Alfred did not have to return to the (previous) refugee camp. Heinz confirmed that Alfred was now indeed interned in Küsnacht, Zurich, and Hilde was on the path to the same place; things were moving rapidly. All officials had announced and supported this change, and the only thing bothering Heinz now was that Hilde could not see it in black and white on paper with her own eyes, and therefore she might not believe the news. Heinz confirmed again: he had seen all the official documents while in Bern. It would take a while for the confirmation to reach her. The final words I found from Heinz to Hilde in this last saved letter in the AfZ archive were that she would very soon be hearing directly from Alfred and Claus.

When I had finished working through all of Heinz's letters and writing this part up, I realised how carefully composed his letters were. He knew a censor was reading them, and he took care not to criticise his country's way of dealing with the Wilhelm family. It was as if he wrote with someone watching over his right shoulder; I could almost feel him weighing each of his sentences before he typed. Yet, at the same time, he sympathised with how Hilde struggled and, to comfort her, shared everything he was undertaking to get the family out of the camps.

The chapters about Grete, Else and Therese were, for me, the most harrowing to write. I thought writing about what had happened to the Wilhelm family would not be so challenging because they had all survived. However, reading the letters drew me deeply into their fate, and I was surprised by how disturbing their tale was to me. I felt sad but also indignant while writing. My heart especially warmed to

Heinz as I studied his letters; he had done much to help the Wilhelm family. He died sixteen months after writing the letter to Hilde in April 1943. I knew from my research on the Gütermann family of his illness and how his death had affected my grandfather, Bruno. Learning how he fell ill just a year and a few months after helping the Wilhelm family touched me intensely.

When I met Heinz's grandson Christoph Gütermann in Vienna in 2019, I gave him copies of the letters from the AfZ archive and they touched him too. He had known nothing of these letters or this phase of his grandfather's life, and he was initially confused about how I had come to possess them. When I explained how I had found them online and been given access, Christoph responded that he had found a film from 1943 and had wondered who the boy in the film was; the letters solved that mystery – it was Claus. There we were, Christoph and I, sorting out what happened to our predecessors during the Second World War, nearly eighty years previously. It bound as close together; we were both moved and astonished by what we had brought to light.

Claus

I found Claus's meticulous drawing with its hopeful subtitle, 'Commemoration of Dad's Birthday on 31 August 1944, the Last in Exile' in the AfZ archive. He had made it for his father as a birthday present that year. It documented the family's flight path to escape the Nazis. Claus was fifteen when he drew it, and some of his developing skills manifested in this sketch. The drawing is geographically pretty accurate, although he drew Belgium a bit too small: he'd studied Europe's geography, drew it carefully, including the French rivers, and presented it aesthetically. The picture focused on France, where the family had spent over three and a half years. He noted how long the family stayed in each location. The numbers and lines document how often the family moved around as they tried to keep safe.

When I studied the Wilhelms' family story during the war, I repeatedly got the impression that being the only child caused strain on Claus. He was the focus of his parents' attention and worries. Claus's letters to Hilde during his stay with Heinz and Erika show that he took great pains to reassure his mother how much he loved her and that he was fine. But here was a teenager – he turned fourteen years old in April 1943 – who had been in a refugee camp for over four months, separated first from his father and later from both parents. Reading the letters gave me the impression that his personal experience took second place behind his expressing consideration of his mother's state of mind. Reading the seventeen letters from Claus to his mother from the archive, I sometimes also felt as if there was a lack of healthy distance between mother and son: 'I am very anxious for you, my dear mother, and when I eat something good, I think of you as well as in the evening when I pray.' After being separated from his mother for two months, Claus was hopeful of seeing Hilde when he accompanied Heinz on a trip to Lausanne. Aware of this possibility, Claus wrote that he could 'think of nothing else' and perhaps he could stay overnight. Writing about his Easter holidays and about not having to watch the time in the morning to get to school punctually, he added: 'But the most beautiful part of the holidays will certainly be the hours that I will spend with you'.

Claus seemed to be trying to support Hilde by doing all he could to reassure her, but his voice doesn't always ring true. In comparison, the letters from my father while he was away at boarding school reveal him to have been more independent, and he sometimes confronted or even challenged his parents. There is little sign of that in Claus's letters. While Claus shared details of his new, everyday life with the Gütermann family, for me as a reader it was as if the real person writing the letters was hidden. An exception is a sentence from Claus's first letter to Hilde after he arrived at Heinz and Erika's house. He wrote about his arrival, his bedroom and what he had eaten. The change of environment compared with the refugee camp seemingly bemused him, and he wrote: 'It was as if I was in a dream'.

Claus did not seem to have a storytelling drive like my father, whose letters were written by someone keen to write; Claus's letters don't have that air about them, and that may have had to do with the promise to write every day that Hilde had wrung from him before he left Bex. Perhaps he felt a sense of duty, and that stifled his writing creativity. I do not doubt that Claus had creative energy, but I did wonder how his time in France with his parents in exile influenced his development. It is clear from the saved school reports that Claus was intellectually a most capable pupil. He spoke German and French; his marks ranged minimally from very good to excellent.

Alfred's letters to his son are warm-hearted and full of anticipation and recollection. They are written sketches of things he wanted to do with his son when they were together again and images of previous happy times. Alfred wove in Latin sentences to encourage Claus with his study of Latin, and there was some correspondence in fluent French too. Alfred also wrote about their shared interest in stamp collecting. Regular and good portions of advice were also included in Alfred's letters, but he formulated this gently. I got the impression that Alfred had inherited some of Therese's warm, good-naturedness that I was familiar with from Marianne. No letters from Claus to Alfred have been saved, but there were several self-made cards in the archives. I found a caricature of Hitler in the suitcase archive. I don't know for certain that Claus drew it, but I feel he did. The artist scratched out the writing on the lower right of the image; it seems to say 'my leader' – the English version of 'mein Führer'.

The Wilhelm family after the war

The 1946 residence permit photos of the family gave me the following impression: Claus was putting on a brave face, Alfred looked thin and anxious, and Hilde had an air of defiance about her. After the war, the family stayed in Zurich. Why is not clear; I wondered if it had to do with wanting to give back some of the support they had received from Heinz and Erika during the war since

Erika had become a widow. Or was it because Alfred had found work? He struggled after the war to be allowed to work in Switzerland, even though he found a position with the Association of Swiss Jewish Welfare/Refugee Aid (VSJF).[10] I found harsh letters in the AfZ archive from the state authorities granting him post-war residence and work permits for only three months and then for six months. The pressure (to exit the country) and strict stipulations must have ground him down. Nevertheless, Alfred navigated this phase and built up his work as a lawyer, and this enabled his family to stay in Zurich – but they remained Austrian citizens. A staged photo taken after the war seems demonstratively cheerful. I don't know where it was taken. Marianne and Bruno might have visited Zurich; or had the Wilhelm family gone to London? It is notable that Alfred has put on weight and no longer looks so gaunt. The photo's message is clear: look! we're here, we're together and we're fine. Cigarettes in hand.

I found a few poignant colour photos in the suitcase archive, which were in an envelope with the words 'return to Vienna' on it, dated 1975. There are old people getting out of a car and pictures of the interior of a flat, which must have belonged to the Wilhelms before they fled in 1938. Perhaps the visit helped Hilde and Alfred to reconcile their losses. Alfred died later that year and Hilde two years later, both aged eighty-three.

I'm convinced that Alfred, the lawyer who implicitly dealt with right and wrong, created the AfZ archive, to document his moral outrage, indignation and the injustice done to his family. Although my grandmother, Marianne, never spoke of him to me, Alfred certainly knew of my existence – but we never met. Alfred could not have had an inkling that his great-niece would find the papers, explore them, integrate the findings into a book and thus bring those injustices to a broader public.

---

10. The organisation today: https://swissjews.ch/en/association/cooperations/vsjf.

15 MELITTA
1893–1950

Lies that perpetuate and engineer violence and teach people to hate each other. Lies that poison nations and dig divides between them that may not even be made up for decades.

Karel Čapek[1]

There is so little to write about Marianne's sister that it makes me sad. The first evidence I found of Melitta's existence was her death certificate in the suitcase at my mother's house. It says that she died in London of a cerebral haemorrhage in 1950.

A photo from the early 1930s shows the siblings arm in arm: Melitta is in the middle, Alfred on her right and Marianne on her left. She has a summer dress on. Perhaps the photo was taken on one of Bruno's birthdays, in July. Therese is standing in front of Marianne, and everyone looks relaxed, content and happy; there is no hint of the turmoil and tragedy to come. It strikes me how different Marianne

---

1. Karel Čapek, 'Prayer for Truth', *Lidové noviny*, 25 September 1938. https://motivago.cz/en/motivation-inspiration/prayer-for-truth.

and Melitta looked: Marianne had a roundish head; Melitta's head was oval, like Alfred's.

I found several records having to do with Melitta. Most of them seem to revolve around preserving evidence of her (possibly) involuntary divorce because she was Jewish. Marianne must have committed the documents to the suitcase at my mother's house, which became the family archive. There is no evidence that Melitta studied at university like Alfred or Marianne, and she may well not have had academic leanings like her siblings. I found her baptism certificate dated 24 June 1916. It seems Melitta converted because of her upcoming marriage, which took place a few days later. This means that she did so earlier than Marianne and Bruno, who were christened in 1938 while in Switzerland. Melitta was twenty-nine when she married Eduard, a German, who was six years younger. The marriage certificate shows that Therese's father – Melitta's grandfather – Ludwig Sonnenblum witnessed the marriage ceremony at the evangelical church in 1916.

I found a copy of the divorce verdict, dated 14 March 1939, and the content makes for disturbing reading. It is aggressively written and based on the Nazis' antisemitism and the Nuremberg Decrees from 1935, which aimed to prohibit or dissolve marriages between Germans (with 'German blood') and persons of 'foreign blood'. The divorce decree has a swastika stamp on it. The translated verdict states:

> *The powerful political events of 1938 made the plaintiff [Eduard Hellmann] understand the importance of the racial difference between the spouses. The defendant [Melitta] had no understanding of the political events. Therefore, marital quarrels arose from which it could be inferred that the spouses were completely estranged from each other. The court accepts this fact as proven, based on the statements of both parties, especially as this situation is supported by a letter from the*

defendant and by the plaintiff's statement that he made during the hearing. He did not want to continue the marriage which would be intolerable for both parties. In such a marriage, there would be no question of mutual love, respect, and support, both spiritual and material, due to the difference in their outlook on life and duties towards the community. The court is convinced that at the time of the marriage, the plaintiff was mistaken about significant circumstances. If he had been aware of the situation at the time of the marriage, namely that racial difference leads to the most vexatious animosity and hinders the plaintiff's participation in society, he would certainly not have married. The divorce claim is, therefore, justified by §37 of the Greater German Marriage Law.

Melitta and Eduard were divorced after twenty-three years of marriage. They had a son, Gerhard, called Gert. It is easy to judge Eduard and suspect that he was divorcing his wife to save his skin and distance himself from his wife's Jewish identity. But Benjamin Frommer points out that this kind of divorce cannot automatically be considered a sign of 'malicious intent or wanton indifference'.[2] Frommer explains that many Czech intermarried couples opted for a 'fake divorce' to save their property or jobs but still lived together. The real situation between this couple will remain obscured in history forever; I cannot know in what spirit the divorce took place. Perhaps Melitta had been prepared to divorce to protect Gert and save him and Eduard's work as a paper merchant? My feeling, though, is that the divorce deeply hurt Melitta, and that Marianne knew that and committed documents to the family archive for this reason.

If so-called 'mixed marriages' were dissolved, the now-divorced Jewish partners were no longer protected and were in danger of Nazi

---

2. Benjamin Frommer, *Privileged Victims: Intermarriage between Jews, Czechs, and Germans in the Nazi Protectorate of Bohemia and Moravia.*

persecution and deportation. This must have been why Melitta also fled to England, and I believe it was another Quaker family who took her in. Melitta's work permit was issued just five weeks after her divorce on 26 April 1939 under the UK 1920 'Aliens Order'. She left for England after Hitler marched into Prague in March 1939. This permit was written in non-gender-neutral language; it reads as if only men were recipients of such permits. Melitta was furthermore referred to in this document, in a language now foreign to us, as an 'alien'. Seven times in only twenty lines, she was called this.

Marianne mentioned in a letter to Irma that Melitta was in Wimbledon and working for a family as a domestic help. Initially, however, the employer's address on her work permit was in the Midlands: Mrs L.E. Simpson, Ringstead, Moor Hill Park, Sutton Coldfield. That was her 1939 address, and her stated surname was the German version: Hellmann. An envelope without content, addressed to Melitta during a visit to Czechoslovakia, shows that she stayed with her son in Opava after the war in 1946. It was addressed to her using the Czech version of her name: Melitta Helmannova (the correct Czech would have been Helmannová), London. However, a different Wimbledon household was noted on her death certificate in 1950: 3 Ridgway Place, Wimbledon. A sense of disruption comes across; Melitta was not at home anywhere. She lived in England for only eleven years, and my father recorded in his letter that she wished to return home. Gert, in Opava, had married; the pair had a son, Peter – Melitta's grandson. Of course she wanted to reunite with her family. Why she did not stay after her visit in 1946 is unclear: it may have been a combination of the unstable political situation and Eduard not welcoming her back.

Two differing UK death certificates document Melitta's death. She died on 7 January. The second document, dated September 1950, was a corrected version of the first from February 1950. Why her death certificate was amended was revealed by a long letter I found to do with Melitta: two pages from Gert, which he wrote to Marianne after his mother had died, dated 22 February 1950. It seems that he did not come over to London for the funeral because, in the first sentence of his letter, he commiserated with his aunt about how much Marianne had to organise for Melitta's funeral. He suggested that the time after losing a loved one is difficult enough, and the last thing one wants is to have to deal with official red tape. Marianne had asked Gert to send certain documents because she had made a mistake while signing the (first) death certificate. It seems that Marianne had signed that Melitta was a widow, this was amended to divorcee on the second death certificate. Seemingly to officially rectify her status, documents had to be obtained from her place of birth. A document issued in Opava, dated 21 February 1950, confirmed her marriage in 1916 a few days after her christening, and the same record confirmed her divorce in 1939. Gert must have requested this official confirmation from the authorities in Opava and sent it to his aunt to iron out Marianne's mistake regarding her sister's status at her time of death. Gert enclosed Melitta's birth and baptism certificates and a certified copy of the marriage certificate. At some point, Marianne committed these documents to the suitcase that eventually came into my mother's possession.

Over half a page of Gert's letter concerned his mother's status (as not a widow but a divorcee) and Marianne's mistake. It was important to Marianne, but above all to Gert, to have the record set straight for the following reasons. Being divorced from a German meant (at least on paper) that she had taken a proactive decision to distance herself. Being widowed from a German entailed no such decision, because it would have been a status she'd passively gained. So, Melitta's 'national reliability' status – a prerequisite for getting her citizenship and legal rights back after the war – was therefore 'proven' by the divorce. Otherwise, she might have been considered an ethnic German and might have been subject to deportation along with other Germans when the revenge started. This fine legal line would also have reflected on Gert's legal status in Czechoslovakia after the war.

It meant that he was the son of a nationally reliable Czechoslovak citizen, and his inheritance would be safe.

The second page of Gert's letter was about his family. His son Peter had been in hospital for ten days with diphtheria. Peter was improving, having received penicillin, and the child wanted to return home. Gert requested something unavailable in Opava from Marianne so that he could continue building Peter's electric train set.

Melitta lost her father when she was six years old. In 1939, she lost her marriage, husband and home to the Nazis, who murdered her mother, Therese. She remained in England, separated from her son and grandson, and was alone. Irma, Marianne and Hanne had their partners with them, and their experience in England during the war must have been easier to navigate with someone by their side. While her younger sister, Marianne, must have been a supportive and stabilising presence, I think of Melitta's life as tragic. I tried to trace the Hellmann family via heritage websites but was unsuccessful; I would have liked to have known more.

16 OPAVA

Reaching for the world, as our lives do,

As all lives do, reaching that we may give

The best of what we are and hold as true:

Always it is by bridges that we live.

Philip Larkin, 'Bridge for the Living'[1]

A thought flashed through my mind again and again in 2015: visit the house – 'the house' being the one the family had left behind in Opava in 1938. I spoke to Julia, and she was captivated. In February 2016, I moved into action and reached out to some of the people working at the Opava Town Hall: the website included email addresses of employees. I explained in English who I was and why I was searching for the house, asking if it was familiar to anyone. I sent a grainy

---

1. Philip Larkin (1922–1984): English poet, novelist and librarian at the University of Hull, UK.

digitised copy of a photo taken in the 1930s. My gut feeling said that the house still stood; Julia was also sure it was still there.

Weeks passed, and nothing happened; I even stopped waiting for an answer. Then suddenly, everything started happening. Martina Věntusová, a secretary in the mayor's office, answered my email, writing to me in English: she had located the house. She wrote that a state calibration institution now used it and attached some pictures of the house she'd taken *the day before*. It had snowed, and ... there I saw it standing quiet, sturdy and strong, braving the chilly weather yesterday! It was an extraordinary and tremendously moving moment. I was stunned and excited, and a cocktail of mixed feelings broke out in me. The new address, Martina wrote, was Gudrichova 41. I contacted Julia immediately, and we just wept with one another over the phone. The news made us speechless, and a battery of emotions overwhelmed us. But a state calibration institute?! I observed prickly, possessive feelings woven into my sadness; Julia did not have that reaction.

When I had centred myself, I wrote back to Martina, heartily thanking her and asking if it would be possible to organise a visit at the end of April, having already checked potential dates with Julia and our respective partners. Freiburg and Opava lie about 1,000km apart, and my partner and I planned to travel by car and spend the first part of the trip in Prague. Julia and her husband, Trevor, would fly from London to Prague and we'd pick them up. Again, I heard nothing for a long time and then, yes, on 23 April, Martina wrote back, the present director of the institute in the house would be happy to show us around. Despite our eagerness to visit and do this adventure together, we remained swamped in sorrow, and we spent quite some time during the weeks before the trip crying (not talking) on the phone. I recognised the strong emotional reaction. It was the 'great Holocaust sadness'; Ariane Neumann in her book *When Time Stopped* writes of experiencing sadness which stupefied her.[2]

April came at last, and we picked up Julia and Trevor at the airport and spent two nights and three days together in a smart holiday flat. Prague was blessed with glorious spring sunshine while we were there, and the beauty and elegance of the city exhilarated us. There were some difficult things to do, though, as well. The addresses on Else and Grete's cards were the same, and we wanted to visit the site. Addresses change through time, and a degree of uncertainty remained as to whether the address was still in use – Jindriska 32a or 34 – but it was still a sombre moment finding the building and standing in front of it. Our partners took some photos.

We visited the Pinkas Synagogue without informing ourselves about it beforehand. We hadn't known that the walls were a memorial to the near 78,000 Jewish victims of the Shoah from Bohemia and Moravia. Václav Boštík and Jiří John had painted their names there in the 1950s,[3] and it was one of the first memorials to the murdered Jews of the Czech lands. So, upon entering, it was with excitement and trepidation that we saw the thousands of names on the walls and started searching for our grandfather's sisters. Most people were surging through the synagogue and not looking for names; it was difficult not to flow with the masses. I realised that the names were in alphabetical order, and yes, there, suddenly, a little above me, on the left side where I was frantically scanning the walls, I saw, and my brain registered 'Eduard Lanzer' and 'Marketa Lanzerova'. I was by now familiar with the Czech versions of the names of my lost relatives, although in my mind the German versions were the right ones. I called urgently to the others, who, fighting their way through the crowd in the opposite direction to the flow, joined me to stare at

---

2. Neumann, Ariane, *When Time Stopped: A Memoir of My Father's War and What Remains*.
3. www.jewishmuseum.cz/en/explore/sites/pinkas-synagogue.

the wall. Pain wrenched my heart, and tears stung my eyes; I fought them back.

Slowly moving on, with tears threatening to brim over, I started searching for Bruno's younger sister, Else, and her husband. And there they were, lower right, among the vast sea of victims' names in another area of the synagogue: Karel Federmann and Elsa. As we knew their dates of birth, we could be sure that these were the lost sisters who had never been spoken of. We did not search for Therese; I had not yet found her documented online, and with a surname beginning with 'W', her name would probably have been under the roof and out of sight. Finding their names made the fate of our great-aunts and their husbands palpable and manifest. It was a further tragic confirmation of their fates.

It was a tedious three and a half hours' drive from Prague the following day, and the four of us arrived in Opava tired but full of anticipation at around 2pm. We had a short rest and a nap at our hotel. We left again at 3:30pm for the brief journey to the house at Gudrichova 41; we had an appointment at 4pm with the director of the calibration institute. His name was Ivo, and he had kindly agreed to give up his time at the weekend, let us into the house and show us around. The house was only a few kilometres from our hotel, so we arrived at 3:40pm.

As I set eyes for the first time upon the large house my grandfather had built, where my father had spent childhood years, tears stung my eyes; I was deeply moved. All was quiet as I slowly got out of the car, a fresh breeze was blowing and the sky was grey. We started exploring the yellow wall surrounding the house and its positioning in the area, and excitedly compared photocopied photos from years ago that Julia had with her. I walked up to the original massive iron gate with a trace of art nouveau about it. Then, to the left of the entrance gate, I saw a sign that tangibly triggered something in my brain. I needed a second to comprehend the interwoven jagged letters; one was upside down. Then I realised I was looking at a stylised B underneath, with an M on top connected with a V in the middle. It was two years later in 2018 that Julia gave me the woodcarving her mother had made – this was the first time I had seen the interwoven initials MBV. Bruno and Marianne Vogel – our grandparents! I called loudly; Julia appeared quickly. I hurriedly explained, she understood instantly, and we both felt sobs well up again as we hugged one another, overwhelmed with emotion. The date underneath was 1929; the family had spent only nine years here before they fled in 1938, a shockingly short length of time.

Something else on the wall around the house gripped us: the outlines of a mammoth moulded into concrete. Julia and I knew that a mammoth skeleton had been found when the house foundations had been dug. My father referred to this 'elephant' in his letter from 1945 upon his return to the house after the war, and it was one of the few harmless pieces of information passed on to us from Opava during our English childhoods. Our grandfather had preserved the skeleton find for posterity by drawing it symbolically into the wall, but only now did I understand why my father said that the elephant had winked at him as he passed by during his visit home in 1945.

Soon it was 4pm; Ivo turned up and, upon seeing us, called someone on his phone, and another car drew up more or less immediately. This was good, because Ivo spoke neither English nor German and we spoke no Czech, but one of the people who arrived in the car, Veronika, spoke English. Her father, Vladimir, had worked in the house for forty years: he knew it well, as we were to discover. We all shook hands, introducing ourselves and thanking them for their time. First, we spent time outside, comparing photos and getting to know one another. Julia and I sat outside on the steps for a weep and a hug. She had a photo of her mum sitting there on the same steps some eighty years previously.

Then we went inside the house. The front door was cheap and new; it seemed to strip the home of some of its memories, and I felt a tinge of annoyance. We stood there scanning the office rooms, the walls lined with files, machines on the desks and piles of paper everywhere. The surroundings were contradictory; behind the files on the shelves were sleek walnut panels. The modest lino flooring bothered me as the door had; it was wrong and jarring because it did not belong. We started puzzling about which room was which. Julia showed copies of photos of the previous living room to the group and Vladimir quickly oriented us, exclaiming excitedly and pointing to a little space in the wall with instruments. He had identified the space, which had previously harboured the sitting room clock in times long gone. We could see the family clock in the wall in Julia's photo. (One morning, several months after my sixtieth birthday in 2018, I woke up with the realisation that the clock in Eva's woodcarving that she made for her parents' twentieth wedding anniversary was that sitting room clock from the family house in Opava.)

Vladimir pointed to glass shelves and asked Veronika to translate to say that they were the original shelves. On the ground floor, one room had been a summer conservatory and could be easily identified from one of Julia's photos. It hurt me how the beautifully furnished space was now a simple storage room; the tasteful spirit of this living space was long dead.

In the basement, Vladimir showed us little signs on the walls with words in German: *Wasch-Küche, Parterre-Küche, Reserve Kamin* and *Keller-Küche*. They were low down and had not been painted over. The signs stood for chimneys no longer in use. It touched me that, through the years, people had painted around the signs, little silent ghosts from the long-gone past. It suggested quiet respect for the previous owners.

The seven of us went up a stylish Art Deco staircase that had remained relatively undisturbed through the decades and onto the first floor. Here our hosts showed us one of the most touching objects. Bruno had designed a dressing table for Marianne, which was still there. Originally, it had probably been the same smart walnut we had seen downstairs; now, it was plain and smooth and had been painted over in white. The functionality was obvious: closed, it was a surface to put things on. Opened, it was a high-quality mirror, and the mirror we looked upon was the original. And what a fantastic view our grandmother had had out onto the plains of Moravia as she had sat there all those years ago. I imagined her starting her days, seeing the lovely countryside and the openness of the space – and imagined her happiness. I heard her hearing her children playing and saw her planning her time, as mothers do. I fleetingly entered her world as I stood there; I looked out through her window into her world all those years ago. As I did that, a parallel awareness opened alongside my everyday one, I briefly had the strange sensation of being Marianne and, momentarily, I actually felt her happiness.

Surrounding this room area were fitted cupboards and small shelves that Bruno had designed. Julia and I recognised his style. Ivo and Vladimir were making internationally understandable sounds of admiration and approval; the quality and ingenuity of the woodwork impressed them. We were shown some more rooms, but we could not know which bedroom had been my father's or Eva's. By now, I was struggling with my emotions; tears were threatening to overwhelm me. Ivo, Veronika and Vladimir generously showed us the house's details, but I was on a different level of experience. I felt permeable to the spirit of the people who had lived here in the past. While I was interested in the material level I was being shown, I was wrestling with the grief that swamped me. I saw that Julia was also suppressing tears but they threatened to overpower us both the longer the afternoon drew on.

Going up another floor to where the nanny (and later the au pair, Mademoiselle) must have lived, Vladimir became enthusiastic about the house's insulation, which he explained with his daughter translating. Warm air, which rises, was collected in a space, and this space could be accessed via tiny openings which he showed us in each of the five small rooms under the roof. Vladimir found that impressive. Yes, it had been well designed. Julia and I smiled knowingly at one another; we were familiar with our grandfather's ingenuity.

After the inside tour, we went into the garden and chatted. We had been together for about an hour, and we were warming to one another. Vladimir eagerly explained that an underground irrigation system had been discovered in the garden, and there had been a pit for inspecting a car from underneath. How we coordinated the house's past in the present gripped all of us. The kindness and generosity with their time of our hosts and guides touched us. Vladimir, who had spent so much time of his working life in our grandfather's house, told us through his daughter that he had always been curious about the people who had previously lived there. They had left so many personal traces; he had noticed them and wondered. Veronika shared that she had visited her father at work as a child and had also been fascinated. They said that they had had the impression it had been a very special house, lived in by special people. They now knew more about the previous owners, and that had made the afternoon memorable for them too.

At one point, Julia nipped to the bottom of the garden. In a quiet moment, she spread a tiny amount of Eva's ashes in the garden that her mum had loved so much and where Eva had played as a child eight decades before.

We gave one another spontaneous and hearty hugs as we took our leave; it had been an emotionally intense afternoon. I was relieved to go so that the sadness I'd been tussling with could have some space. But within, I now felt curiously lighter and unburdened – as if something that had long been in the way of the light had moved aside. I mentioned this to Julia, and she felt the same. And there the house quietly stood as I turned to look at it one last time before we left: still majestic but a little tainted and time-battered. It stood there simply on its mound overlooking the area and watching us people, as it had steadily done for the last eighty-seven years.

I had found a picture of my father taken during his 1991 visit to Opava. He was standing next to a memorial to Therese, murdered in Treblinka, and the grave of her husband Leopold, Marianne's father, in the Jewish cemetery. And so I, too, sought out this place on the evening of our visit. The inscription, translated from German reads: 'Who ever lives in the memory of loved ones is not dead, he only lingers far away'. I wondered who had carefully ensured that Therese would not be forgotten and thought that it must have been her son, Alfred.

17 JULIA AND NICOLA
*1959; *1958

... lost stories must be told again and again because that is the only way to assemble the traces of identity and fuse the fragments of a crumbled world.

David Grossmann[1]

I spoke to Julia about her mother and our shared family history in February 2022. I recorded our meeting so that I could transcribe it. Julia had prepared herself and dug up numerous documents to do with her mother's life to share what she had found. The most emotional part of our conversation was how Julia experienced the traumatic loss of her father when she was six years old. Julia called my father Peter; my mother's name is Pam. Towards the end of the conversation, Julia was trying to understand and piece together unknown parts of the family's story. We had started chatting informally, and my first pre-considered open question was to ask her

---

1. https://royallib.com/read/grossman_david/writing_in_the_dark_essays_on_literature_and_politics_.html#o.

to share something about the unspoken Jewish heritage in her – our – family.

> Julia: *I think Granny and Grandpa brought Eva and Peter up as Catholics because Grandpa particularly had experienced such antisemitism in his life. They were not Orthodox, and they didn't practise. Mum and Peter went to the local school and were … er… Catholic … Mum refused to talk about her memories as Hitler's power increased. Peter said he knew that everyone was saying that he was Jewish, and that he knew they were a rich Jewish family in that area. Mum seems to have successfully blocked that information. So, you know, Granny and Grandpa, by the fact that they went to Switzerland* [in 1938 on the way to England] *and converted to Catholicism as a safety mechanism, sort of illustrates they were trying to protect themselves, and more importantly, the children. I don't know if Irma and Alfred* [Karplus] *converted. So Mum came to Britain as a Czech refugee, but she would never have called herself that. Her story was that Grandpa got a job in England. Therefore, they came to England, they were not running away. Now, how much was she protecting herself by thinking that or how much Granny and Grandpa kept that from her, that's really the sort of question you would have had to ask Peter. He was younger, but he had much more of a perception of what was going on. So, as Peter said, she was a victim of Hitler's propaganda. My mother did not like Jews very much, and I think that she, purely out of fear, when all this stuff came up and I found out, she blew up absolutely, 'None of your fucking business, it's irrelevant! It's not your story!' And I said* [speaking quietly], *'Yes, it is my story' and she said, 'You know, I never wanted you to be burdened by this' and that is very telling. She was burdened with it and never wanted anyone to know that she was Jewish.*

> Nicola: *And when she reacted like that, how was that for you?*

Julia: *Well, first of all, I just asked that casual question, 'Oh Mum, so many people say I look Jewish, is there any Jewish blood in the family?' You see, Mum was not a liar, she just did not tell, there is a difference. So, she sort of looked incredibly uncomfortable ...* [mumbling, imitating her mum, shaking her head] *'Well, might have been ... might be' and I said, 'Well, who – what!?' And she said: 'Well, you know, Granny and Grandpa' so I said, 'WHAT! that means you're Jewish!' and she said, 'Don't be so RIDICULOUS!' You know, literally like that and ... deeply upset ... and it accounted for so much when I was a child. If I used my hands as a child, she'd say, 'Don't use your hands like that!' Now I don't know if that is just general etiquette not to express yourself using your hands, but going in for stereotypes, I would think it's quite a Jewish thing to do to talk with your hands. So, I'm interpreting like that, and it might be just Mum thinking I was ill-bred.*

Nicola: *So, she knew she was Jewish, she suppressed it, she comes to England, she lives in England, carries 'the burden' of being Jewish, she doesn't want her daughter to know anything about the Jewish legacy of the family out of fear. But I'm picking up a bit of disgust as well.*

Julia: *Well, like Peter said, she was a victim of Hitler's propaganda. Because I suppose, Granny and Grandpa, when Eva and Peter were children, they didn't say, 'You are Jewish and we are going to hide it, you're going to be Catholic'. All the locals must have known that the Vogels were rich Jewish people, Grandpa ran the sewing silks* [factory], *didn't he? It was obviously extreme to her, and I was like: 'Did Daddy know that you are Jewish?!' Look, she just did not want to talk about it; she would not talk about it ...*

Nicola: *So, she didn't answer that question as to whether your father knew?*

Julia: *Not really, he must have known, though, and the whole family* [on her father's side] *knew. She wouldn't have shared with her friends in Thames Ditton back then that she was Jewish, but people can't be that stupid. Out of respect for that, I haven't really talked about it to many of her friends. I just feel I need to respect her and what she would have felt because you can say, 'How ridiculous!' and 'how stupid!' and 'what's the matter with her'? But the shock of being part of a race that has been persecuted and went through that horrendous annihilation is difficult to bear. If you think, 'Christ, that could have happened to me'.*

Nicola: *So, she put down the shutters; she just separated from it.*

Julia: *Yes, and where she stayed in England and the various jobs she did, the people she mixed with, she placed herself* [gestures a circle] *in the upper middle classes. I'm sure that drove Pam and Peter around the twist, and I'm sure that was one of the – who did she think she is?! Margaret Tha-?! But you know, Mum did that. She wasn't the sort of person who could analyse, she wasn't into analysis; she would sit on the stairs and talk with me and my friends till 3am in the morning about the meaning of life, debate stuff, but she didn't focus on herself and analyse too much.*

Nicola: *You've shared with me how your mum dealt with her Jewish heritage, a lot of unspoken stuff; how do you think that influenced you growing up with her?*

Julia: *I didn't even think about it because, as far as I knew, mum was Catholic, and I was nothing. I had been christened, but religion never meant anything to me.*

Nicola: *Me neither.*

Julia: *All I was aware of, desperately, was class. I think this whole thing of mum wanting to be so 'uber-British' was quite a burden on me as well. Mum was horrified when I first met Trevor, and I was marrying someone who was older than me, and he was working class. She grew to absolutely love Trevor; I've got no doubt about that. She saw what a good person he was. But when she first clapped eyes on him, she said: 'Don't you think he looks a bit like Hitler?'*

[Laughter]

Nicola: *And he has a northern accent, not a Conservative posh accent! Let me come back to how it affected you because Eva had her share of tragedies, four miscarriages before she got pregnant with you, her husband died when you were six years old, but she was outspoken, she was full of energy, but she wasn't dealing openly with her tragedies, was she?*

Julia: *No.*

Nicola: *I have 'the unspeakable' and 'the unspoken' in my book – the more I write, the more I have the feeling of how much I picked up [as a child], but I had no idea what it was. So again, how did the unspoken affect you?*

Julia: *Well, I think what I picked up from mum is that she wasn't a safe person. She was late for everything, and she didn't make one feel safe and that it was all going to be 'all right', because I think she was tainted with the fact that it isn't going to be all right. I think, if I look back on it, I never, ever felt not loved, I know I was enormously loved by her, but she wasn't a safe person. In a way I suppose she was unlike a 'normal mother'. She would go: 'I just wouldn't know why you want to tell me these things'. Very much: you're an independent human being, why would you want to talk to your mother about this? She adored Granny, she didn't really like Grandpa very much, she didn't have this 'I'm-going-to-*

miss-my-mummy-and-daddy' kind of thing. It's hard ... to describe ... she was not a safe person.

[Pause]

Nicola: *I knew my aunt, I knew your mum, there was this kind of hovering on the surface: lots of vitality, energy,* [she was] *outspoken, and below* [the surface] *there was all this stuff, and that is what a child will pick up.*

Julia: *Well, I suppose going through such a terrible grief* [of losing her husband] *which you don't share with the child, which wounded you so deeply, mum always said, 'If I hadn't had a child I would have just starved to death'; she had no interest in going on after Michael died, but she had to plough on. In that way, I admire her: plunging into the bloody Tories ... this making a life for herself which didn't rely on me, which was brilliant, but she was extremely difficult to navigate, she'd go from nought to sixty in a way that can even make my tummy turn now. You know, I look and think: I loved her, but did I like her? And that will always be a puzzle to me: did I like her? I don't know how much I liked her if I'm honest, although I'd defend her to the nth degree. I distanced myself from her once I left university, I didn't go home and nor did she impose herself upon me. She would say her opinion and then let me get on with my life. She didn't say, 'If you marry Trevor, I will disinherit you'. So, she was liberal but scary. I remember sitting in the kitchen and thinking* [after hearing that Eva was Jewish]:*'This makes so much sense: her whole mania for fitting in'. I could feel that she didn't feel she fitted in – in so many ways.*

Nicola: *And she was trying so hard to fit in, and that's a kind of tension, isn't it?*

Julia: *That's a very good way of putting it: I was tense about so many aspects of living with her. You know, it wasn't a pleasant experience when I look back at it. But just imagine, her husband died, the child goes bonkers.*

Nicola: *So, tell me about this, you went 'bonkers'. You shared with me your mum only told you six months later that your father had died.*

Julia: Yes.

Nicola: *Do you remember that time? Did you realise he was ill?*

Julia: *Well, I knew he was ill because there were nurses coming to the house all the time. Particularly one nurse was completely lovely with me, I remember her. But nobody said, 'Daddy is ill'. And he kept going to hospital. What I do remember is that mum said, 'He's going to the hospital again' and I'm* [rubs her hands, childish voice]: *'Oh, I'll watch the ambulance go' which is what I usually did, and Mum went* NO YOU CAN'T WATCH – GET BACK TO BED!!! *and you know, I was tiny ... And what had happened is that he'd died and then she was waiting for him to be hoiked away by the undertakers ... so ...*

Nicola: *It wasn't an ambulance; it was the undertakers that were coming –*

Julia: Yes.

Nicola: *Wow.*

Julia: *So she didn't want me to look out of the window, she said, 'Daddy's going now' and I wanted to say goodbye to the ambulance, and she shrieked at me, and it did not make sense to me. And I remember that so clearly that it did not make sense: why is she shouting at me? Normally, I can look at the ambulance, but she was obviously in such a state of horror.*

Nicola: *She was deeply upset because he'd died, and she didn't know how to deal with you at that moment.*

Julia: *Well, she had to deal with herself, imagine.*

Nicola: *But while he was so ill, were you still visiting him in his bedroom?*

Julia: *Sometimes. It was interesting, I went to a ninetieth birthday party recently, and there was a darling woman there who was one of my many second mummies, and we were talking. She's got all her marbles and she said to the assembled: 'You know Julia's father died when she was only a little girl', and she said it was so awful: 'Your mother didn't even let you go in to see him when he was ill'. So even then it was like: 'How was Eva dealing with Julia and her father?' Mum didn't know any better, and she thought she was doing what was right. So, I could never chastise her for that because it's been and gone.*

Nicola: *You must have realised he was thin and weak? Can you remember seeing that he was ill?*

Julia: *Oh, I remember peeking through the door.*

Nicola: *Oh ... so you weren't in contact with him and talking to him?*

Julia: *No.*

Nicola: *Oh, Jules ...*

Julia: *No, nothing. I was kept well away ... and then, you know: 'Where's Daddy?', 'He's still in hospital', 'Where's Daddy?', 'He's still in hospital'. 'Where is he? Where is he?' I remember sitting on the stairs* [some time later] *and Mum saying, 'I have to tell you Michael died about six months ago' and then Winston Churchill died, and I imagined that*

Michael's funeral was exactly like Winston Churchill's, which was quite good.

[Laughter]

Julia: *Not any allusions of grandeur or anything ...*

Nicola: *Well, you were only six, six and a quarter ... Did you cry?*

Julia: *No.*

Nicola: *Did you cry about your dad? No mourning?*

Julia: *No.* [shaking head]

Nicola: *What a way to deal with losing your dad at the age of six.*

Julia: *I know, it was kind of the time, people did that.*

Nicola: *But it's also part of this not speaking, the unspoken in our family, not addressing things.*

Julia: *Not speaking, you know, your grandmother that you love beyond anything died in a concentration camp. And all Mum could do ... She did talk about Therese but didn't say what happened to her:* [speaking curtly] *'She died in the war'.*

In this part of the conversation, a parallel struck me between Therese's fate and how Eva dealt with (not) communicating to her daughter that her father had died. These were traumatic events, the loss of a close family member, but the details were shrouded in silence and the closer circumstances of the death were suppressed; the losses were not dealt with openly. Therese had also just 'disappeared'. The family in England was not notified that she had been transported and then killed in Treblinka – of course not. Michael also (from Julia's point of view) just 'went away'. I thought that Eva's four miscarriages belonged to the same pattern. Embryos don't have funerals – at least, they did not in the 1950s, and dealing with the trauma of multiple miscarriages was even less possible in those times than today.

Nicola: *What did she share about Therese?*

Julia: *Oh, that she was liberal, marvellous, loving, and gorgeous: None of them liked Johanna very much. She remembered Therese taking her to the solarium [in Troppau], you know, they were all the liberal, sort of middle-class women [who] went to sunbathe, naked – and she took Mum in, and I got her to tell me the story loads of times. All these naked women were screaming 'GET THAT CHILD OUT OF HERE!' [Laughter] Get her out of here, get her out of here! And Therese was completely unperturbed, didn't give a monkey's, and she was the one who sent Granny to grammar school.*

But poor Mum ... Auntie Pam, just incandescent. When I went over to Freiburg for your sixtieth birthday [in 2018], and we were talking, Pam said, 'Who do you think organised Michael's funeral?! It wasn't your mother!' I hadn't even thought that Mum hadn't organised it! Who organised it? Well, I don't know; Pam knew who had organised it, but it definitely wasn't Mum. To Mum a funeral was meaningless, she never went to funerals, what's the point? They're dead: the end. And I'm totally different; I love a funeral.

While transcribing this part, I saw another parallel: Therese had had no funeral and Eva was renowned for 'not doing funerals'. She didn't go to her parents' funerals in 1979 and 1980, and she hindered Julia from going too – something Julia later regretted. This seemed to be part of Eva's denial and blocking-pain-off strategy.

Nicola: *Well, you still have to say goodbye, there are some rituals among Homo sapiens, you don't just – they might be dead and gone but you still have to do something with the body, don't you?*

Julia: *Exactly, exactly.*

Nicola: *So, Michael died, it was summer 1965.*

Julia: *August.*

Nicola: *And you used the word 'bonkers'. What happened?*

Julia: *After all that, Mum was just constantly late picking me up from school and I was not just like a normal person: 'Oh, Mum is late'; it was instantly: dead, she is dead. I remember this feeling of unease started when I went to stay with my godmother, sort of not feeling right. It was basically deep anxiety. I didn't want to go to school. I couldn't say I consciously felt that if I left Mum out of my sight she'd never come back, but that must have been it, like somebody leaves* [speaking softly] *and they never come back. And I still feel that to this day, although it's more controlled. If I'm at an airport, I don't really like it if Trevor says, 'I'm going to get a paper'. I'll have to say to myself: 'He's just gone to get a paper; he's not going to disappear'.*

Nicola: *So there's no kind of natural understanding that people come and go, a deep fear permeated you as a child, and it can still be activated?*

Julia: *Totally,* [nodding] *you know, they go, and they never come back.*

Nicola: *And you didn't go to school for three years, is that right?*

Julia: *Yes.*

Nicola: *From what age to what age?*

Julia: *It must have been from about eight and a half to about twelve.*

Nicola: *And it was in that phase, as a child, I picked that up, my dad started being more there for you, wasn't he?*

Julia: *Yes.* [tears, shakes head, moved, holds her hand to her mouth].

Nicola: [gently] *Have a cry ... me too.* [We both have tears in our eyes].

While transcribing this bit, I was struck by contrast. Julia was touched and tears came as she remembered my father's care and attention in a very difficult phase of her life. Remembering the death of her father a few minutes beforehand, though, had not awoken emotions. Eva's strategy of blocking off the pain of traumatic events for herself and her daughter seemed still to be echoing decades later.

Julia: *Yes, he was so lovely to me, you know, and I just knew he cared, and I knew he kept an eye on me. He was so kind to me, he really was, despite Mum's rudeness to him. When she didn't want to face something, she'd just clam up, she never opened any of the letters from Austria* [about inherited property from Martha, Bruno's aunt, and Eva's great-aunt], *she never got on top of it; she felt deep guilt that she had the properties, so she did nothing with them, and that's the reason why Peter stepped in. But he was mindful; he was so kind of 'big' because even though there was friction, he was loyal to her and what Mum and Peter had in common was an enormous sense of right and wrong from Granny and Grandpa, and that is where they empathised, it was the right and wrong of stuff in terms of your actions, and I think that – Mum was – I think – yeah ... yeah ...*

[Pause]

While transcribing this part, I thought that Julia was reaching the edge of trying to understand and make sense of her mother's behaviour, hence the hesitation in an otherwise very flowing dialogue.

> Julia: *But she couldn't, as I said, bring herself to say thank you to Peter properly for dealing with Austria.*
>
> Nicola: *What I'm understanding is that she held a lot of stuff in herself. Saying 'thank you' means being soft and open, and she was holding much, much more in than my dad did.*
>
> Julia: *Oh, much more than your dad. He'd been to Israel, he'd said, 'I am Jewish', you know, he'd done all that. Mum, I think, looked at him like an alien; she felt she had nothing in common with him. Except just that sort of blood tie. And how much that meant to her or not, I don't know.*
>
> Nicola: *Was that 'looking at him like an alien' connected to this horror of being Jewish and maintaining distance to being Jewish?*
>
> Julia: *Maybe. We saw Granny and Grandpa every week, it wasn't ... It was such an unspoken thing, maybe Peter had talked about it, who knows the conversations they had about it. But I know there was a deliberate not mentioning 'it' whenever Eva and I were over at your parents' place.*
>
> Nicola: *With 'it' you mean Jewishness?*
>
> Julia: *Yes, there was no sort of – ummm ...*
>
> Nicola: *... confronting the past and dealing with it and your identity and tidying the past up?*

Julia: *She was, 'This Jewish thing has NOTHING to do with you!' and I was, 'But it has, it has everything to do with me'.*

Nicola: *That was her way of coping with the past, and I do deeply believe that Granny and Grandpa had a major role in this because I didn't know that Grandpa had two other sisters, I didn't even know that Irma was his sister. I didn't know that Marianne had a brother and a sister, I didn't know that my father had cousins. So, they dealt with it in a much less demonstrative way; your Mum was sort of out there dealing with it* [gestures energetically with hands] – *it was like a front, wasn't it? But Granny and Grandpa were quiet people with the unspoken–*

Julia: *Yes.*

Nicola: *This thing about not speaking about where we came from, the source of it was not Eva; it was Granny and Grandpa: they cultivated it.*

Julia: *And their parents, not just Granny and Grandpa, Johanna divorced her husband, didn't she?*

Nicola: *Yes, they were assimilated Jews, I think, but I have come to believe that Therese was a little bit observant–*

Julia: *Oh, was she? What happened to Granny's sister?*

Nicola: *Her name was Melitta; she married Eduard Hellmann, and he divorced her on racial grounds –*

Julia: *Oh yes, oh God –*

Nicola: *They had a child, Gerhart. And he was in the family house when my father went over after the war in 1945. The Hellmann family lived in Troppau, and Melitta wanted to go back.*

Julia: *Where was she? Where did she go?*

Nicola: *She got into England, to London –*

Julia: *Did she!*

Nicola: *I've got the envelope of a letter to her in London, she died in 1950. I've got a copy of her death certificate.*

Julia: *In London?*

Nicola: *Yes. It's interesting because there is so much out there when you analyse the data, but this unspoken thing is quite loud.*

Julia: *Yes, I mean, if we had known that whole visceral story of coming to England through Switzerland* [Nicola: nodding] *surviving there and ... where did Granny and Grandpa go before they had a flat? Was it a refugee camp? What was it?*

Nicola: *Averard House at Lancaster Gate.*

Julia: *And was that like ... small apartments?*

Nicola: *No! Like a luxury hotel!*

[Laughter]

Nicola: *So how do you see our shared grandparents?*

Julia: *Well, they were much more sort of a place of security than Mum. They were completely loving, and Granny was full of laughter – she had the sort of laughter that bubbled; and she would laugh, with a slight cough. Grandpa and her obviously got on well, and she was so sweet and kind and warm, and she cooked. I just loved being in that house. I always thought Granny was good at cooking because she was a chemist* [pharmacist] *and was able to mix things. She seemed to have a really happy life; they went off on their Alpine holidays, Granny would play bridge all the bloody time ...*

Nicola: *How's your view on this writing project of mine?*

Julia: *I think it a really important part of our lives: We're the last generation who will have had contact to the people who had to radically alter their lives. We might not have existed. It is absolutely horrifying what they could have gone through, I suppose it is like nearly having a car crash and you think, 'What if, what if ...' Thinking that your relatives had died in a concentration camp is so much more enormous than thinking I-could-have-smashed-the-car kind of thing. But you find that people who come out of Auschwitz* [referring to a recent BBC documentary], *despite the enormous trauma they went through, despite the tremendous horror they went through, the grief and the loss, they still manage to come out of that as loving and kind people, but they are who they are: they are Jewish people. My mum was not who she was. I think the horror might have been that she was sold a lie all her life because she'd grown up carefree, Catholic, terrified about Saint This and Saint That and the Devil coming to your window, and you suddenly discover that you are actually a Jew. And you might be killed for it. How do you cope with that?! It was traumatic.*

Nicola: *You were told that Therese, you mum's grand mum, died of tuberculosis.*

Julia: *Oh, I think she just said, 'She was just ill' but then Peter said, she died in Theresienstadt during a typhoid outbreak. But she died in a concentration camp.*

Nicola: *Yes, I found out summer 2021 that she was murdered in Treblinka, as a seventy-six-year-old.*

Julia: *That is just unbearable.*

Nicola: *And when did you find out about Grandpa's sisters, one died in Auschwitz, the other sent to the Łódź ghetto?*

Julia: *When you told me.*

> Nicola: *So, you had no idea that Bruno had sisters?*
>
> Julia: *Well, I knew he had sisters but as far as I knew, the only people who came to Britain were Irma and Alfred, and I just thought the others stayed in Czechoslovakia ... Where does all this anger about being Jewish come from?! It's fear, absolute fear. Eva was sooo exhausting!*
>
> Nicola: *I don't think it was only fear, if I'm honest with you. When Eva was confronted with facts that she 'didn't belong', when you break the narrative of the stuff 'on top' she got angry – she was not herself, she was not calm, she was not clear, it was psychological tension. So, I don't agree with you that it was all fear, there was lots of stuff she hadn't addressed.*

I'm referring indirectly here to the psychological concept of congruence and suggesting that Eva was incongruent. That means she had not integrated her experiences in her self-concept and that was a source of tension.

> Julia: *I absolutely agree with you: a big bit of it was fear, but there was denial, and if somebody is trying to dig, someone is going to get defensive. You know, I told you, I sometimes ragged her: she said, 'I TOLD YOU A HUNDERT TIMES!!' And I'd go: 'Hundred – hundred, you can't even speak the language'. That really bugged her ...*
>
> [Laughter]

Julia and I then debriefed with small talk, having spoken for one and half hours. I remembered that my father also couldn't say 'hundred', and he'd pronounce finger without the 'g', which is how it is pronounced in German.

Julia knew from her mother, Eva, that Bruno, our grandfather, had lost half of his middle finger through an accident in the factory in

Troppau, but she said she did not reach out as a child to touch the stump as I had. Julia also knew that when Marianne, our grandmother, 'escaped' from her care home, she returned to 13 Castlebar Hill – to Bruno.

I never met Martha, our great-great-aunt. Julia did; twice, Eva visited Vienna and Martha at her house with her daughter, and Julia recalls Martha as 'ancient and like someone from a different era'.

Julia noticed while reading a draft of this manuscript that Therese was transported to Treblinka on Marianne's birthday, a tragic fact that had escaped me. Julia shared Eva's story, and valuable documents Eva had kept contributed to this story. When I interviewed Julia, new facets of the hushed narrative emerged that helped to break decades of family silence and bound us close together. When in 2011 we started going deeper into the past, it was clear how little we knew about the history of our European family. Julia quite soon became a sounding board for my research and was the first to react when I sent my father's 1945 letter from his return to Opava. She was fascinated. Together, as time passed and this project progressed, we developed a sharper awareness of our Jewish roots and became sisters.

18 CONNECTING LINKS

It would be impossible to write a book – fiction or nonfiction – that captured the scope of the Holocaust as a whole.

Ruth Franklin[1]

In the following, I connect various aspects of my family's story, try to synthesise the narrative, and look at things that have arisen through the research and writing.

The first thing I want to point to is the *use of terminology*. I think *émigrés* is a more suitable term for my father's family than *refugees*: they decided to emigrate due to political and racial developments; they were in exile. They were uprooted when they left Troppau in late 1938, and *émigrés* points to that, whereas the term *refugee* focuses on the safety of that status. The connotations of the word *uprooted* are interesting. Botanically, a root gives stability, it holds a plant in place and nurtures it as water and minerals are drawn from

---

1. Franklin, p. 144.

the earth. Roots are unseen; they are underground and vast. Roots take time to develop. Stefan Zweig speaks of being 'torn loose from all roots that held us'.[2] That imagery gives a sense of what Marianne, Bruno, Eva and my father, and the Wilhelms, Alfred, Hilde and Claus, went through, as well as Melitta, Irma and Alfred, Hanne, Frank, and Susi. Academic studies, books and films such as *Schindler's List* and *The Pianist*, and works about Anne Frank often focus on the horror that people experienced at the hands of the Nazis. However, a large group of Jews managed to escape in time. Their lives were totally disrupted, and they lived through years of fear and insecurity as they fled and started anew far from their loved ones and their true homes. This is the quieter, less dramatic side of the Holocaust, but it too deserves attention.

A word I have avoided using in this book is *perished*, because it is general and doesn't assign responsibility to the persecutors and murderers. Therese was gassed in Treblinka, Grete may have died of illness, desperation and starvation before facing the gas chamber at Auschwitz, or she may also have been gassed. Eduard was a victim of the wretched, inhuman conditions in Theresienstadt. I will never find out how Else died in the Łódź ghetto, but it was probably from starvation and illness. Karl was almost certainly gassed at Kulmhof. All of them were persecuted as Jews and were killed or died as a result.

The Gütermann Company and IVO Tapestries

Now a word about the two companies that were part of this book.

Gütermann was sold to American & Efird in 2014 and is now called AE Gütermann. The factory in Gutach, which my father and grandfather visited on business trips, is still there and remains visually unchanged on the outside; internally, there must have been

---

2. Zweig, *The World of Yesterday*, p. 43.

profound changes as a result of the international merger. I approached the company in spring 2022, explaining who I was and why I was interested in the past, and asked if the company archive had anything on my grandfather and the Troppau branch that Bruno set up. In a terse phone call I was told that nothing had been saved. As Alexandra Gütermann has three books on the market about her family's history, this answer surprised me, and I don't find it credible. Alexandra must have drawn on the company archives to write her books; everything she needed could not possibly have been in her own possession. I would have liked to have the emotional letters Bruno wrote about Heinz after Heinz's death that were quoted in Alexandra's books. So why the Gütermann Company rejected me remains a puzzle.

The company IVO Tapestries, founded by Bruno's mother, Johanna, and run by his sister Irma from 1931 to 1965, was dissolved on 10 May 2016. My mother had taken over the company after Irma's death and had sold it in 1990. When it was finally dissolved, it had been trading for 123 years.

I now turn briefly to religion. My father had no patience with any kind of religion. I am not religious; thirteen years at the convent cured me for life of that. As Judaism is traditionally handed down through the mother, I am not considered Jewish. Julia is though, through her mother, Eva, but she does not identify with it. My relationship with Judaism is as an outsider. However, when I visited Israel in 1993, I was stunned that, when the plane landed, tears suddenly came into my eyes. I had not been prepared for that reaction, as I was 'only' visiting my Alexander Technique trainers, who were all Israeli. I wondered in that moment if the tears were possibly triggered by an unconsciously inherited past connected with the horror of the Holocaust. The speed and ease with which I learned German and my affinity with the Black Forest also speaks for such a theory.

The relics of the past

It is intriguing that my paternal family saved so much from their lives. All of these things meant something to somebody: they were the building blocks of the puzzle that enabled parts of long-forgotten stories to be retrieved, and to a certain extent reconstructed. It seems to me that the rich data I could draw on had been patiently waiting for decades for precisely that to happen. Many members of my paternal family put pen to paper (or finger to typewriter) to record their experiences, and without their writing this book would not have been possible. I want to mention Heinz Gütermann in this context too.

The search and discovery of a legacy I was only vaguely aware of made me understand what research (re-search) means. Some people I talked to while writing this book had wanted to know more about their own family history and had searched but found little or nothing. How different their experience was: wanting to know more but facing a void. I hadn't previously wanted to know anything because I didn't know there was anything to know. When Grete's passport entered my life, I started to search and encountered waves, then an avalanche, of family history. It's as if the stories cascaded towards me. But I needed years to go in deeply.

There is, though, a difference between me reconstructing history and my father and my grandparents directly knowing the people I've been writing about. I have come to sense all of the never-mentioned relatives a little as I encountered their different fates. But I'm aware that only the story owners knew the true version of the stories; I do not. Narratives can break or maintain dialogue between generations, and my connections were severed.

I have gained access to the past my grandparents didn't want to acknowledge. Marianne's avoidance when I asked her how old she was ('as old as my tongue, a bit older than my teeth') was teasing, but I now believe there was also secrecy in her answer. I wanted to know something about her, and she avoided answering. The extent to which the past was avoided also showed in Bruno's missing half-finger. He couldn't say anything about it to his inquisitive little granddaughter, such as: 'I had an accident in a factory in the place called Troppau, where we used to live'. Instead, he recoiled when I touched the stump; he pulled his hand away from me sharply, and even now I remember the jerky (and surprising) quality of his movement and how that puzzled me. I now understand that I had literally touched the past – a place he didn't want to visit.

Although I am not religious, I celebrate Christmas and still have some baubles that Bruno hung on his Christmas trees years ago during my childhood. Year in, year out, I decorate my tree with them, and annually I tell my children that they are from Bruno, one of their great-grandfathers. Soon my grandchildren will be old enough for me to explain whom these baubles came from and why they are special. We'll build a bridge between the decades.

Personal and public remembering

Most children born in Germany after the end of the war had fathers (and mothers) who, in some way, had been involved in violence: fighting as soldiers, Nazism, murdering, and persecuting Jews or other minorities. Their parents had lived and grown to adulthood during the hostile indoctrination of Nazism in Germany. Many soldiers returning home after the war had been Soviet prisoners of war, and the brutality of Soviet (Russian) prison camps was – and still is – renowned. German families also sustained various traumas: of being forced to flee their homes during or after the war, enduring months of hunger, and being dislocated before resettling. Thus, German history includes perpetrating crimes against humanity but also being victimised by the conditions during and after the war. And yet, how little it is talked about. I know only four people who openly say that their fathers were Nazis. This is the German side of *the unspeakable*.

On a national, political level, *Erinnerungskultur* (the culture of remembrance) is lived out in Germany with great responsibility and seriousness. However, it seems to me that individual stories need more space in the public realm: the impact of personal narratives is greater than speaking abstractly about the vast numbers of people murdered during the Holocaust. The ritualised days of remembrance for the Shoah, with speeches and wreaths laid at memorials, need to be intensified with the telling of personal stories.

My story is about German-speaking Jewish-European citizens who made their homes in areas spanning Czechoslovakia, Austria and Switzerland. It is a story that raises questions about the relationship between the language spoken in a geographical area and national identity. In simplified terms, Hitler got the Sudetenland because German speakers lived there, and the Austrian Anschluss happened for a similar reason. National identity is sometimes – perhaps often – associated with language. But it's not as straightforward as that. A common cross-border language creates entanglement; we forget that human language is transnational. I see a sorry parallel in Putin's invasion of Ukraine on 24 February 2022. Simply put, Putin started his war because Russian speakers live in Ukraine. (That is not the only reason, but this is not the place to elaborate.) Thinking about how language and identity have a bearing on political conflicts that have led to war, I'm reminded of the sense of clear country borders I had while growing up England: the British Isles ended where the sea started.

I visited the Arolsen Archives, the International Centre on Nazi Persecution, in central Germany in summer 2022. Information on over seventeen million victims of the Nazis is documented there; it is the most comprehensive collection in the world. Christiane Weber, who works there, kindly gave me a guided tour to show how the Archives had developed from the International Tracing Service, which the Allies set up in central Germany after the war. Christiane had detailed and comprehensive knowledge, and she told me that of the millions of people documented there, information on the fate of over thirteen million people had not (yet) been requested, although on average twenty thousand requests for information are received by the Archives each year. I also came to know Axel Braisz, who had researched Else and Karl's address in the Łódź ghetto and Grete's fate after arriving at Auschwitz in December 1943 for me. I experienced Axel (who told me when I asked that he'd been working for forty years at the Archives) as gentle and mindful when sharing traumatic family history facts. When I arrived and met him and Christiane, the first thing that happened was that I become very teary. They both gave me some space to let the sadness ebb; they were understanding, and I sensed I was not the first to experience a little emotional upheaval upon arriving at the Archives. I felt in good hands and was grateful that they gave their time and expertise.

Questions about people

I tried to trace Hanne, Else's stepdaughter, who had migrated with her husband Frank to Australia, as my father noted in Grete's passport. While we are not related, she belongs to my story, and I would have been interested to know what became of her and her family. Heritage sites document Hanne's children, but there was no response when I reached out. I managed to indirectly contact a cousin of Hanne's mother, but unfortunately no exchange started up. I let it go.

Months later, after I had finished the second draft of the book's manuscript, I contacted the Pinkas Synagogue in Prague, including Grete and Else's dates of birth to gain permission to use photos from their walls. That turned out to be unnecessary, but Dr Lenka Šindelářová, historian and curator of digitised records at the Jewish Museum in Prague, stunned me by answering and sending me Karl and Else Federmann's family tree. My inquiry email had been passed on to her and that connection enabled me to find Hanne's descendants. Once more, out of nowhere, data was again tumbling out of the internet.

With a snippet of information I received from Lenka, I used the internet to find Hanne's children in Australia, and we met online, which was extraordinary. My father had mentioned that Hanne was pregnant in a letter from September 1944 and now, seventy-eight years later, I was talking to the baby Hanne had carried all those decades ago, plus her younger brother's son, Matt. It was a wonderful experience to find them alive and well. However, Hanne's children wanted to retain distance from all things having to do with the Holocaust (which I respect and hence I have not shared their names). I realised how 'the unspoken' has staying power, and everyone has different reasons for keeping it like that. However, Matt did want to connect and have a deeper exchange. I was delighted to have found one of Karl Federmann's great-grandchildren, and he too was excited to connect with me; we have stayed in contact. From him I received further details about Hanne's half-sister, Susi, and her suicide.

In June 2022, I traced Alice Trier-Samuel, Haidi Wilhelm's friend whom I'd met in 2014 when I went to Zurich to fetch the archive suitcase belonging to the Wilhelm family. Alice, who is Jewish, was born in 1938. She told me about her friendship with the Wilhelm family. For years after the war, she had lived in the same house as Claus and Haidi, and she knew them well. She also knew Hilde and Alfred, and I asked her about her impressions of them. She remembered both Claus and Alfred as quiet and described Claus as reserved. Haidi and Claus, Alice recollected, checked in daily with Hilde and were attentive and caring towards her. Nevertheless, Hilde was quite demanding. Claus knew nothing about Judaism and had once asked Alice when Yom Kippur was. (The 'Day of Atonement', Yom Kippur, the holiest day in Judaism, is a moveable date, as are all Jewish holidays, as they are based on a lunisolar calendar; Yom Kippur takes place in September or October.) Kaddish, a prayer chanted as part of the mourning rituals in Judaism, was spoken for Claus at his funeral, which Alice remembered as very moving. I forgot to ask during our exchange who made the decision about this given that Claus knew nothing about Judaism.

I have nearly finished my narrative, but the story is not complete. Holocaust stories can never be complete. Among the other relics in the suitcase at my mother's house I had found an envelope from 1937 addressed to a Dr Helene Lemberger in Chicago. I'd sometimes wondered who this was. I assumed that Helene was someone else who had left Czechoslovakia in time to escape the Nazis. The envelope was from a letter Therese had sent to the USA, but it had been returned, perhaps because of the franked stamps: there were several stamp collectors in the family. Therese's name and address in her bold and spirited handwriting were on the back of the envelope. However, there was so much to research about the main people in this book that I hadn't tried to find out who Helene was; I'd repeatedly put the envelope aside, not wanting to get sidetracked.

Then, one day in November 2022, after I'd finished the second draft of the manuscript and was still feeling relieved to be out of the unspeakable Nazi zone, I spontaneously decided to research Helene Lemberger via the various websites I'd become used to working with. I quickly discovered that Helene's mother was Ida Lemberger, and Ida's maiden name was Sonnenblum, like Therese's. Ida was Therese's sister, born on 30 April 1869 in Troppau; she was three years younger than Therese. Helene was Therese's niece, and they had written to each other. 'Lemberger' as a surname simply means someone from Lemberg, and there is a connection because Freiburg (where I live in south-west Germany) is Lemberg's partner town. I know Lemberg as Lviv; it now lies in western Ukraine, and donations and support during Putin's brutal war against Ukraine have been going directly there from Freiburg by lorry, several times a week.

Ida's card in the Arolsen Archives documenting her fate showed that she had fled to Holland but was interned in the Westerbork camp on 30 May 1943, from where she was transported to Theresienstadt on

4 September 1944. I needed help from Axel Braisz at the Archives to decipher Ida's card; it was not the 'usual' card like Else's, Therese's or Grete's, which I'd found online. I learned that Ida and Therese had two brothers called Ludwig and Wilhelm (as a first name, not a surname as in 'Therese Wilhelm'). Wilhelm was born in 1864 and died aged thirty-eight after a short illness. I found his death announcement online, with Therese and Ida's names on it as his sisters. He had a law doctorate like his nephew, Alfred Wilhelm. Later, after completion of this book, I found further details about Ludwig, who survived the war. Ida's son, Helene's brother, was Paul Lemberger, born on 7 May 1900, which is noted on the card. Ida, Therese, Ludwig and Wilhelm's mother was Regina Sonnenblum; I'd found a photo of Regina's grave in the suitcase at my mother's house that my father must have taken when he visited Opava in the mid-1990s after the fall of the Iron Curtain. Regina had lived from 1838 to 1915. Now I knew that Therese had had three siblings; I'd often wondered about her family during my research.

More spoken and unspoken stories

In October 2022, I posted a story summary with photos of Else, Therese and Grete on the Jewish Genealogy Portal Facebook page.[3] I wrote that the Holocaust had been hushed in my family and asked if others had had similar experiences. I was overwhelmed with the response: seven hundred and fifty 'like', 'hug' and 'love' emojis and three hundred comments later, I knew that hushing the Holocaust in families was a common phenomenon. Via this post, I met Rick Pinard, an American who lives in Prague. He approached me via a comment and asked for the names of my family who had lived in Troppau all those years ago. He owns a 1936 telephone book for Moravia-Silesia. And there they all were. Rick kindly sent me photos he'd taken of the entries for Bruno, Therese, Eduard Lanzer and IVO

---

3. www.facebook.com/groups/641559152559001/search/?q=nicola%20hanefeld.

Tapestries (Johanna Vogel). To say that this was moving is an understatement. I was deeply touched by Rick's gesture and by seeing their names in an old, innocuous telephone book. It was evidence of their everyday lives all that time ago.

As we became friends, I slowly discovered that Rick was not 'just' a hobby historian (as I had wrongly assumed) but an authority who had done doctoral research on the Nazis' broadcast policy on Czech radio in the so-called Protectorate. He offered to check my manuscript for historical facts, and his first suggestion had to do with Grete. I'd thought she had corrected her name on her ID application. Rick thought that most unlikely. He suggested that a civil servant had reviewed the information that Grete had provided, which had been typed, and that, in combination with her opting for Czechoslovak (later 'Protectorate') citizenship, amending her name to German made the statement: 'she may have Protectorate citizenship, but culturally, she's German – that is, one of ours'. As Grete would hardly have miswritten her mother's name (Johana instead of Johanna), it became clear that my idea was uninformed and wrong. Furthermore, Rick who is fluent in Czech, explained the details of the complicated background regarding whether people opted for citizenship after the Munich Agreement. Rick added further details about discrimination against Jewish people in Prague:

> *By decree from 12 November 1940 issued by the Police Directorate of Prague, in city trams, Jews were only allowed to use the last car, the one pulled by the engine car. If the car only had one entrance, Jews were allowed only to use the back half of the car. Jews were not permitted to use trams consisting of only one car.*

The information that the only post office Jews were allowed to use now houses the Václav Havel Library also came from Rick, who also explained about the Vlajka and how the Czech fascists related to the Nazis. When I asked him what Jewish people had lived on in Prague if they were no longer allowed to work, he answered that it was savings or, riskily, by selling possessions. Further additions came from Rick, such as the diacritics in my father's letter when he returned to Opava, and a suggestion as to why Eva moved to the third person in her 'Return of the Native' account and her description of herself in the night club as the 'gracious lady'. He translated Czech words and suggested additional interpretations of my father's aggressive letter to his sister, and he contacted the university my father went to (Mendal University in Brno) and discovered when he'd studied. As my father had not signed up to the winter 1947/1948 term, that helped us to understand when he had left Czechoslovakia for ever. (I was amazed that these records still existed.) Rick also discovered that Else had been a part-owner of IVO Tapestries. As the company had done and was doing well, my idea that perhaps the Federmanns did not have the financial possibility to emigrate seemed incorrect. Why they did not leave remains a mystery.

Two final things. First, Grete, Irma, Martha and Haidi didn't have any children. Else's only child killed herself. That is a chilling, silent message: the next generation did not follow on; there was nothing from these family lines. And second, I also see Susi and Irma as victims of the Nazis, if not directly.

Through my rediscovering and assembling of the stories of Grete and Eduard, Else and Karl, and Therese, it feels as if these family members have regained some of the dignity that the Nazis stole. The murdered, lost relatives have their identity back: they are there again. They can be found, and their stories and fates have been documented. With that, and looking through the window to the past, I can honour them. That contrasts with the disdain, spite and murderous hatred Nazis had for them, but it is not enough to balance their cruel fate.

EPILOGUE

I was the hinge between these generations, but what did that mean?

Esther Safran Foer[1]

My biggest question, and my motivation for researching my great-aunts and great-grandmother, was how to understand why I had never heard of Grete, Else or Therese while growing up. When I was forty-six years old and my father sent me Grete's passport in 2004 with details of family members who'd been victims of the Nazis, I'm sure he never dreamed that I would unlock family history to the extent of writing a book. At that point, he knew his life was ending; he had terminal cancer. I think he just sent me the passport to make sure that something important to him was not forgotten. Through the years, Grete's passport took up a role in my life; it mutated, from something that 'simply' revealed tragic information about my family to becoming an assignment. I wanted to understand what the

---

1. Esther Safran Foer, *I Want You to Know We're Still Here: A Post-Holocaust Memoir*, pos. 1284 (chapter 7, paragraph 7).

information it contained meant. On the one hand, Grete's passport broke the silence surrounding the people my father had noted as victims of the Nazis. But on the other hand, as he sent it to me only shortly before he died, it also seemed to contain a message regarding the silence itself. As I later discovered, my brothers were somewhat informed on some aspects of the tragedies that had befallen our family – but we too had not spoken about it.

As I tried to try make sense of why my family never mentioned the fates of my grandfather's sisters or my grandmother's mother to me, the silence appeared heavily laden with meaning: anguish, sorrow, loss, shame, anger, denial and much more. Traumatic events can get put away in people's minds as they manage their everyday lives. Silence protects and can be part of a coping mechanism: repressing grief means not experiencing it. Not dwelling on negative experiences, moving on, can be a healthy human reaction, to avoid bitterness linked to trauma. I suspect each surviving family member may have protected themselves from their own wartime trauma: a combination of the loss of family members, their personal experiences of escape and starting anew in England, and the larger experience of living through the Second World War. I also think that my paternal family did not have the means to address trauma; they had no personal resources with which to deal with the unspoken past. They were not able to do anything to help Grete, Else and Therese after the war started; that helplessness alone is a lot to deal with.

Most probably, they also wanted to avoid burdening the younger generation and to protect their offspring from the details of horrific war happenings. Furthermore, it seems difficult to separate the silence around their relatives' fate from the silence about the family's Jewish roots. Bruno and Marianne had the financial possibility of escape, but other family members seemingly did not. Notably, Quakers did not take my grandparents in. While Bruno worked hard for his assets, he might have felt uncomfortable about being wealthy, which may have led him and Marianne to keep quiet about their

Jewish roots. In light of the cliché about 'rich Jews', coupled with a more sinister reason for not speaking about their roots, this might have been their way of avoiding antisemitism, widespread in the UK when they arrived in 1939. (And yes, antisemitism still exists, and a wave reared its ugly head when Israel retaliated after the unspeakable Hamas attack on Israel on 7 October 2023. And no, I don't think the Israeli government's plan to decimate Gaza and its population was the right response.)

My grandparents probably also took the pragmatic stance of putting the past behind them and getting on with their new life in England. Possibly it was for a combination of all these reasons that my grandparents did not speak about the past and their relatives lost to persecution during the Second World War.

Shortly after my mother's eighty-eighth birthday in 2022, I was musing on the phone with her on the issue of silence in my father's family. She said, 'We didn't talk about *any*thing'. After a short pause she added, 'Mind you, the silence was one way'. She told me how Marianne had rigorously questioned her during a twenty-minute taxi ride across London, shortly after my parents had met in the early 1950s. I could vividly imagine the scene, and I smiled as I listened.

Bruno's sisters, Marianne's sisters-in-law, all died in tragic circumstances: Grete aged sixty, Else aged fifty-four and Irma at seventy-two. Bruno's niece, Susi, killed herself after coming to England aged only nineteen. Marianne left her mother, Therese (Bruno's mother-in-law), behind in Troppau when the family emigrated to England, and Therese was murdered in Treblinka's gas chambers. Marianne's sister, Melitta, died in 1950. The shock of Irma and Alfred's deaths in 1965 and then the death of Bruno and Marianne's son-in-law, Julia's father, Michael, in the same year must have also played traumatically into the unspoken non-narrative. The death of Heinz Gütermann, Bruno's best friend, was a further loss. There was nothing about Heinz in the various family suitcase archives that revealed how close Bruno and Heinz were, and that also suggests a blotting-out strategy to overcome sorrow and pain. I discovered my grandfather's anguish about the death of his best friend via the Gütermann family history books; it had not, until my research, been part of my family history, although the family archives were there, waiting to be explored. Taken together, there were so many tragedies that they simply could not be put into words, but my grandparents reacted quietly and without bitterness. The film of them on their fiftieth wedding anniversary shows two happy – not soured – old people. I have come to believe that Marianne and Bruno did not forget Grete, Eduard, Else, Karl or Therese but that these relatives were rather shrouded in silence. As Hadley Freemann says in her novel, *The House of Glass*, 'Suppressing the past does not mean you don't think about it'.[2]

How much there was in my grandparents' hidden narrative of the past, and how I respect Marianne and Bruno's decision to emigrate when they did. If I could ask them one thing, it would be: what was it like to make your decision to leave? I now understand what strength of mind it would have taken to leave their house and home, family, possessions, friends, and work. I admire their sense of agency and believe that Marianne and Bruno made the momentous choice more easily than Irma did. Irma wrote in 1943 that she had begged Alfred 'to end it all' before emigrating. I admire how they managed the upheaval, their immigration experience and putting their lives together again once in England. I see now how I played a role in that process along with Julia and my brothers.

The Nazis murdered unutterable numbers of people, whose lives and unspeakable fates cannot be reconstructed because there are no survivors who could search for them, or documents are missing, or descendants are not aware it is possible. As I write, tears fill my eyes again: Grete, Eduard, Else, Karl and Therese are only five of the

---

2. Hadley Freeman, *The House of Glass: The Story and Secrets of a Twentieth-Century Jewish Family*, pos. 4403 (chapter 14, paragraph 14).

murdered millions, and most of those millions of people's lives, their pasts and fates, have vanished forever into the dark history of Nazi Germany. For this reason, I've included in the appendices the link to the list of people transported to Auschwitz with Grete in 1943, which the Arolsen Archives sent me when I requested information about Grete in 2022. Behind every name on this list there is a biography, a family and a tragic story. But again, the 2,500 names on that list represent only a fraction of the murdered. Ruth Franklin calls the endlessly echoing, ever terrifying, infinitely variable stories of the Holocaust 'a thousand darknesses', making this into the title of her book about Holocaust literature.

I understand now why I felt attracted to the farming life: my father had felt that attraction too. But even that remained unspoken: I had no idea that he'd started studying agriculture in Brno. I admire how my father navigated his numerous setbacks without getting despondent. I've gained insight into his schooling difficulties, and I think he managed so well. Studying his letters helped me to understand him on a deeper level. (I have forgiven him for getting his secretary to type his letters to me while I was away at university, from dictations done on the way to work. Perhaps that was his way of dealing with his spelling issues.)

My overwhelming feeling, now that I've completed this book, is one of relief, as if a weight has been lifted from my shoulders. That relief is imbued with a sense of clarity and more understanding about the unspoken in my family. I sense a deep peace of mind, having puzzled the things together that my predecessors saved in albums, suitcases, letters or official archives.

On a more global, less personal scale, the senselessness of war has again become shockingly clear to me. The only certain thing that war does is to create destruction and immense human suffering. The similarities between Czechoslovakia's place in Europe and its fate as it was torn between East and West, and the brutal war against Ukraine that Putin started on 24 February 2022, are glaringly obvious. Likewise humankind's inability to compromise and find solutions to decades-long conflicts; the Israel–Hamas war which started on 7 October 2023 but has a hundred-year-old history comes to mind. Two populations with different religions struggling over a sliver of land in the Middle East, using violence to try to solve their 'issues' – how stupid, unwise and incapable of learning is *Homo sapiens*?

What a tragic but rich legacy I have found in the shadows and brought into the light, and how immensely my perspective has changed. I've become aware of the complexity of my origins. Suppressed stories have been uncovered, and I'm still surprised as I regard them all. My family has grown in my mind, and I've discovered my father, my aunt, my grandparents, and Irma and Alfred as different people to the ones I knew. Delving into the past has been a surprisingly therapeutic and meaningful journey of discovery that seems to have come from making sense of family experiences and addressing and clarifying some of my cloudy thoughts and memories, and shadowy family feelings. How much I see now that I hadn't seen before 2004, when Grete's passport fell into my life. I have become personally aware of how trauma is passed on to the next generation: it became stunningly clear in my interview with Julia. I've realised, though, that I don't belong anywhere. My home is in Freiburg, but I am English, although I also have German nationality, but I would never say I'm German. Am I half Czech? I do not speak or understand a single word of Czech beyond *dobrý den*, which means 'good day'.

I believe the third generation of descendants of Holocaust survivors and people who escaped in time have a responsibility to span the bridge to the next generation to make sure that we never forget the Shoah. Soon, all first-generation survivors' voices will go quiet forever when they leave us. I want my children and grandchildren to ask and to know. My children are the fourth generation to speak English and German; I hope my grandchildren will become the fifth. I look at them, born in 2020, 2021 and 2022, and it touches and moves me beyond words to know they are Therese's (and Johanna's) great-great-great-grandchildren.

My family has grown in my mind as I have found Grete, Else and Therese and as my grandchildren have been born. Embracing the larger family fills me with wonder and joy, but the inescapable reality of the Holocaust means that the sadness can still flood over me. It is no longer quite so sudden and intense as the unexpected flare-ups of a few years ago – but it has not left me. As I look again at the photos of the three women I drew out of history, I notice for the first time that only Else was looking at the camera when she was photographed decades ago; and now it is as if she is looking at me. I don't recall when or how I at last found a photo of her. I see something gentle but a little wary in her expression. I sense her vulnerability, and my great-aunt, who was the most remote while I was writing this book, is suddenly the closest.

A mystery remains: how did Grete's passport get to England? The only certain thing is that the Nazis didn't get their hands on it, otherwise it would have been either destroyed or committed to an archive after the war. Is it possible that my father reclaimed it at a police station in Prague or found it at Grete's house upon his return to Opava in 1945? I will never know. This seems the great irony of this story; Grete's passport is now with me in Germany, where it lies quietly on my desk.

APPENDICES

Link to the list of people transported to Auschwitz with Grete in December 1943

www.holocaust.cz/de/transport/43-ds-theresienstadt-auschwitz/page/8/

Timeline of significant events

1914–1918: First World War

1918: collapse of the Austro-Hungarian Empire and founding of the First Czechoslovak Republic

1920: Bruno Vogel returns from POW camp and sets up a Gütermann branch in Troppau/Opava

1922: Bruno and Marianne marry

1923: Eva is born

1925: my father, Hans-Peter, is born

1929: the family house in Troppau/Opava is completed

1933

January: Hitler becomes Chancellor of Germany

March: public book burning; antisemitism as part of state policy; establishment of first concentration camps Oranienburg and Dachau

1935: antisemitic and racist Nuremberg Laws are enacted

1937: Buchenwald concentration camp is set up

1938

March: Anschluss (incorporation) of Austria into Germany

September: the Munich Agreement; German-speaking parts of Czechoslovakia are ceded to Nazi Germany

October: the Vogel family leave their home in Troppau for Prague and then move on to Zurich

November: pogroms – Reichskristallnacht

1939

The Wilhelm family flees to Paris

February: Irma and Alfred Karplus arrive in England

March: Hitler invades the remaining part of Czechoslovakia; founding of 'The Protectorate of Bohemia and Moravia'

Susi Federmann and the Vogel family arrive (separately) in London

September: start of Second World War

1940

The Łódź ghetto in German-occupied Poland is cordoned off with 165,000 people in 1.6 square miles

May: Susi dies by suicide

1941

July: Reinhard Heydrich becomes responsible for the *Endlösung*; the extermination of Europe's Jews

September: Heydrich becomes 'Acting Reichsprotector' of the Protectorate of Bohemia and Moravia, what is left of Czechoslovakia

September: Jews are forced to wear the Star of David

October: Else and Karl Federmann are transported to the Łódź ghetto in German-occupied Poland; Auschwitz II (Birkenau) is set up to murder Jews, Romani, Poles, homosexuals and Russians

November: Theresienstadt ghetto/concentration camp is set up

December: Grete and Eduard Lanzer are transported to Theresienstadt

1942

May: Operation Anthropoid; Reinhard Heydrich dies a week after an assassination attempt

June: Therese Wilhelm is transported to Theresienstadt

Treblinka killing centre is set up

August: Eduard Lanzer dies in Theresienstadt

September: the Wilhelm family enter Switzerland illegally after three years in France; Karl Federmann is transported to Chełmno/Kulmhof

October: Therese Wilhelm is transported to Treblinka

1943

December: Grete Lanzer is transported to Auschwitz

1944

June: D-Day Allied invasion at Normandy

September: Heinz Gütermann dies of sepsis in Zurich aged 56

1945

May: the war ends with the total defeat of Germany

September: my father returns to Czechoslovakia

1945–1946: about three million mostly indigenous ethnic Germans are expelled from Czechoslovakia

1947: my father leaves Czechoslovakia forever

1948

February: the Communists stage a putsch and take over in Czechoslovakia

1955: my parents marry

1958: I am born

1959: Julia is born

1989: the Berlin Wall falls; democracy returns to Czechoslovakia

1993, January: break-up of Czechoslovakia into the Czech Republic and Slovakia

2016: Julia and I visit the Vogel family house in the Czech Republic in Opava

LITERATURE AND SOURCES

In English

Aarons, Victoria, 'A Kaddish for History: Holocaust Memory in Ehud Havazelet's *Bearing the Body*', in *Studies in American Jewish Literature*, Vol. 29, edited by Carole Kessner and Ann Shapiro (Ashland, OH: Purdue University Press, 2010).

Albright, Madeleine, *Prague Winter A Personal Story of Remembrance and War, 1937–1948* (New York: Harper Collins, 2012).

Becker, Jurek, *Jacob the Liar, a Novel* (New York: Arcade, 2021; anniversary edition).

Bessel, Richard, *Germany 1945 From War to Peace* (London: Simon & Schuster, 2009).

Bonyhady, Tim, *Goodliving Street: The Fortunes of My Viennese Family* (Sydney: Allen & Unwin, 2011).

Boyd, Julia, *Travellers in the Third Reich: The Rise of Fascism through the Eyes of Everyday People* (London: Elliot and Thompson Ltd, 2018).

Davis, Angela, 'Belonging and "Unbelonging": Jewish Refugee and Survivor in 1950s Britain', *Women's History Review*, 26:1 (2017), 130–146.

De Waal, Edmund, *The Hare with the Amber Eyes: A Hidden Inheritance* (New York: Picador, 2011).

Defalque, Ray J. and Amos J. Wright, 'The Puzzling Death of Reinhard Heydrich', *Bulletin of Anesthesia History*, 1:1 (2009), 4–7.

Dobroszycki, Lucjan (ed.), *The Chronicle of the Łódź Ghetto, 1941–1944* (New Haven, CT, and London: Yale University Press, 1984).

Epstein, Helen, *Where She Came From: A Daughter's Search for Her Mother's History* (Lexington, MS: Plunkett Lake Press, 2010).

Fine, Ellen, *Third Generation Holocaust Representation Trauma, History, and Memory* (Evanston, IL: Northwestern University Press, 2017), p. 47.

Franklin, Ruth, *A Thousand Darknesses: Lies and Truth in Holocaust Fiction* (New York: Oxford University Press, 2011).

Freeman, Hadley, *The House of Glass: The Story and Secrets of a Twentieth-Century Jewish Family* (London: Fourth Estate, 2020).

Friedländer, Saul, *When Memory Comes* (Vancouver: The Noonday Press/Harper Collins, 1979/1991).

Frommer, Benjamin, *Privileged Victims: Intermarriage between Jews, Czechs, and Germans in the Nazi Protectorate of Bohemia and Moravia* (Lincoln: University of Nebraska Press, 2020).

Gilbert, Shirli, *From Things Lost: Forgotten Letters and the Legacy of the Holocaust* (Detroit: Wayne State University Press, 2017).

Groag Bell, Susan, *Between Worlds. In Czechoslovakia, England and America: A Memoir* (London and New York: Willian Abraham-Dutton Books, 1991).

Grossman, Wassili, 'The Hell of Treblinka', in *The Road: Short Fiction and Essays* (London: MacLehose Press, 2011).

Hájková, Anna, *The Last Ghetto; An Everyday History of Theresienstadt, 1941–1945* (New York: Oxford University Press, 2020).

Hawes, James, *The Shortest History of Germany* (Exeter, Devon: Old Street Publishing Ltd, 2018).

Holzer Schirm, Joanie, *Adventurers against Their Will: Extraordinary World War II Stories of Survival, Escape, and Connection – Unlike Any Others* (Orlando, FL: PeliPress, 2013).

Levi, Primo, *If This Is a Man* (London: Abacus, 2014).

London, Louise, *Whitehall and the Jews: British Immigration Policy, Jewish Refugees and the Holocaust* (Cambridge: Cambridge University Press, 2020).

Manchester, William, *Winston Spencer Churchill: The Last Lion, Volume 2: Alone, 1932–1940* (London: Little, Brown, 1989).

Neumann, Ariane, *When Time Stopped: A Memoir of My Father's War and What Remains* (London: Scribner, 2021).

Pinard, Peter Richard, *Broadcast Policy in the Protectorate of Bohemia and Moravia: Power Structures, Programming, Cooperations and Defiance at Czech Radio 1939–1945* (Frankfurt am Main: Peter Lang GmbH Int. Verlag der Wissenschaften, 2015).

Nicholson, T.A.J., 'Producing a Product Range: Perivale Gütermann Threads', in *Managing Manufacturing Operations: A Casebook* (London: Palgrave Macmillan, 1978).

Rajchmann, Chiam, *The Last Jew of Treblinka 1942/43: A Survivor's Memory*, translated from Yiddish by Ulrike Bokelmann and Evita Wiecki (New York: Pegasus, 1945/2012).

Safran Foer, Esther, *I Want You to Know We're Still Here: A Post-Holocaust Memoir* (New York: Crown Publishing/Penguin Random House, 2020).

Tippner, Anja, 'Postcatastrophic Entanglement? Contemporary Czech Writers Remember the Holocaust and Post-War Ethnic Cleansing', *Memory Studies*, 14:1 (2021), 80–94.

Zweig, Stefan, *The World of Yesterday: Memoirs of a European*, translated from German by B. Huebsch and H. Rippergerb (ebook: Plunket Lake Press, 1943/2011).

In German

Grossman, Wassili, *Die Hölle von Treblinka* (Blaudfelden: New Academic Press, 2020).

Gütermann, Alexander, *Die Gütermanns: Eine Familiengeschichte, Band 1 und 2* (Gutach: Eigenverlag, 2009 and 2011).

Heim, Susanne and Maria Wilke (eds), *Die Verfolgung und Ermordung der europäischen Juden durch das nationalsozialistische Deutschland 1933–1945.*

Band 6: *Deutsches Reich und Protektorat Oktober 1941 – März 1943* (Berlin: De Gruyter Oldenburg, 2019).

Klüger, Ruth, *Unterwegs Verloren: Erinnerungen* (München: Deutscher Taschenbuch Verlag 2010). Also available in English.

Klüger, Ruth, *Weiter Leben: Eine Jugend* (München: Deutscher Taschenbuch Verlag 2013). Published in English as *Still Alive: A Holocaust Girlhood Remembered* (New York: The Feminist Press at CUNY, 2003).

König, Maria and Antje Leetz, *Marisha – mehr als ein Wunder: Eine Überlebensgeschichte* (Göttingen: Wallstein Verlag, 2021).

Maxim, Leo, *Wo wir zu Hause sind: Die Geschichte meiner verschwundenen Familie* (Köln: Kiepenheuer & Witsch, 2021).

Reiners, Ludvig (ed.), *Der ewige Brunnen* (München: C.H. Beck, 1955).

Von Bechtoldsheim, Sophie, *Mein Großvater war kein Attentäter* (Freiberg: Herder Verlag, 2019).

Von Bechtolsheim, Sophie, *Staufenberg: Folgen. Zwölf Begegnungen mit der Geschichte* (Freiburg: Herder Verlag, 2021).

Zelkowicz, Józef, *In diesen albtraumhaften Tagen: Tagebuchaufzeichnungen aus dem Getto Łódź/Litzmannstadt, September 1942*, edited by Angela Genger, Andrea Löw and Sascha Feuchert, translated into German from Yiddish by Susan Hiep (Göttingen: Wallstein Verlag, 2015).

Websites

www.afz.ethz.ch
www.arolsen-archives.org
www.auschwitz.org/en
www.geni.com
www.holocaust.cz
www.jewishmuseum.cz (Pinkas Synagogue)
www.opava-city.cz/en
www.yadvashem.org
Additional material and photos can be found on my website, www.speek.de

ACKNOWLEDGMENTS

Numerous people helped me with this book's completion. You were a reliable, highly engaged, caring and ever-expanding international network. With gratitude and heartfelt thanks ...

To my cousin, Julia Waring, in London, who gave me love, support and encouragement. We talked a lot throughout the months of writing and became very close. You added numerous facts, memories and documents. Without you, this book would not have been possible. You were with me and always (instantly) ready to discuss what I was working on if I reached out.

To my father, H. Peter Vogel, who started me on this journey into the past in 2004 by sending the passport of his aunt, Grete Lanzer. I'm sorry we didn't speak more about where you came from during your lifetime. I've had many quiet conversations with you in my mind while writing this book, and sometimes it's as if you're still here. I miss you.

To my mother, Pam Vogel, in England, who filled me in on numerous details about her parents-in-law and her husband, my father. Thank you for your excellent memory for details I couldn't know. Your interest in this project was motivational, and I think the historian in me comes from you.

To Antigone Kiefner, who has a degree in history, and was the first person in Freiburg (where I live) to support my research and writing.

You were there for me when the going was tough, for example while researching Grete and Therese's fate.

To Dr Robert Neisen, historian, Freiburg. Your open ear, interest, insight and backing were an incentive to get to grips with this project. You are familiar with the darkness of the subject, and talking to you helped me into the light again. Your knowledge of the local scene facilitated my getting to know Julia Wolrab, director of the Documentation Centre for the History of National Socialism in Freiburg.

I met Julia Wolrab for the first time at Freiburg's Platz der Alten Synagoge. We sat besides the 'mirror of water' which serves as a memorial for the old synagogue that was destroyed during the Reichskristallnacht in November 1938. Thank you, Julia, for your openness, warm heart, empathy and interest regarding my family's history. That motivated me and played a significant role in the book's completion.

Thank you to Sabine Hohn-Neumann, Bruno Schnaider, Malcolm Hart and David Harrowes for your friendship, support, feedback and input on early drafts of the manuscript. Thank you to friend and colleague Sabine Graton for her close reading of the final manuscript.

To Dr Christoph Gütermann, Heinz Gütermann's grandson, Vienna. You corrected historical facts and contributed input and knowledge of your family. We were bound through history and our grandfathers' friendship and that brought us close in a special way.

To Lesley Cooke, England, my Bach flower remedy colleague and friend. (I am a Bach Foundation Registered Practitioner as well as a teacher of the Alexander Technique.) You went through the first draft with professional conscientiousness; this led to numerous improvements. You had a deep understanding of how emotionally draining the research was. We journeyed together for two and a half months, chapter by chapter, as the second draft of the manuscript grew. You pointed out that the Nazis' strategy of making women strip off their clothes before they were sent to the gas chambers was a further unspeakable degradation that they subjected their victims to; these were Victorian women who had probably never stood naked even in front of their husbands, let alone strangers.

To Ruth Rootberg, my Alexander Technique colleague and friend in the USA. You supported me wholeheartedly and became my developmental editor. Your meticulous work transformed the second draft of the manuscript into the third in only three months. I sensed your deep interest in the project and commitment. On the technological level, your competence with MS Word was a blessing, as I have absolutely no patience with that kind of stuff.

Thank you to Martina Věntusová for making our trip to Opava possible. When I reached out in 2016 to employees at the Opava Town Hall, I had no idea what would happen. It was one of the extraordinary moments in my life when you answered and sent photos you had taken *on the previous day* of the house my family had left in 1938. You organised our visit and took time to meet us, and we were delighted by the presents the mayor of Opava gave us through you. Thank you, Veronika Kalusová, for translating for your father, Vladimir, and Ivo during our visit to the house in Opava. It was heart-warming meeting you all in Opava.

Thanks to Nikola Faltynková for digging up the detail of when my father was enrolled at the Masaryk University, Brno, which helped to pinpoint when he left the country before the communists took over.

Thank you to 'my' branch of the Gütermann family for accepting me with such ease into your family in the 1970s. The head of that family had worked for the company for many years and knew my father, my grandfather and the Gütermann factory in England. We spoke on the phone in summer 2022, and I encountered his agile and clear mind. When asked what he remembered of Bruno, he answered without hesitation: 'the garden and his collection of alpine flowers.' For the first time I heard the following story: Bruno had been disappointed that a planned visit to the Troppau factory by the company management in the mid-1930s was cancelled because everything was in an excellent state. A visit wasn't necessary.

To Alice Samuel Trier, Zurich (born 1938), for a lively chat in the summer of 2022 which made Hilde, Alfred and Claus (whom she knew) come alive as people.

Special thanks to Axel Braisz at the Arolson Archives Bad Arolsen in Germany for your careful and prompt answers to my requests for information about Else, Grete and Therese. Likewise, to Dr Lenka Šindelářová from the Jewish Museum in Prague. Here were professionals at work with deeply disturbing material, creating the link between the Nazis' unspeakable crimes and the victims' descendants. How you interacted with me was heart-warming, and I sensed how much you cared. Thank you to Hana Vebrová, Development and PR Department at the Jewish Museum in Prague, for clarifying the free use of my photos from the Pinkas Synagogue (on my website). Thanks to Rosina Berger and employees at the Archiv für Zeitgeschichte in Zurich, Switzerland, for digitising and sending the Wilhelm family archive. Your quick and no-nonsense passing on of the documents was encouraging and motivating.

To Prof. Benjamin Frommer, Illinois, USA, for your warm, friendly, quick and helpful answer when I inquired about enforced marriages in Moravia. As I reached out and connected with people I did not know via the internet, people who lived thousands of miles away, their prompt, friendly responses while I grappled with the data repeatedly amazed me.

To Michael Simonson from the Leo Baeck Institute (LBI), New York, for your helpful input on the term 'survivor'. Thanks to the LBI for organising webinars with Anne Hájková, Ariane Neuman and Helen Epstein. It was inspiring to learn from these women who've already been to the unspeakable place (Terezín) that I had to (metaphorically) visit.

To Jessica Case, Deputy Publisher at Pegasus Books, USA, for permission to use the excerpts from Rachjmann's book on Treblinka. Your speedy answer and good wishes for my work heartened me. Many thanks to Lena Hartmann from Wallstein Publishers in Germany for permission to use the excerpts from Jozef Zelkowicz's diary.

To Prof. Elizabeth Harvey, Department of History, University of Nottingham and Leibniz Institute for Contemporary History, Munich-Berlin. Prof. Harvey is leading the momentous translation project on the definitive work, *Persecution and Murder of the European Jews by Nazi Germany, 1933–1945* (*VEJ*). Your friendly response when I spontaneously reached out, our chat in English (although we both live in Germany) and your interest in my research were heart-warming. Elizabeth liaised with publisher De Gruyter for permission to use the translated excerpts from volume 6 of the *VEJ* series, on the persecution of the Jews of Bohemia and Moravia. The series comprises sixteen volumes, around 5,280 documents and approximately 12,800 pages.

Serendipity sent Dr Peter Richard Pinard, a multilingual US historian living in Prague, into my life as I worked during the final months of writing. We met via my social media post in October 2022 on the Facebook Jewish Genealogy Portal. With your support, the third draft developed into the fourth, which was greatly enriched by your corrections, additions and sharp editing skills. Thank you, Rick, for being reliable, understanding and present. As a historian, you are familiar with the thousands of unspeakable facets of Nazi terror, and your sheer endless knowledge of the era and events in Czechoslovakia repeatedly amazed me. After reading Grete's chapter, your chilling comment haunted me: 'the intent and effect of the Holocaust was to take perfectly lovely, decent people like Grete, deceive them, rob them of everything, abuse them and then turn them into a pile of ash and bone chips. Imagine having a mindset that considered such a project a good idea.'

Last but certainly not least, a huge thank you to Liesbeth Heenk from Amsterdam Publishers (AP) for your support, guidance, and huge commitment to publishing this and dozens of other Holocaust memoirs. Your work ensures that the two words 'never forget' become filled with meaning. Luke Finley polished the manuscript for AP to its final version. Thank you, Luke, for your attention to detail and for being so careful and attentive over the accurate use of words and the flow of the narrative and towards me as an author. I felt seen by both of you.

Marianne and Bruno had the courage and means to leave Troppau in 1938 and set up a new life in England. They left behind everything familiar to them. That decision was facilitated through Heinz and Bruno's friendship and Bruno's esteemed position within the Gütermann company. I believe that gave them the confidence and a sense of security that emigrating would work out well, which it did. Thinking of Marianne and Bruno now, over forty years after they died, I'm flooded with love for them. Besides the fact that I have my life because of their actions back then, I'm struck by how they navigated the change and their losses and how they adapted. Deep gratitude fills my heart. You were wonderful grandparents.

ABOUT THE AUTHOR

Nicola Hanefeld was born in 1958 in London and grew up in England, unaware of her Jewish heritage. She has lived in Freiburg in south-west Germany since 1981. Shortly before her father died, he shared never previously mentioned facts about his family. Her father's revelations sent Nicola on a heart-breaking journey to discover the Holocaust trauma silently embedded in her family. As she is fluent in German, she could understand the historical documents in German which surprisingly came to light during her research. Nicola has a degree in biology, a PhD in maternal health and is a freelance Alexander Technique coach. She's a mother of three grown-up children and has three grandchildren.

AMSTERDAM PUBLISHERS HOLOCAUST LIBRARY

The series **Holocaust Survivor Memoirs World War II** consists of the following autobiographies of survivors:

Outcry. Holocaust Memoirs, by Manny Steinberg

Hank Brodt Holocaust Memoirs. A Candle and a Promise, by Deborah Donnelly

The Dead Years. Holocaust Memoirs, by Joseph Schupack

Rescued from the Ashes. The Diary of Leokadia Schmidt, Survivor of the Warsaw Ghetto, by Leokadia Schmidt

My Lvov. Holocaust Memoir of a twelve-year-old Girl, by Janina Hescheles

Remembering Ravensbrück. From Holocaust to Healing, by Natalie Hess

Wolf. A Story of Hate, by Zeev Scheinwald with Ella Scheinwald

Save my Children. An Astonishing Tale of Survival and its Unlikely Hero, by Leon Kleiner with Edwin Stepp

Holocaust Memoirs of a Bergen-Belsen Survivor & Classmate of Anne Frank, by Nanette Blitz Konig

Defiant German - Defiant Jew. A Holocaust Memoir from inside the Third Reich, by Walter Leopold with Les Leopold

In a Land of Forest and Darkness. The Holocaust Story of two Jewish Partisans, by Sara Lustigman Omelinski

Holocaust Memories. Annihilation and Survival in Slovakia, by Paul Davidovits

From Auschwitz with Love. The Inspiring Memoir of Two Sisters' Survival, Devotion and Triumph Told by Manci Grunberger Beran & Ruth Grunberger Mermelstein, by Daniel Seymour

Remetz. Resistance Fighter and Survivor of the Warsaw Ghetto, by Jan Yohay Remetz

My March Through Hell. A Young Girl's Terrifying Journey to Survival, by Halina Kleiner with Edwin Stepp

Roman's Journey, by Roman Halter

Beyond Borders. Escaping the Holocaust and Fighting the Nazis. 1938-1948, by Rudi Haymann

The Engineers. A memoir of survival through World War II in Poland and Hungary, by Henry Reiss

Spark of Hope. An Autobiography, by Luba Wrobel Goldberg

Footnote to History. From Hungary to America. The Memoir of a Holocaust Survivor, by Andrew Laszlo

Farewell Atlantis. Recollections, by Valentīna Freimane

The Mulberry Tree. The story of a life before and after Holocaust, by Iboja Wandall-Holm

The Boy in the Back. A True Story of Survival in Auschwitz and Mauthausen, Fern Lebo

The Courtyard. A memoir, by Benjamin Parket and Alexa Morris

Beneath the Lightless Sky. Surviving the Holocaust in the Sewers of Lvov, by Ignacy Chiger

Run, Mendel Run, by Milton H. Schwartz

The series **Holocaust Survivor True Stories**
consists of the following biographies:

Among the Reeds. The true story of how a family survived the Holocaust, by Tammy Bottner

A Holocaust Memoir of Love & Resilience. Mama's Survival from Lithuania to America, by Ettie Zilber

Living among the Dead. My Grandmother's Holocaust Survival Story of Love and Strength, by Adena Bernstein Astrowsky

Heart Songs. A Holocaust Memoir, by Barbara Gilford

Shoes of the Shoah. The Tomorrow of Yesterday, by Dorothy Pierce

Hidden in Berlin. A Holocaust Memoir, by Evelyn Joseph Grossman

Separated Together. The Incredible True WWII Story of Soulmates Stranded an Ocean Apart, by Kenneth P. Price, Ph.D.

The Man Across the River. The incredible story of one man's will to survive the Holocaust, by Zvi Wiesenfeld

If Anyone Calls, Tell Them I Died. A Memoir, by Emanuel (Manu) Rosen

The House on Thrömerstrasse. A Story of Rebirth and Renewal in the Wake of the Holocaust, by Ron Vincent

Dancing with my Father. His hidden past. Her quest for truth. How Nazi Vienna shaped a family's identity, by Jo Sorochinsky

The Story Keeper. Weaving the Threads of Time and Memory - A Memoir, by Fred Feldman

Krisia's Silence. The Girl who was not on Schindler's List, by Ronny Hein

Defying Death on the Danube. A Holocaust Survival Story,
by Debbie J. Callahan with Henry Stern

A Doorway to Heroism. A decorated German-Jewish Soldier who became an
American Hero, by W. Jack Romberg

The Shoemaker's Son. The Life of a Holocaust Resister, by Laura Beth Bakst

The Redhead of Auschwitz. A True Story, by Nechama Birnbaum

Land of Many Bridges. My Father's Story, by Bela Ruth Samuel Tenenholtz

Creating Beauty from the Abyss. The Amazing Story of Sam Herciger,
Auschwitz Survivor and Artist, by Lesley Ann Richardson

On Sunny Days We Sang. A Holocaust Story of Survival and Resilience,
by Jeannette Grunhaus de Gelman

Painful Joy. A Holocaust Family Memoir, by Max J. Friedman

I Give You My Heart. A True Story of Courage and Survival,
by Wendy Holden

In the Time of Madmen, by Mark A. Prelas

Monsters and Miracles. Horror, Heroes and the Holocaust,
by Ira Wesley Kitmacher

Flower of Vlora. Growing up Jewish in Communist Albania, by Anna Kohen

Aftermath: Coming of Age on Three Continents. A Memoir,
by Annette Libeskind Berkovits

Not a real Enemy. The True Story of a Hungarian Jewish Man's Fight for
Freedom, by Robert Wolf

Zaidy's War. Four Armies, Three Continents, Two Brothers. One Man's
Impossible Story of Endurance, by Martin Bodek

The Glassmaker's Son. Looking for the World my Father left behind in Nazi Germany, by Peter Kupfer

The Apprentice of Buchenwald. The True Story of the Teenage Boy Who Sabotaged Hitler's War Machine, by Oren Schneider

Good for a Single Journey, by Helen Joyce

Burying the Ghosts. She escaped Nazi Germany only to have her life torn apart by the woman she saved from the camps: her mother, by Sonia Case

American Wolf. From Nazi Refugee to American Spy. A True Story, by Audrey Birnbaum

Bipolar Refugee. A Saga of Survival and Resilience, by Peter Wiesner

In the Wake of Madness. My Family's Escape from the Nazis, by Bettie Lennett Denny

Before the Beginning and After the End, by Hymie Anisman

I Will Give Them an Everlasting Name. Jacksonville's Stories of the Holocaust, by Samuel Cox

Hiding in Holland. A Resistance Memoir, by Shulamit Reinharz

The Ghosts on the Wall. A Grandson's Memoir of the Holocaust, by Kenneth D. Wald

Thirteen in Auschwitz. My grandmother's fight to stay human, by Lauren Meyerowitz Port

The series **Jewish Children in the Holocaust** consists of the following
autobiographies of Jewish children
hidden during WWII in the Netherlands:

Searching for Home. The Impact of WWII on a Hidden Child,
by Joseph Gosler

Sounds from Silence. Reflections of a Child Holocaust Survivor, Psychiatrist
and Teacher, by Robert Krell

Sabine's Odyssey. A Hidden Child and her Dutch Rescuers,
by Agnes Schipper

The Journey of a Hidden Child, by Harry Pila and Robin Black

The series **New Jewish Fiction** consists of the following novels, written by Jewish authors. All novels are set in the time during or after the Holocaust.

The Corset Maker. A Novel, by Annette Libeskind Berkovits

Escaping the Whale. The Holocaust is over. But is it ever over for the next generation? by Ruth Rotkowitz

When the Music Stopped. Willy Rosen's Holocaust, by Casey Hayes

Hands of Gold. One Man's Quest to Find the Silver Lining in Misfortune, by Roni Robbins

The Girl Who Counted Numbers. A Novel, by Roslyn Bernstein

There was a garden in Nuremberg. A Novel, by Navina Michal Clemerson

The Butterfly and the Axe, by Omer Bartov

To Live Another Day. A Novel, by Elizabeth Rosenberg

The Right to Happiness. After all they went through. Stories, by Helen Schary Motro

Five Amber Beads, by Richard Aronowitz

To Love Another Day. A Novel, by Elizabeth Rosenberg

Cursing the Darkness. A Novel about Loss and Recovery, by Joanna Rosenthall

The series **Holocaust Heritage** consists of the following memoirs by 2G:

The Cello Still Sings. A Generational Story of the Holocaust and of the Transformative Power of Music, by Janet Horvath

The Fire and the Bonfire. A Journey into Memory, by Ardyn Halter

The Silk Factory: Finding Threads of My Family's True Holocaust Story, by Michael Hickins

Winter Light. The Memoir of a Child of Holocaust Survivors, by Grace Feuerverger

Out from the Shadows. Growing up with Holocaust Survivor Parents, by Willie Handler

Hidden in Plain Sight. A Family Memoir and the Untold Story of the Holocaust in Serbia, by Julie Brill

The Unspeakable. Breaking my family's silence surrounding the Holocaust, by Nicola Hanefeld

Eighteen for Life. Surviving the Holocaust, by Helen Schamroth

Austrian Again. Reclaiming a Lost Legacy, by Anne Hand

The series **Holocaust Books for Young Adults** consists of the following novels, based on true stories:

The Boy behind the Door. How Salomon Kool Escaped the Nazis. Inspired by a True Story, by David Tabatsky

Running for Shelter. A True Story, by Suzette Sheft

The Precious Few. An Inspirational Saga of Courage based on True Stories, by David Twain with Art Twain

Dark Shadows Hover, by Jordan Steven Sher

The Sun will Shine Again, by Cynthia Goldstein Monsour

The series **WWII Historical Fiction** consists of the following novels, some of which are based on true stories:

Mendelevski's Box. A Heartwarming and Heartbreaking Jewish Survivor's Story, by Roger Swindells

A Quiet Genocide. The Untold Holocaust of Disabled Children in WWII Germany, by Glenn Bryant

The Knife-Edge Path, by Patrick T. Leahy

Brave Face. The Inspiring WWII Memoir of a Dutch/German Child, by I. Caroline Crocker and Meta A. Evenbly

When We Had Wings. The Gripping Story of an Orphan in Janusz Korczak's Orphanage. A Historical Novel, by Tami Shem-Tov

Jacob's Courage. Romance and Survival amidst the Horrors of War, by Charles S. Weinblatt

A Semblance of Justice. Based on true Holocaust experiences, by Wolf Holles

Under the Pink Triangle. Where forbidden love meets unspeakable evil, by Katie Moore

Amsterdam Publishers Newsletter

Subscribe to our Newsletter by selecting the menu at the top (right) of **amsterdampublishers.com** or scan the QR-code below.

www.ingramcontent.com/pod-product-compliance
Lightning Source LLC
LaVergne TN
LVHW091706070526
838199LV00050B/2293